The Political Economy of Taxation in Latin America

Paying taxes is one of the least popular activities worldwide. Latin America in particular is notorious for having low direct taxes, weak compliance and enforcement, and high levels of inequality. Although fiscal extraction has gained renewed interest among governments in recent years, with the end of the commodity boom adding special urgency, the successful adoption and implementation of tax reforms is easier said than done, even when tax policy prescriptions are widely shared. This volume provides the first comprehensive, region-wide assessment of the role of political factors, including public opinion, democratic institutions, natural resources, interest groups, political ideology, and state capacity.

What explains the region's low levels of taxation? What explains the low progressivity in its tax structure? And what explains considerable differences across countries? In addressing these questions, each of the volume's chapters makes original theoretical and empirical contributions toward understanding how to overcome the political challenges to taxation.

Gustavo A. Flores-Macías is Associate Professor of Government at Cornell University. He is the author of *After Neoliberalism: The Left and Economic Reforms in Latin America* (2012), which received the Latin American Studies Association Tomassini Book Award. He is a faculty fellow at Cornell's Atkinson Center for a Sustainable Future and core faculty at the Cornell Institute for Public Affairs. In 2017–2018, he was the recipient of Princeton University's Democracy and Development Fellowship.

The Political Economy of Taxation in Latin America

Edited by

GUSTAVO A. FLORES-MACÍAS
Associate Professor of Government
Cornell University

CAMBRIDGE
UNIVERSITY PRESS

CAMBRIDGE
UNIVERSITY PRESS

University Printing House, Cambridge CB2 8BS, United Kingdom

One Liberty Plaza, 20th Floor, New York, NY 10006, USA

477 Williamstown Road, Port Melbourne, VIC 3207, Australia

314-321, 3rd Floor, Plot 3, Splendor Forum, Jasola District Centre, New Delhi - 110025, India

103 Penang Road, #05-06/07, Visioncrest Commercial, Singapore 238467

Cambridge University Press is part of the University of Cambridge.

It furthers the University's mission by disseminating knowledge in the pursuit of education, learning and research at the highest international levels of excellence.

www.cambridge.org
Information on this title: www.cambridge.org/9781108464994
DOI: 10.1017/9781108655934

First published 2019
First paperback edition 2022

A catalogue record for this publication is available from the British Library

Library of Congress Cataloging in Publication data
NAMES: Flores-Macias, Gustavo, editor.
TITLE: The political economy of taxation in Latin America / edited by Gustavo Flores-Macias.
DESCRIPTION: Cambridge, United Kingdom ; New York, NY : Cambridge University Press, 2019. | Includes bibliographical references and index.
IDENTIFIERS: LCCN 2019006488 | ISBN 9781108474573 (hardback)
SUBJECTS: LCSH: Taxation – Latin America. | Latin America – Economic policy.
CLASSIFICATION: LCC HJ2460.5 .P66 2019 | DDC 336.20098–dc23
LC record available at https://lccn.loc.gov/2019006488

ISBN 978-1-108-47457-3 Hardback
ISBN 978-1-108-46499-4 Paperback

Contents

Figures

Tables

Contributors

Marcelo Bergman is a sociologist and a professor at Universidad Nacional Tres de Febrero in Buenos Aires, Argentina, and an affiliated professor at CIDE (Research Center for Teaching Economics) in Mexico City. He holds BA and MA degrees in Political Science from the Hebrew University of Jerusalem, and a PhD from the University of California at San Diego. His recent books include *Tax Evasion and the Rule of Law in Latin America: The Political Culture of Cheating and Compliance in Argentina and Chile* (2009) and *More Money, More Crime: Prosperity and Rising Crime in Latin America* (2018).

Juan A. Bogliaccini is Associate Professor of Political Science at the Department of Social and Political Sciences, Universidad Católica del Uruguay. He holds a PhD in Political Science from the University of North Carolina at Chapel Hill. His research focuses on the political economy of redistribution and inequality, in particular in the areas of comparative capitalism, skills formation, and welfare states.

Tasha Fairfield is Associate Professor of International Development at the London School of Economics, and 2017–2018 Mellon Foundation Fellow, Center for Advanced Study in Behavioral Sciences, Stanford University. She is the author of *Private Wealth and Public Revenue in Latin America: Business Power and Tax Politics* (Cambridge University Press, 2015; winner of the LASA Donna Lee Van Cott Award, 2016). Her recent articles include "Explicit Bayesian Analysis for Process Tracing" in *Political Analysis* (winner of the Sage Best Paper Award, APSA-QMMR 2017).

Gustavo A. Flores-Macías is Associate Professor of Government at Cornell University. He is the author of *After Neoliberalism: The Left* *and Economic Reforms in Latin America* (2012), which received the Latin American Studies Association Tomassini Book Award in 2015. He is a member of the core faculty at the Cornell Institute for Public Affairs and a faculty fellow at Cornell's Atkinson Center for a Sustainable Future. In 2017–2018 he was awarded Princeton University's Democracy and Development Fellowship at the Princeton Institute for International and Regional Studies.

Mark Hallerberg is Professor of Public Management and Political Economy at the Hertie School of Governance in Germany and Director of Hertie's Fiscal Governance Centre. He is the author of *Domestic Budgets in a United Europe: Fiscal Governance from the End of Bretton Woods to EMU* (2004), coauthor of *Fiscal Governance in Europe* (Cambridge University Press, 2009), and coeditor of *Who Decides the Budget? A Political Economy Analysis of the Budget Process in Latin America* (2009). He publishes articles and book chapters on fiscal governance, tax policy, and exchange-rate choice.

Juan Pablo Luna is Professor of Political Science at the Pontificia Universidad Católica de Chile (Instituto de Ciencia Política & Escuela de Gobierno) and Associate Researcher at the IMFD-Chile. He earned his PhD in Political Science from the University of North Carolina, Chapel Hill. He is the author of *Segmented Representation: Political Party Strategies in Unequal Democracies* (2014).

James E. Mahon, Jr. is Woodrow Wilson Professor of Political Science at Williams College. His recent work includes the codirection of a project with the Woodrow Wilson Center in Washington, DC, which produced the edited volume *Progressive Tax Reform and Equality in Latin America* (2015). He holds a BA from Dartmouth and a PhD from the University of California, Berkeley.

Francisco J. Monaldi is Fellow in Latin American Energy Policy at the Baker Institute for Public Policy; Lecturer in Energy Economics at Rice University; Fellow at the Center on Global Energy Policy at Columbia University; Visiting Professor at Tecnológico de Monterrey; and Founding Director of the Center on Energy and Professor at Instituto de Estudios Superiores de Administración (IESA).

Gabriel Ondetti is Associate Professor of Political Science at Missouri State University. He is the author of *Land, Protest and Politics: The Landless Movement and the Struggle for Agrarian Reform in Brazil*

(2008). His recent articles include "The Roots of Brazil's Heavy Taxation" in *Journal of Latin American Studies*, and "The Power of Preferences: Economic Elites and Light Taxation in Mexico" in the *Revista Mexicana de Ciencias Políticas y Sociales*.

Carlos Scartascini is Principal Economist at the Research Department of the Inter-American Development Bank. His areas of expertise include political economy, public finance, and behavioral economics. He has published seven books and more than thirty articles in specialized journals and edited volumes. He is Associate Editor of the academic journal *Economía*. A native of Argentina, he holds a PhD in economics from George Mason University.

Aaron Schneider is Leo Block Associate Professor of International Studies at the University of Denver, where he also directs the Latin America Center and co-directs the International Development Degree Program. He is the author of *State-building and Tax Regimes in Central America* (Cambridge University Press, 2012). Previously, he served as advisor to the chief economist for Central America at the Inter-American Development Bank.

Acknowledgments

This book was born out of an effort to inform tax policy. It responds to the concern that the bulk of existing scholarship on the topic has focused on the design of the appropriate tax policies, but has neglected the political considerations that promote or hinder those policies. A central motivation for the project was the firm belief that the best economic reforms are doomed to failure in the absence of the right political conditions to adopt them and sustain them over time. Although its focus is on Latin America, the volume seeks to inform our understanding of common political challenges beyond the region.

This endeavor benefited from the generosity of several centers around Cornell. The Mario Einaudi Center for International Studies and the Institute for the Social Sciences contributed funds to hold in Ithaca the seminal conference on taxation that paved the way for this volume. The Latin American Studies Program provided support for the logistics of the conference. The Princeton Institute for International and Regional Studies at Princeton University provided a rich intellectual environment to work on the volume during my time as the 2017–2018 Democracy and Development Fellow.

I am especially grateful to Robert Kaufman, Kenneth Roberts, and Ben Ross Schneider. Their feedback at the taxation conference considerably improved the volume, and their encouragement throughout the project was key in turning it into a book. I am also grateful to Sarah Kreps, Jim Mahon, Mick Moore, Vicky Murillo, Gabriel Ondetti, Tom Pepinsky, Will Prichard, Nic van de Walle, and Deborah Yashar for helpful comments and discussion about the topics in this volume. David de Micheli, Whitney Taylor, and Jimena Valdez provided invaluable assistance with organizing the conference. Finally, I thank Sara Doskow and her team at Cambridge University Press for their enthusiasm and support for the project, and Richard and Maritza Williamson for their generosity.

1

Introduction: The Political Economy of Taxation in Latin America

Gustavo A. Flores-Macías

As the scandal of the Panama Papers – the leak of millions of records in 2016 from a law firm's list of clients with shell companies in offshore tax heavens – revealed, individuals will go to great lengths to avoid taxation. In one case, a wealthy Mexican businessman had established a half-dozen offshore corporations to evade taxes, and, in the aggregate, his unpaid taxes on foreign accounts are estimated at around US$100 million. The government of Costa Rica found at least 410 offshore companies set up by that country's nationals. Overall, 22% of Latin America's financial wealth is believed to be offshore, representing about US$21 billion in foregone government revenue (Zuckman 2015). By most accounts, the leak revealed only the tip of the iceberg.

Although the prominence of the Panama Papers might imply that only economic elites engage in this behavior, resistance to paying taxes takes place at all levels. As former Guatemalan finance minister, Juan Alberto Fuentes Knight (2012, 22), laments about recent efforts to integrate business units of all sizes into the fiscal system: "It is well known that in practice, many companies keep three books: what they show to the tax authority that reflects extremely low profits or losses in order to pay low taxes; what they show to the banks to get loans, where they increase their profits to appear very successful; and the true accounts, that are secret." These examples are emblematic of a long-standing challenge in the political economy of development: how to make taxation palatable.

In spite of this generalized animosity, however, there is an increasing consensus about the salutary consequences of taxation in terms of state capacity, government accountability, and economic development. For example, taxation is considered a fundamental source of resources that can translate into state strength (Brautigam et al. 2008; Schneider 2012). It can generate links of accountability between citizens and rulers that make governments more responsive (Paler 2013; Tilly 2009). It can contribute to addressing inequality (de Ferranti et al. 2004; Mahon Jr. 2012) and promoting growth (Bird 2012; Canavire-Bacarreza et al. 2013), and, for these reasons, taxation is considered an essential tool for development (Evans 1995; Inter-American Development Bank 2013). Not surprisingly, calls by think tanks (e.g., Council of Foreign Relations 2014) and international organizations (e.g., CAF Banco de Desarrollo de América Latina 2012; Inter-American Development Bank 2013) for increasing fiscal extraction in the developing world have gained momentum in recent years.

Yet, in spite of the importance of taxation for these different areas, the attention on taxation has been largely concentrated in the design of tax systems (Santos de Souza 2013). Existing scholarship on the design of tax systems has been extensive at presenting a diagnostic of the state of taxation in the region and the nature of the reforms needed. For example, we know that extraction in Latin American countries is low compared to that of other countries at similar stages of development; that although taxation is generally low, there is considerable variation in fiscal extraction across countries; that the region's tax structures tend to favor indirect over direct taxes; and that evasion tends to be high compared to other places (OECD 2016). Given these considerations, common prescriptions have been the simplification of tax systems, the modernization of tax revenue administrations, and the elimination of exceptions and tax incentives – to name a few – in order to promote efficiency and minimize distortions in the economy.

This emphasis, although an important step in identifying the direction of reform, has come at the expense of the political factors associated with the successful adoption of reforms. With notable exceptions, most studies on fiscal policy in Latin America have tended to ignore the political underpinnings of taxation. This is a significant oversight because political conflicts are at the heart of the obstacles to reforming tax systems. As Wagner Faegri and Wise (2011, 246) have noted,

> Despite the central role of taxation in economic development and growth, political economists have yet to develop a program of research that fully captures the politics of tax reform in emerging-market economies. Although legislative coalitions for economic reform have emerged in even the most contentious political environments, tax reform remains one of the more contested and understudied issues in Latin America.

This volume explores the role that political factors play in addressing the region's fiscal challenges. In particular, it tackles three main questions of the political economy of taxation in Latin America: What explains the region's low levels of taxation? What accounts for the region's tax structure? What explains differences across countries? By answering these questions, this book can inform efforts to address the region's taxation shortcomings.

In particular, the volume shows that commodity prices generate strong incentives for cycles of resource nationalism – encouraging certain governments to make poor tax decisions when entering into contracts – but also suggests that there is room for less structural factors to shape the levels and incidence of tax collection. For example, levels of taxation are shaped by the strength of economic elites, state capacity and compliance, and patterns of economic incorporation. Further, electoral rules, interest groups, and public opinion can play an important role in explaining differences in the tax structure, although there is significant crossover between groups because much of the region's low tax collection is related to the "missing share" of direct taxes. Differences in government's commitment to public spending, institutional strength, elite power, and electoral rules are helpful to account for considerable variation across countries, from Brazil's remarkable 34% at the top to Mexico's paltry 11% at the bottom.

Naturally, different courses of action often involve important tradeoffs. A policy that makes taxes politically palatable may increase fiscal revenue but at the same time affect other important considerations in the design of tax systems, such as efficiency or equity. For example, while there is evidence that earmarking taxes reduces animosity toward increasing the tax burden (Flores-Macías 2015; 2018), these taxes might reduce efficiency in the tax system (Buchanan 1963; Goetz 1968). Yet, it is important to know the full spectrum of options and their tradeoffs to know what governments can draw on given each country's particular circumstances. Technically desirable courses of action can only go so far without the ability to generate the political conditions for their approval.

FROM RESOURCE BOOM TO FISCAL PINCH: THE RENEWED IMPORTANCE OF TAXATION

Paying taxes is perhaps one of the least popular activities for people across the world. In the United States, for example, public opinion surveys consistently show the percentage of people who believe their taxes are too high at about 50%, whereas only 3% express that the tax burden is too low (Riffkin 2014). Attitudes toward taxes are similar in Latin America. In Chile, for example, 64% of respondents in a nationally representative survey suggested the tax burden should be lowered, compared to 9% who stated it should be increased (Fundación Jaime Guzmán 2011). In Mexico, only 5% of respondents in a similar survey suggested that taxes should be raised, whereas 64% stated they are too high (Centro de Estudios Sociales y de Opinión Pública 2013). These percentages have remained remarkably stable over time.

In spite of the continuous unpopularity of taxes, however, fiscal extraction has gained renewed interest in Latin America due to governments' newfound urgency to find sustainable sources of revenue. The commodity boom that began in 2003 and ended in 2014 became a major source of revenue for governments across the region (Monaldi 2014). The revenue windfall from exports of hydrocarbons, minerals, and agricultural products – often at record prices – greatly benefited government coffers. It allowed governments to improve budget balances and expand expenditures.[1] It also allowed them to increase official reserves and pursue countercyclical measures to cushion the impact of economic crises (Ardanaz et al. 2015, 4; IMF 2015).

However, commodity prices declined sharply in 2014, with many commodities by 2019 valued at less than half of their peaks during the decade-long boom. A prominent case is the price of oil, which stabilized at about $40–50 per barrel by mid-2015 – less than half of its value a year earlier, and a fraction of its peak of $143 in 2008.[2] This experience of oil – along with other hydrocarbons more generally – is not atypical; metals such as nickel, copper, silver, and gold – important exports for Andean countries such as Peru, Colombia, and Chile – have followed similar trends. The price of agricultural products such as soybeans – important for Argentina, Brazil, and Paraguay – have seen comparable decreases. Although current prices are not as low as those prevailing in the early 2000s before the onset of the boom, they have discouraged production, resulting in turn in lower revenue from royalties and taxes.

In Colombia, for example, where oil revenue represented a fifth of government revenue (Schipani 2015), oil production has plateaued after

[1] For example, governments across the region engaged in significant fiscal stimulus programs as a response to the 2008–2009 global economic recession.

[2] Constant prices in 2015 US dollars: www.macrotrends.net/1369/crude-oil-price-history-chart

a period of sustained growth between 2004 and 2013. In 2015, drilling declined by 25%, and the government is considering exempting oil companies from paying income taxes to address a decline in production, which is expected to drop below the government's target of 1,000 million of barrels per day (Willis 2015). In Mexico, where more than a third of government revenue comes from oil and the expected investment interest in the recently privatized oil industry has not materialized, production has steadily declined to its lowest point (1.9 million barrels per day [mb/d] in 2017) in at least two decades (Paraskova 2018) – a 24% decline since 2014 and 50% since its peak of 3.85 mb/d in 2004 (Flores-Macías 2016; Lajous 2014, 8). In both places there were high fiscal expectations riding on commodity prices before the panorama changed significantly.

A problem the region now faces is that increases in government spending based on temporary sources of revenue, while generally beneficial while they last, become difficult to roll back once the sources of revenue dry out (IMF 2015; World Bank 2016). People quickly get used to the higher levels of government expenditure, which become perceived as entitlements rather than temporary measures. In the aftermath of the global recession and the end of the commodity boom, governments have, by and large, failed to pare down the increases in spending since 2009 (IMF 2015). According to the International Monetary Fund (2015), spending-to-GDP ratios are about four percentage points of GDP higher on average today than their pre-crisis levels in 2007.

Due to the combination of reduced revenue from commodity exports and increased spending to cope with the global recession, fiscal balances across the region have deteriorated in spite of the sustained economic recovery following the crisis. Although several countries have adopted measures that have ameliorated the negative effects of the decline in commodity prices – including greater flexibility in the exchange rate and fiscal policy rules – the decline was so sudden and pronounced that it has had negative consequences across the board (Caceres and Gruss 2015, 51). As Figure 1.1 shows, the average fiscal balance as a share of GDP reached its lowest point in 2015 since the start of the boom. The difference is considerable when compared to the peak of the boom right before the 2008 crisis, when the region even experienced a surplus.

Although commodity prices behaved similarly for a number of goods, including metals, food, and oil (Figure 1.1), there is variation across countries as to the importance of the commodity boom for government coffers. As Figure 1.2 suggests, several countries leveraged the commodities boom to achieve surpluses between 2003 and 2012, including Argentina, Chile,

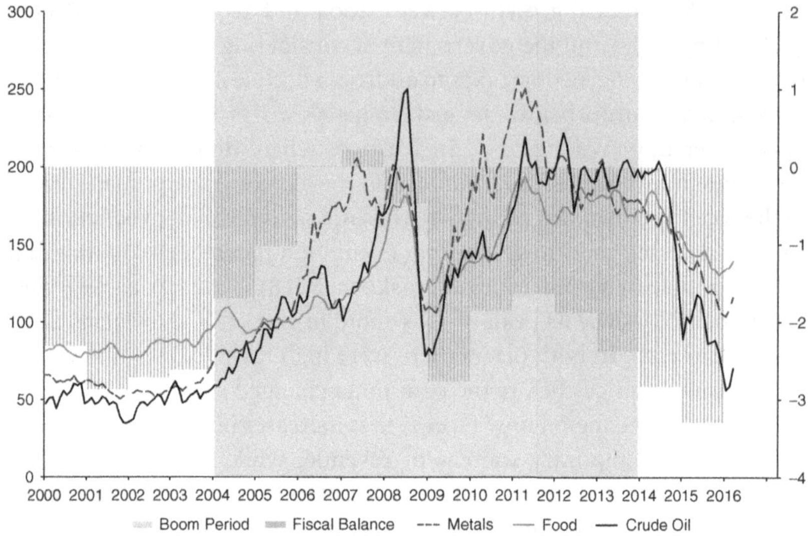

FIGURE 1.1 Commodity prices and Latin America's fiscal balance
NB: Left axis corresponds to the Indexes for Metals, Food, and Crude Oil (2005=100). Right axis corresponds to fiscal balance as a share of GDP. Fiscal Balance for 2015 is estimated with latest data available.
Source: Generated by the author with data from the IMF World Economic Outlook Database and CEPAL

Ecuador, Paraguay, and Peru. Others, such as Brazil, Colombia, Mexico, and Uruguay, did not achieve an average surplus during this period but improved their fiscal balances. However, all countries' bottom lines have suffered since the end of the boom. Whereas fiscal balances in Colombia, Nicaragua, and Peru have deteriorated by less than 1.2 percentage points of GDP since 2013, Argentina, Chile, and Ecuador have suffered decreases of more than 3.7 points. Although Venezuela is not included in Figure 1.2 because of lack of data, the impact of the end of the commodity boom is likely worst in that country, where oil generates more than 80% of the country's export revenue and about 45% of the government's revenue.[3]

Contrary to the favorable international outlook during the first decade of the twenty-first century, this bleak fiscal outlook for Latin America is taking place in the context of much less favorable international conditions. The global economy has decelerated, and perspectives for the

[3] There has been little transparency in Venezuela's reporting of government data since Hugo Chávez's presidency.

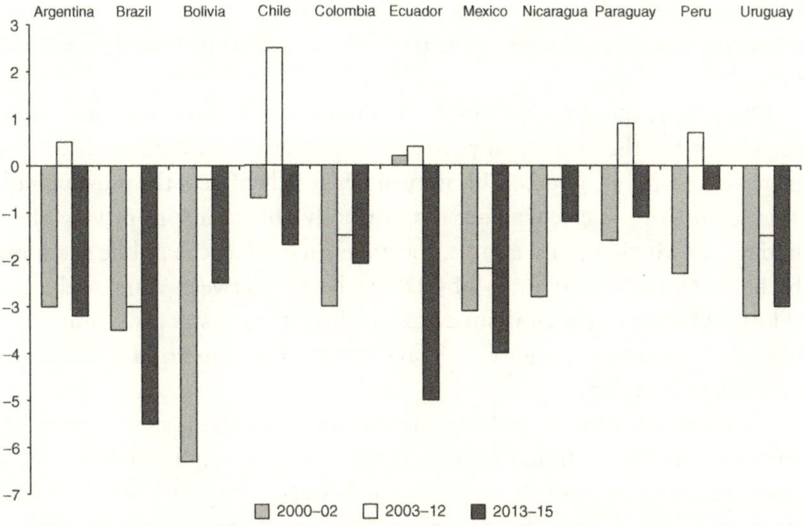

FIGURE 1.2 General government balance, selected countries (% of GDP)
Source: Zhang (2016)

region's economic performance are much less rosy than over the previous decade due to tightening interest rates and higher borrowing costs. Growth in emerging economies is showing signs of less dynamism, with China and India struggling to maintain the spectacular rates of recent years. China's economy has grown at rates below 8% for five years in a row since 2013. The rates of 6.7% for 2016 and 2017 are the country's lowest since 1990 – far from its peak growth of 14% in 2007 (Magnier 2016; Hsu 2017). India's growth has also decelerated from a high of 10% in 2010 to 7.1% in 2016, and 6.8% in 2017 (BBC 2016; Times of India 2017). The decreased dynamism of these two countries has not only contributed to the end of the commodity boom, but also to a decrease in demand for Latin American exports more generally.

At the same time, the US Federal Reserve has begun to raise interest rates. This will lead to higher borrowing costs, translating into both a greater burden from servicing existing debt denominated in US dollars and an increased cost of borrowing in the future. These factors, along with US president Donald Trump's proclivity toward protectionism, are likely to further decelerate the global economy. In 2016, for example, the region contracted by 1% on average, with Brazil and Venezuela contracting by 3.5 and 8.3% respectively (World Bank 2016). In 2017, regional growth was a meager 0.9%. This leaves Latin America in the unenviable situation of having to look for sources of revenue beyond those from natural resources at a time of international economic turbulence and low growth prospects.

Otherwise, the deteriorating fiscal situation will have important consequences for the region. In particular, spending cuts tend to affect the provision of public goods. This in turn negatively affects the most vulnerable sectors of society, who are not normally able to afford private alternatives. In Mexico, for example, the government has cut public spending by between 0.5% and 1.5% of GDP each year between 2015 and 2018 (Flores-Macías 2016; Graham 2017). In Brazil, a drastic provision limiting government spending for 20 years was approved in 2016 (Paraguassu and Marcello 2017).

Further, governments will become less able to address sudden crises by engaging in fiscal stimuli to soften the blow through countercyclical measures, as they did in 2008–2009. Instead, they are likely to find themselves faced with the conundrum of having to respond to a crisis but also having to put the fiscal house in order, which would likely worsen the crisis. This increases the chances that governments disregard existing fiscal rules in order to face short-term spending needs (IMF 2015). Fiscal buffers must be rebuilt before the next real crisis hits. Otherwise, the same tool used effectively during the 2008–2009 recession will not be available in the future. As the Latin American experience clearly shows, procyclical policies have been found to undermine growth (Ardanaz et al. 2015).

BEYOND COMMODITY BOOMS: LATIN AMERICA'S PENDING FISCAL ASSIGNMENTS

While the end of the commodity boom has brought the need for increased fiscal extraction to the fore of the region's policy agenda, it also serves as a reminder of unaddressed fiscal problems with which Latin American countries have struggled for decades. In particular, two main pending assignments are low levels of fiscal extraction and the tax structure's low contribution to addressing inequality.

Extraction Levels

First, while there has been some improvement over the last quarter century, the region's fiscal extraction remains lower than would be expected for its level of economic development. To be sure, the region has come a long way compared to the period of large fiscal imbalances coupled with high inflation – which eroded the real value of tax revenue – that resulted from the debt crisis during the 1980s. At the time, countries across the region responded to the crisis by slashing public expenditures and adopting policies aimed at generating fiscal revenue.

Since then, governments have made important strides in modernizing their tax revenue administrations, simplifying tax systems, broadening tax bases, and reducing the number of exceptions and tax incentives (Prichard and Moore 2018; OECD 2016, 25). For example, many countries have expanded their tax systems to include all labor and capital income – including dividends – and introduced minimum taxes based on presumptive taxation along with controls for transfer prices (Tanzi 2008; OECD 2016, 25).

This trend is encouraging, but much remains to be done. Even with these important strides in tax collection, Latin American countries generally collect less than their potential. With a handful of notable exceptions, most countries' tax-to-GDP ratios range between 10 and 20%. As Figure 1.3 shows, this is not only lower than what most OECD countries collect, but also below the expected ratio for middle-income countries. The majority of the region's countries are a full five percentage points below their expected levels of taxation.

Yet, in spite of Latin America's generally low levels of taxation, there is variation across the region in terms of revenue generation. Whereas

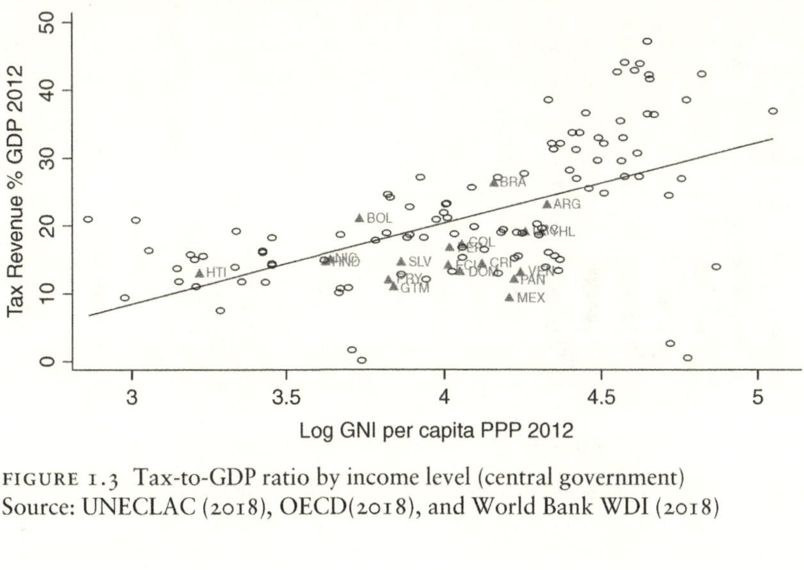

FIGURE 1.3 Tax-to-GDP ratio by income level (central government)
Source: UNECLAC (2018), OECD(2018), and World Bank WDI (2018)

Guatemala and Mexico record extremely low levels of fiscal extraction with tax-to-GDP ratios of around 11%, Argentina and Brazil boast ratios comparable to those of many development nations – more than 30%. Other countries, including Bolivia, Honduras, Nicaragua, and Uruguay, have managed to collect tax ratios generally in line with expectations.

Inequality

In addition to the deficit in tax collection, another pending assignment is to generate tax systems that contribute meaningfully to addressing disparities in the region with the worst income inequality in the world. As Figure 1.4 shows, the wealthiest 10% of the income distribution concentrates 30% of income on average across countries in the region; by comparison, the average for the OECD is 24% of income. This concentration ranges from 40% of income in Brazil and 38% in Guatemala, on the higher end of the spectrum, to 20% in Uruguay and 23% in Venezuela, at the lower end. Conversely, the bottom 40% of the income distribution takes home 24% in Uruguay and 21% in Venezuela, compared to 15% in Brazil and 14% in Guatemala.

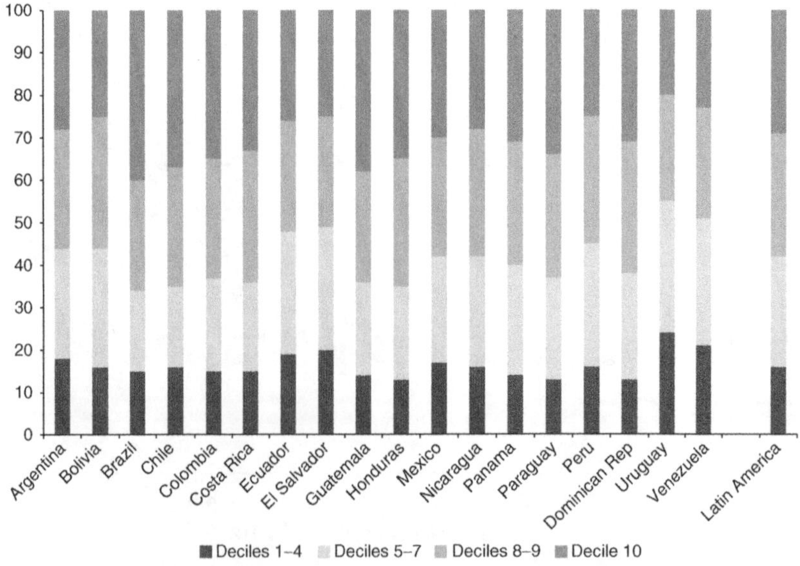

FIGURE 1.4 Latin America income share by decile group (%)
Source: Hanni et al. 2015, with data from ECLAC. Data ca. 2012

The region's inequality is problematic because, beyond moral considerations, inequality has negative consequences on growth and development. As Mahon Jr., Bergman, and Arnson (2015, 1) have pointed out, "Over the course of more than a generation of vibrant and mostly uninterrupted electoral democracy, Latin American governments have done almost nothing about the fact that the region suffers from the highest levels of inequality, on average, in the world."

In particular, there are two parts to the problem. First, fiscal redistribution is ineffective in Latin America in part because of the low levels of tax collection discussed earlier (Goñi et al. 2011, 1559). Second, most of the redistribution that does take place is conducted through transfers – particularly those in kind – rather than through taxes. The little that has been done corresponds mostly with efforts on the spending side, such as those related to conditional cash transfer programs – as with Brazil's Bolsa Família or Mexico's Progresa – or universal noncontributory pensions – as with Bolivia's Renta Dignidad or Mexico's Pensión Universal. On the taxation side, however, the region has been characterized by generally regressive tax systems that contribute little to addressing inequality and are a far cry from the highly redistributive European and even US systems (Mahon, Jr. 2012).

As Figure 1.5 shows, Latin American countries underperform considerably compared to their European counterparts – whose levels of market income inequality (46 versus 50) are not very different – regarding the redistributive effect of taxes. Although transfers play a more significant role in reducing inequality than taxes in some countries, the ability to carry out transfers hinges on the ability to collect taxes. Further, the effect of direct taxation in reducing inequality can be significant, as the European experience shows, but its potential has been unrealized in Latin America. Whereas in Europe income inequality measured as the Gini coefficient decreases by 5 points – from a gross income coefficient of 0.36 (after transfers) to a disposable income (after direct taxes) coefficient of 0.31, in Latin America the reduction amounts to one point – from 0.48 to 0.47. Although there is some variation across the region, from Mexico's reduction of 2.5 points at the high end to Paraguay's 0.3 points, the entire region stands to increase substantially the contribution of direct taxes to ameliorate inequality.

Clearly, there is a lot of room for improvement in leveraging tax collection to address inequality the way other countries do. Although the goal of increasing revenue has historically been pursued through indirect rather than direct taxes, there is increasing awareness that direct taxes can contribute to both increasing revenue and decreasing inequality.

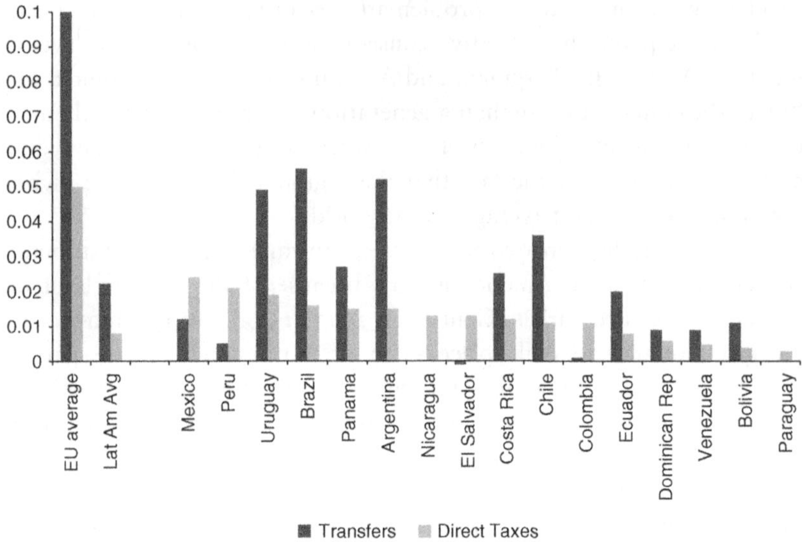

FIGURE 1.5 Change in inequality measured as Gini coefficient, *ca.* 2011
NB: Transfers correspond to changes from market income to gross income due to transfers and pensions. Direct taxes reflect changes from gross income to disposable income after direct taxes.
Sources: Data for Latin America from Hanni et al. 2015; Data for the European Union from Goñi et al. 2011

Indirect taxes have been considered a reasonable path to fiscal extraction in places where state capacity is low because they are comparatively easier to collect than direct taxes. They also have the advantage of not discouraging economic activity by reducing disposable income. Following this logic, reforms between the 1960s and early 1990s relied heavily on indirect taxes – first to fund rampant government spending and later to compensate for the foregone revenue from trade liberalization and the elimination of tariffs in the transition from an import-substitution development model to a free-market oriented one (Lora 2012; Mahon Jr. et al. 2015, 3).[4] Further, between the 1990s and mid-2000s taxes on income were simplified – under the argument that their progressivity discouraged economic activity in the form of labor supply and investment (Cornia et al. 2014, 295).

[4] For example, Brazil and Uruguay were early movers introducing the VAT in 1967 and 1968, respectively (Tanzi 2008).

As Figure 1.6 shows, on average, the vast majority of the gains in extraction during the 1990s took place due to indirect taxes – about 90% of total gains – with less than 10% of gains corresponding to taxes on income and profits (OECD 2016, 26). Today, Latin American levels of VAT collection are comparable to those of the OECD at about 7% of GDP (Gómez et al. 2014, 18).

However, indirect taxes tend to be regressive and therefore do little to address inequality. In fact, they make it worse. In Latin America, for example, after consumption taxes are subtracted from disposable income the Gini coefficient worsens by one point (Goñi et al. 2011, 1560). Consequently, beginning in the mid-2000s, some tax reforms have sought to pay attention to redistributive considerations, as in Uruguay in 2006 (Rius 2015), Mexico in 2013 (Romero 2015), Chile in 2014 (Fairfield 2015b), and Colombia in 2014 (Flores-Macías 2015). As Figure 1.6 shows, the gains have been considerably more balanced between 2000 and 2014, with gains on taxes on income and profits greater than those of VAT.

Still, in spite of these gains, the importance of income taxes in Latin America is considerably smaller than in other parts of the world. Whereas in developed economies in Europe and the United States income taxes are the largest contribution to tax revenue, indirect taxes are the main

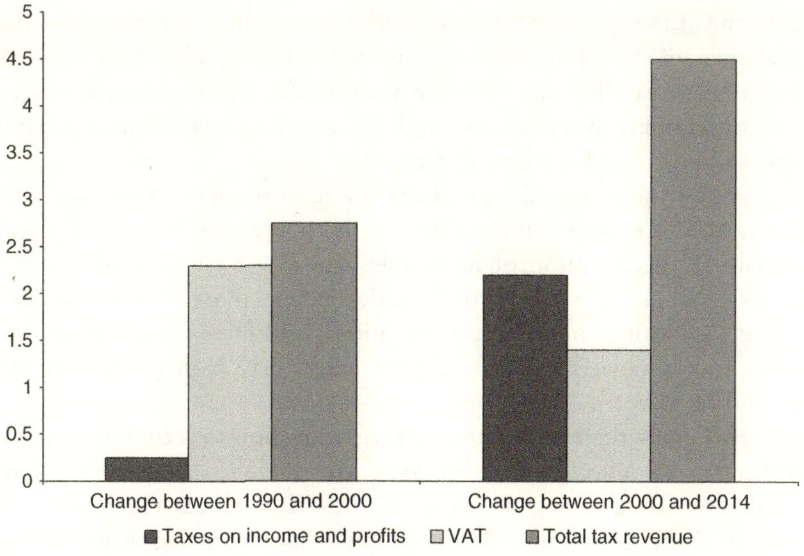

FIGURE 1.6 Change in total tax revenue (% of GDP)
Source: OECD 2016 ch. 1, fig. 1.3

generators of tax revenue in Latin America. Taxes on income and profits represent 12% of GDP on average for OECD countries – excluding Chile and Mexico – but only 6% in Latin America. Conversely, consumption taxes represent about 11% of GDP on average in both the OECD and Latin America (OECD 2016). In other words, whereas income taxes represented 27.8%, on average, of all tax revenue in Latin America, consumption taxes accounted for close to half (43%) (OECD 2016). While there is variation in personal income tax collection in Latin America – from Bolivia (0.20% of GDP) and Guatemala (0.5) at the low end of the spectrum, to Uruguay (3.4) and Brazil (3.6) at the high end (Mahon Jr. et al. 2015, 8) – the regional average lags behind Eastern Europe, Africa, and Asia, so there is ample room for the personal income tax to play a larger role.

BRINGING POLITICS BACK IN TO CONTRIBUTE TO REFORMS

The gloomy fiscal outlook for the region in the wake of the bust of the commodity bonanza has made addressing Latin America's pending fiscal assignments even more pressing. International organizations and scholars have called for the adoption of so-called second-generation reforms (Naím 1994; UN Economic Commission for Latin America 2014) – those aimed at addressing pending issues after the period of structural adjustment that preceded the commodity boom. In order to address the challenges of increasing extraction and reducing inequality, these reforms seek to increase efficiency, promote horizontal and vertical equity, reduce evasion, simplify the tax system, and eliminate loopholes (Gómez Sabaíni and Morán 2013; Ter-Minassian 2012).

Some of the technical ingredients for reform appear fairly straightforward. For example, if the objective is to strengthen countercyclical measures, the adoption of fiscal rules and the formation of autonomous fiscal councils that provide independent, more objective assessments of existing conditions, assumptions, and forecasts can go a long way. If the objective is to address inequality, higher progressivity should be adopted.

Other times, there is no agreement regarding how to accomplish a goal. In the case of collecting more in taxes, for example, the debate between those advocating raising marginal tax rates (Krugman 2012; Institute on Taxation and Economic Policy 2012) and those reducing them (Moore 2014) – i.e., whether there is any truth to the Laffer curve and where the inflection point might lie – remains unresolved.

Even when prescriptions are shared widely, successful implementation is easier said than done. As the literature on economic reforms has shown, even the best-designed policies are bound to fail when the political factors necessary for implementation are neglected (Haggard and Webb 1994; Haggard and Kaufman 1995). Compared to other economic reforms, research on the political determinants of fiscal extraction has taken a back seat, and important questions remain far from being resolved. At the most general level, for example, why and how are reforms successfully undertaken in some countries but not others? What is the role of factors such as public opinion, democratic institutions, natural resources, interest groups, ideology, and state capacity in hindering or facilitating fiscal extraction? Although recent efforts to address these issues in the Latin American context are encouraging (e.g., Arce and Wibbels 2003; Castañeda 2017; Fairfield 2015a; Fairfield and Garay 2017; Focanti et al. 2013; Mahon Jr. et al. 2015; Ondetti 2017; 2015; Sánchez 2011; Schneider 2012), many of these topics are only beginning to receive the attention they deserve. To be sure, many of the claims about the political factors affecting taxation still await a first evaluation or a systematic discussion in the Latin American context.

The lack of understanding of these topics has impaired our ability to improve tax systems. This does not mean that tax reforms do not take place in the region. Quite the opposite: in many countries they take place fairly often, as Hallerberg and Scartascini (Chapter 6 in this volume) show. In places such as Colombia or Mexico, they might even take place every handful of years. However, without knowledge of the political factors that might be conducive to reform, reforms often end up being fairly cosmetic because of the difficulty of overcoming political obstacles. In spite of the frequency of reforms, Mexico's tax intake as a share of GDP has consistently hovered around 10% of GDP over the last fifty years (Tello and Hernández 2010; Ondetti, Chapter 4 in this volume). Other times, they might even turn out to be detrimental to a reform's original objectives.

Given these impediments, this volume seeks to improve our understanding of the different avenues through which reform may become possible. These include the study of structural aspects – from historical legacies to resource dependence – that have made reforms difficult and are worth taking into account when designing strategies for reform. Other less permanent factors, such as levels of state capacity and compliance, institutional arrangements, and electoral cycles, are also important in shaping strategies for reform and the likelihood for success. Finally, the study of interest groups, business–government relations, and public opinion at the mass level can play a key role in facilitating tax reform.

For example, the expansion of income taxes has tended to face important political obstacles. Although this course of action makes sense in highly unequal societies because of the taxes' progressivity, inequality is also what makes its adoption difficult in practice (Agosín et al. 2008). In countries where wealth tends to be highly concentrated, the taxpayer base tends to be fairly narrow. Governments have to rely on this narrow base for increases in income taxes, but these sectors begrudge having to carry the weight of the fiscal burden. Moreover, the wealthiest sectors are also those best able to avoid additional tax obligations through lobbying or finding loopholes in the tax code (Castañeda 2017; Fairfield, Chapter 7 in this volume; Moore 2013).

The difficulty in expanding income taxes and making them progressive is not new; it has been current for decades, and not because of lack of technical expertise. During the 1950s and 1960s, in the context of the Alliance for Progress, the United States, the Organization of American States, the Inter-American Development Bank, and the United Nations promoted the expansion of income taxes, but governments were reluctant to rely on them meaningfully because of political obstacles and electoral considerations (Tanzi 2008).

More recently, explanations for the low productivity of income taxes have ranged from the high share of informal sector that characterizes Latin American countries – at more than 50% in some countries – to the weakness of tax administrations in collecting revenue that is not withheld at the source (Bergman, Chapter 3 this volume; Tanzi 2008). Indeed, the share of total income that corresponds to nonwage income is fairly high in the region. Wage income is less than 30% in some places – as in Mexico, with 28% – compared to 70% in some industrialized countries (Tanzi 2008, 8). How to tax adequately salaried workers, and especially how to tax the large majority whose income is not withheld at the source, remains a significant challenge.

The animosity toward expanding the tax base and increasing the progressivity of the tax system can be especially strong in resource rich countries. In places where natural resources are available, resource wealth often generates perceptions of wealth among the population, undermining efforts to increase the tax burden because of the expectation that the government will fund its expenditures through taxes on natural resource extraction and royalties, especially if these companies are foreign (Tanzi 2008). The result is that resource-dependent countries tend to engage in procyclical policies, spending in the boom and retracting during the bust.

Electoral politics also makes the adoption of meaningful reforms difficult. Campaign season reduces incentives for incumbents to introduce reforms deemed unpopular among the general population or among financial patrons of political campaigns. The incentive is for incumbents not to formulate any reform initiatives, or, if they do, to formulate them in ways that dilute any real fiscal impact because of fear of retaliation on election day.

Beyond elections, shaping public opinion more generally is another important challenge behind the adoption of reforms. Due to the unpopularity of taxation, convincing people to pay more in taxes is difficult (Mahon Jr. et al. 2015). Additionally, because of the extreme inequality that exists in Latin America, economic elites resent the narrow basis for fiscal extraction and look to incorporate broad sectors of society into sharing the tax burden. Conversely, the general public looks to the wealthy to shoulder more in taxes. Both sectors begrudge being targeted whenever the government looks for additional revenue.

As a result, not only are citizens generally opposed to increases in the tax burden, but many will also go out of their way to circumvent their tax obligations (Prichard 2016). Latin American countries' tax compliance tends to be lower than in other parts of the world (Bergman 2009). Compliance at times has to do with attitudes and practices that persist in society. At other times, compliance is a function of willingness to enforce regulations based on political considerations. Yet others, it is contingent on the state's capacity to enforce such tax laws. It is important to take into account these considerations when devising strategies to make the adoption of reforms feasible and their sustainability possible.

ORGANIZATION OF THE BOOK

This book is intended to address several gaps in the literature on the political economy of taxation in Latin America. In particular, it provides a big-picture perspective of the relationship between taxation and the key actors and forces in Latin America based on topics that generally cut across countries and areas of interest to the entire region. Chapters studying mainly levels of taxation are presented first, followed by those focusing mainly on progressivity in the tax structure, although the emphasis is often shared.

In Chapter 2, Francisco Monaldi studies the determinants of tax policy related to hydrocarbons. It answers the question of why some countries increase the fiscal intake through greater state intervention during commodity booms, while others reduce government control over the industry and turn to the private sector. In particular, it points to the role that certain characteristics of the oil sector – including rents, sunk costs, and the risk profile of a project – along with geological endowments and the price and investment cycles play in determining tax policy in the hydrocarbons sector.

Marcelo Bergman (Chapter 3) focuses on tax compliance in the region and points to a recent paradox. Typically, gains in compliance take place when economies are growing, since taxpayers are less inclined to rely on evasion during good times. However, although Latin America recently enjoyed one of its most prosperous decades since WWII, tax compliance remained fairly stable at mediocre levels. Based on several indirect measures of compliance, this chapter both identifies this pattern and evaluates potential explanations. It suggests that a combination of commodity boom benefits, political variables, and cultural factors account for the lack of improvement of tax compliance rates.

Gabriel Ondetti (Chapter 4) offers insight into the question of why there is so much variation in levels of fiscal extraction across the region. Recognizing that natural resources can only go so far in explaining this variation, he points to the historical legacies of early redistributive attempts as a key factor in understanding why countries have experienced different tax burdens over time. Based on a comparison of Brazil, Chile, and Mexico, he points to early reforms that gave rise to an enduring antistate ideology among key sectors of the economic elites in Chile and Mexico, which was institutionalized in important political organizations and became an impediment to the heavier taxation observed in Brazil.

Aaron Schneider (Chapter 5) focuses on the relationship between taxation and patterns of economic incorporation. Based on a historical overview of the Brazilian case, it shows that the country's ability to extract more in taxes than any other country in the region, and as much as some developed countries, has not always been the case. The chapter suggests that variation over time is due in part to the nature of the interaction between the type of developmental model and federalism. The adoption of different federal arrangements that accommodated the shifting fortunes of rising and falling elite and popular sectors – associated with new patterns of international insertion – explain variation in that country's level of taxation over time.

Mark Hallerberg and Carlos Scartascini (Chapter 6) explore the determinants of tax reforms in the region. In particular, they examine whether the electoral rules that bring legislators to office – determining how "personal" or narrow a constituency elects them – shape the neutrality of reforms. They find that legislatures with rules favoring narrow constituencies favor reforms that compromise the neutrality of the tax system. They also find a diffusion effect: reforms affecting the neutrality in the system are more likely to take place following those adopted by other countries in the region.

Tasha Fairfield's chapter (Chapter 7) also contributes to our understanding of both extracting fiscal revenue and addressing inequality. Contrary to traditional median-voter approaches (Meltzer and Richard 1981; Boix 2003; Acemoglu and Robinson 2006), she finds that economic elites play a central role in the politics of tax policy. Instead, her chapter highlights the role of the business sector's instrumental and structural power as a central component in explaining why economic elites' wealth has been targeted in some countries but not others. Drawing on evidence from experiences in Argentina, Bolivia, and Chile, she finds that efforts at elite taxation are least successful when either instrumental or structural power is strong, especially institutionalized partisan linkages in the former and organizational robustness in the latter.

James Mahon, Jr. (Chapter 8) advances our understanding of how to make tax systems more progressive by exploring the role of property and income taxes in the liberal tradition. Placing experiences in the region in a global and historical perspective, the chapter focuses not only on revenue generation, but also on the control and programmatic orientation of spending. It finds that Latin America's low reliance on property taxes is consistent with a fiscal-contract notion in which a relative weakness in personal income and property taxation corresponds to a similar weakness in policy outcomes.

Juan Bogliaccini and Juan Pablo Luna (Chapter 9) explore preferences on taxation and redistribution in Latin America. Their analysis identifies variation across the region in the degree to which preferences for progressive taxation are consistent with individuals' political ideology, economic well-being, and class. Drawing on survey research from ten Latin American countries, they find that there is strong support for progressive taxation across the region. However, with the exception of Guatemala and Mexico, in most Latin American countries political ideology, perceptions of economic well-being, and class are not determinants of attitudes toward progressive taxation.

The concluding chapter addresses the volume's findings and discusses their potential impact for the region. In particular, it discusses their implications for levels of taxation and the nature of the tax structure. It suggests that several of the factors covered in this volume can play an important role in making the adoption of fiscal reforms more likely and sustainable over time. The Conclusion also discusses the tension between path dependence and the role of ideology, as well as between elites and the public for taxation. Finally, the Conclusion offers potential avenues for future research.

References

Acemoglu, Daron, and James Robinson. 2006. *Economic Origins of Dictatorship and Democracy*. New York: Cambridge University Press

Agosín, Manuel, Alberto Machado, and Aaron Snyder. 2008. "The Struggle for Tax Reform in Central America," in Diego Sánchez-Ancochea and Iwan Morgan (eds.), *Political Economy of the Public Budget in the Americas*, London: Institute for the Study of the Americas.

Arce, Moises and Erik Wibbels. 2003. "Globalization, Taxation, and Burden-Shifting in Latin America," *International Organization* 57 (1): 111–136.

Ardanaz, Martín, Ana Corbacho, Alberto Gonzales, and Nuria Tolsa Caballero. 2015. "Structural Fiscal Balances in Latin America and the Caribbean: New Dataset and Estimations," *IDB Working Paper Series* 579, Washington, DC: Inter-American Development Bank.

BBC. 2016. "India Outpaces China in 2015 Economic Growth," *BBC Online*, February 8: www.bbc.com/news/business-35519671.

Bergman, Marcelo. 2009. *Tax Evasion and the Rule of Law in Latin America*. University Park: Penn State University Press.

Bird, Richard. 2012. "Taxation and Development: What Have We Learned from Fifty Years of Research?" Working Paper 1, International Center for Tax and Development, UK.

Boix, Carles. 2003. *Democracy and Redistribution*. New York: Cambridge University Press.

Brautigam, Deborah, Odd-Helge Fjeldstad, and Mick Moore (eds.). 2008. *Taxation and State-Building in Developing Countries*. New York: Cambridge University Press.

Buchanan, James. 1963. "The Economics of Earmarked Taxes," *Journal of Political Economy* 71 (5): 457–469.

Caceres, Carlos and Bertrand Gruss. 2015. "The Commodity Price Bust: Fiscal and External Implications for Latin America," in International Monetary Fund, in *Regional Economic Outlook: Western Hemisphere*, Washington, DC: IMF: 43–53.

CAF Banco de Desarrollo de América Latina. 2012. *Finanzas públicas para el desarrollo: fortaleciendo la conexión entre ingresos y gastos*. Bogotá: Panamericana Formas e Impresos.

Canavire-Bacarreza, Gustavo, Jorge Martínez-Vázquez, and Violeta Vulovic. 2013. "Taxation and Economic Growth in Latin America," *IDB Working Paper Series* 431, Washington, DC: Inter-American Development Bank.

Castañeda, Néstor. 2017. "Business Coordination and Tax Politics," *Political Studies* 65 (1): 122–143.

Centro de Estudios Sociales y de Opinión Pública. 2013. *Encuesta telefónica acerca de la reforma hacendaria.* Mexico: CESOP.

Cornia, Giovanni Andrea, Juan Carlos Gómez-Sabaíni, and Bruno Martorano. 2014. "Tax Policy and Income Distribution during the Last Decade," in Giovanni Andrea Cornia (ed.), *Falling Inequality in Latin America: Policy Changes and Lessons.* Oxford: Oxford University Press, 295–317.

Council of Foreign Relations. 2014. "Mexico's Oil and Taxes," CFR Latin America's Moment Blog: www.cfr.org/blog/mexicos-oil-and-taxes.

De Ferranti, David, Guillermo Perry, Francisco Ferreira, and Michael Walton. 2004. *Inequality in Latin America: Breaking with History?* Washington, DC: The World Bank.

Evans, Peter. 1995. *Embedded Autonomy: States and Industrial Transformation.* Princeton: Princeton University Press.

Fairfield, Tasha. 2015a. *Private Wealth and Public Revenue: Business Power and Tax Politics in Latin America.* New York: Cambridge University Press.

2015b. "The Political Economy of Progressive Tax Reform in Chile," in Mahon Jr., Bergman, and Arnson (eds.), *The Political Economy of Progressive Tax Reforms in Latin America,* Washington, DC: Woodrow Wilson Center, 30–56.

Fairfield, Tasha and Candaleria Garay. 2017. "Redistribution under the Right in Latin America: Electoral Competition and Organized Actors in Policy Making," *Comparative Political Studies* 50 (14): 1871–1906.

Flores-Macías, Gustavo. 2015. "The Political Economy of Colombia's 2012 and 2014 Fiscal Reforms," in Mahon Jr., Bergman, and Arnson (eds.), *The Political Economy of Progressive Tax Reforms in Latin America.* Washington, DC: Woodrow Wilson Center, 101–126.

2016. "Mexico's Stalled Reforms," *Journal of Democracy* 27 (2): 66–78

2018. "Building Support for Taxation in Developing Countries: Experimental Evidence from Mexico," *World Development* 105: 13–24.

Focanti, Diego, Mark Hallerberg, and Carlos Scartascini. 2013. "Tax reforms in Latin America in an era of democracy," *IDB Working Paper Series* 457, Washington, DC: Inter-American Development Bank.

Fuentes Knight, Juan Alberto. 2012. *Rendición de Cuentas.* Guatemala: F&G Editores.

Fundación Jaime Guzmán. 2011. *Encuesta sobre la reforma tributaria: Agosto 2011.* Chile: FJG.

Goetz, Charles. 1968. "Earmarked Taxes and Majority Rule Budgetary Processes," *American Economic Review* 58 (March): 128–136.

Gómez Sabaíni, Juan Carlos and Dalmiro Morán. 2013. *Política tributaria en America Latina: Agenda para una segunda generación de reformas.* Comisión Económica Para América Latina. Chile: Naciones Unidas.

Goñi, Edwin, Humberto López, and Luis Servén. 2011. "Fiscal Redistribution and Income Inequality in Latin America," *World Development* 39 (9): 1564–1566.

Graham, Dave. 2017. "Mexico to Slow Pace of Budget Cuts in 2018: Finance Minister," *Reuters*, June 20.

Haggard, Stephan and Robert Kaufman. 1995. *The Political Economy of Democratic Transitions*. Princeton: Princeton University Press.

Haggard, Stephan and Steven Webb (eds.). 1994. *Voting for Reform*. New York: Oxford University Press.

Hanni, Michael, Ricardo Mdartner, and Andrea Podestá. 2015. "The Redistributive Potential of Taxation in Latin America," *CEPAL Review* 116 (August): 7–26.

Hsu, Sara. 2017. "China's GDP Numbers: Can We Trust the Data?" Forbes, Jan 23.

Inter-American Development Bank. 2013. *More than Revenue: Taxation as a Development Tool*. Washington, DC: IADB.

IMF. 2015. *Fiscal Policy in Latin America: Lessons and Legacies of the Global Financial Crisis*. Washington, DC: IMF.

Institute on Taxation and Economic Policy. 2012. "*High Rate Income Tax Rates Are Outperforming No-Tax States*," ITEP: Washington, DC, February: https://itep.org/wp-content/uploads/junkeconomics.pdf.

Krugman, Paul. 2012. "More Laffering," New York Times, May 25.

Lajous, Adrián. 2014. *Mexican Energy Reform*, Center on Global Energy Policy, New York: Columbia University: https://energypolicy.columbia.edu/sites/default/files/CGEP_Adrian%20Lajous_Mexican%20Energy%20Reform_Final.pdf.

Lora, Eduardo. 2012. "Structural Reforms in Latin America: What Has Been Reformed and How to Measure It." IADB Working Paper 346. Washington, DC: Inter-American Development Bank.

Magnier, Mark. 2016. "China's Economic Growth in 2015 Is the Slowest in 25 Years," *Wall Street Journal*, January 19.

Mahon, Jr., James. 2012. "Tax Incidence and Tax Reforms in Latin America," Woodrow Wilson Center Update on the Americas, November: www.wilsoncenter.org/sites/default/files/WWC_LAP_MahonReport.pdf.

Mahon, Jr., James, Marcelo Bergman, and Cynthia Arnson. 2015. "The Political Economy of Progressive Tax Reform in Latin America: Comparative Context and Policy Debates," in Mahon Jr., Bergman, and Arnson (eds.), *The Political Economy of Progressive Tax Reforms in Latin America*, Washington, DC: Woodrow Wilson Center, 1–29.

Meltzer, Allan and Scott Richard. 1981. "A Rational Theory of the Size of Government," *Journal of Political Economy* 89, 5 (October): 914–927.

Monaldi, Francisco. 2014. *Is Resource Nationalism Fading in Latin America? The Case of the Oil Industry*, Baker Institute Issue Brief, September 3.

Moore, Mick. 2013. "Obstacles to Increasing Tax Revenue in Low Income Countries," ICTD Working Paper 15, International Center for Tax and Development.

Moore, Stephen. 2014. "The Laffer Curve Turns 40: The Legacy of a Controversial Idea," *Washington Post*, December 26.

Naím, Moises. 1994. "Latin America: The Second Stage of Reforms," *Journal of Democracy* 5 (4): 32–48.

OECD. 2016. *Revenue Statistics in Latin America and the Caribbean 2016*. Paris: OECD.

Ondetti, Gabriel. 2015. "The Roots of Brazil's Heavy Taxation," *Journal of Latin American Studies* 47 (4): 749–779.

2017. "The Power of Preferences: Economic Elites and Light Taxation in Mexico," *Revista Mexicana de Ciencias Políticas y Sociales* 62 (231): 47–76.

Organization of Economic Cooperation and Development. 2018. Revenue Statistics (Online Resource): www.oecd.org/tax/tax-policy/revenue-statistics-2522770x.htm

Paler, Laura. 2013. "Keeping the Public Purse: An Experiment in Windfalls, Taxes, and the Incentives to Restrain Government," *American Political Science Review* 107 (4): 706–725

Paraguassu, Lisandra and Maria Carolina Marcello. 2017. "Brazil Senate Leader sees 30 Billion – 35 Billion Reais Spending Freeze," *Reuters*, March 21.

Paraskova, Tsvetana. 2018. "The Revival of Mexico's Oil Industry," *Oilprice.com*, January 25.

Prichard, Wilson. 2016. "Reassessing Tax and Development Research: A New Dataset, New Findings, and Lessons for Research," *World Development* 80 (4): 48–60.

Prichard, Wilson and Mick Moore. 2018. "Tax Reform for Low-Income Countries: Five Ideas for Simplifying Tax Systems to Fit Local Realities," Summary Brief 17, International Center for Tax and Development.

Riffkin, Rebecca. 2014. "More Than Half of Americans Say Federal Taxes Too High," Gallup Online, April 14. Available at www.gallup.com/poll/168500/half-americans-say-federal-taxes-high.aspx

Rius, Andrés. 2015. "The Uruguayan Tax Reform of 2006: Why Didn't It Fail?" in Mahon Jr., Bergman, and Arnson (eds.), *The Political Economy of Progressive Tax Reforms in Latin America*, Washington, DC: Woodrow Wilson Center, 64–100.

Romero, Vidal. 2015. "The Political Economy of Progressive Tax Reforms in Mexico," in Mahon Jr., Bergman, and Arnson (eds.), *The Political Economy of Progressive Tax Reforms in Latin America*, Washington, DC: Woodrow Wilson Center, 161–188.

Santos de Souza, Saulo. 2013. "The Political Economy of Tax Reform in Latin America: A Critical Review," *Woodrow Wilson Center Update on the Americas*, February.

Sánchez, Omar. 2011. *Mobilizing Resources in Latin America: the Political Economy of Tax Reform in Chile and Argentina*. New York: Palgrave Macmillan.

Schipani, Andrés. 2015. "Oil fall shuts Colombia's 'Door to Paradise,'" *Financial Times*, August 7.

Schneider, Aaron. 2012. *State-Building and Tax Regimes in Central America*. New York: Cambridge University Press.

Tanzi, Vito. 2008. "Introduction," in Luigi Bernardi, Alberto Barreix, Anna Marenzi, and Paola Profeta (eds.), *Tax Systems and Tax Reforms in Latin America*. New York: Routledge: 1–16.

Ter-Minassian, Teresa. 2012. "More than Revenue: Main Challenges for Taxation in Latin America and the Caribbean," *IDB Policy Brief* 175, Washington, DC: Inter-American Development Bank.

Tello, Carlos and Domingo Hernández. 2010. "Sobre la Reforma Tributaria en México," *Economía* 7 (21): 37–56.

Tilly, Charles. 2009. "Foreword," in Isaac William Martin, Ajay K. Mehrotra, and Monica Prasad (eds.), *The New Fiscal Sociology: Taxation in Comparative and Historical Perspective*, New York: Cambridge University Press, xi–xiv.

Times of India. 2017. "India's GDP Growth to Fall at 7.1% in 2016–17, Estimates Government," January 7.

UN Economic Commission for Latin America. 2014. *Tax Policy in Latin America: Assessments and Guidelines for a Second Generation of Reforms*. Chile: CEPAL.

UN Economic Commission for Latin America and the Caribbean (UNECLAC). 2018. CEPALSTAT (Online Resource): http://estadisticas.cepal.org/cepalstat/portada.html?idioma=english

Wagner Faegri, Cristina and Carol Wise. 2011. "Economic and Fiscal Policy in Latin America," Latin American *Research Review* 46 (1): 240–250.

Willis, Andrew. 2015. "Colombia Oil Target Seen Slumping below Target as Wells Drop," *Bloomberg Online*, November 10.

World Bank. 2016. *The Commodity Cycle in Latin America: Mirages and Dilemmas*, Washington, DC: The World Bank.

2018. *World Development Indicators* (Online Resource): https://data.worldbank.org

Zhang, Hongrui. 2016. "Gauging Latin America's Dependence on Commodities," *BTMU Focus Latin America*, January 5.

Zuckman, Gabriel. 2015. *The Hidden Wealth of Nations*. Chicago: University of Chicago Press.

2

The Political Economy of Oil Taxation in Latin America

Policy Volatility and Untapped Potential

Francisco J. Monaldi

In 2013–2015 Mexico opened up its oil industry to private investment, following seventy-five years of exclusive state control. The minimum government-take in the new private contracts is significantly lower than the one paid by PEMEX. Other Latin American governments, including Argentina, Brazil, Colombia, Ecuador, and even Venezuela, covering all political tendencies, are also enthusiastically courting foreign investment in oil, offering increasingly attractive fiscal conditions, with lower government-take. This trend would seem to proclaim a new liberalization cycle in the industry. Although the trend started even before the oil price collapse, it was clearly strengthened by the fall in oil prices in 2014.

In contrast, during the previous decade, under an oil price boom, the region had witnessed a resource nationalism cycle. Most countries in the region significantly increased the government-take on hydrocarbons and the government control over the industry. Still, there were notable exceptions, such as Colombia and Peru, and to some extent Brazil. What are the determinants of these swings in oil policy, and in particular in hydrocarbon taxation policy? What explains policy variation among countries? This chapter argues that structural factors, such as the characteristics of the oil sector (rents, sunk costs, risk profile of projects), the countries' geological endowments, and price and investment cycles are key determinants of oil taxation policy. These factors interact with the broader institutional environment of a country to define oil policy. Ideology usually plays a role in how policy change is enacted, particularly regarding the degree of government control, but the general direction of oil taxation policy is largely determined by the incentives provided by structural factors and market conditions.

There are many examples in which structural conditions trumped ideology. In the 1950s, Juan Domingo Perón, the populist leader of Argentina, opened the oil sector in attractive terms to international companies. The same can be said of the leftist-Peronist Cristina Kirchner, after the nationalization of the energy company YPF in 2012. The new oil law in 2014 included significant fiscal benefits for private investors, and she invited Chevron in. Similarly, despite his fiery rhetoric, Hugo Chávez did not tighten fiscal conditions in Venezuela until 2005, six years after he came to power. Nicolás Maduro, his heir, has offered a variety of fiscal incentives to foreign companies. Enrique Peña Nieto in Mexico implemented the oil opening that his party, the PRI, which nationalized the oil sector in 1938, did not allow the previous president to implement. In Ecuador, the leftist Lenín Moreno is opening the oil sector with production sharing contracts, reversing his same-party predecessor's dramatic government-take hikes.

To understand the phenomenon, let's take a closer look at recent history. As highlighted in the Introduction to this volume, the first decade of this century witnessed one of the largest resource windfalls for commodity exporters. Latin American countries benefited tremendously from the large and persistent increase in commodity prices. The price of oil rose from a low of around $10 in 1998 to more than $100 per barrel ten years later, generating a revenue boom for the region's net exporters of hydrocarbons: Venezuela, Mexico, Ecuador, Colombia, Bolivia, and even Argentina, a declining net exporter. It also significantly benefited Brazil's oil industry, which went from third-largest to largest producer, but is still not a relevant net exporter.

As in the 1970s, the oil boom was accompanied by a wave of resource nationalism – government encroachment on the property rights of foreign investors. In the period 2002–2012, taxes were significantly increased, contracts forcefully renegotiated, and foreign investors outright nationalized. Four out of the five hydrocarbon exporters with foreign investment in oil and gas – Venezuela, Bolivia, Ecuador, and Argentina – decided to nationalize their resources in this period; Mexico, until recently the largest oil producer in the region, maintained its oil industry as a state monopoly until 2013.

As recently as 2012, the Argentine government renationalized YPF, the formerly privatized national oil company, closing a decade of eroding conditions for oil investors in the region. There were some exceptions.

Brazil, Colombia, and Peru, for instance, did not follow the same expropriation pattern. Still, Latin America was the leading example of a global phenomenon of increased taxation, state intervention, and nationalization. Outside the region, Russia was the most notable example, but many others could be found throughout the world. The government-take on profits increased in most oil exporting countries, even in developed countries such as Canada and the United Kingdom. In fact, even Brazil, a model of long-term energy policy in the region, showed clear symptoms of resource nationalism.

In contrast, during the last few years we have witnessed a strong countercurrent of government efforts to attract foreign oil investment to the region. Venezuela, the leader of the nationalizing movement, announced in 2009 that it would auction new areas for joint ventures with foreign companies in extra-heavy oil projects. This took place only two years after completion of the nationalization process, initiated in 2005. Since then, PDVSA, the Venezuelan national oil company, signed seven major extra-heavy oil joint-venture projects, with foreign partners, including Chevron, CNPC, ENI, Repsol, and Rosneft. These projects would require more than US$60 billion in investment. When completed, they would yield more than one million barrels a day in production. PDVSA also pursued other smaller partnerships with foreign companies in conventional oil production, and a major offshore natural gas project with Repsol and ENI. Even though Venezuela did offer lower government-take for the new projects, it was still very high and very little investment actually materialized. As a result, after the decline in oil prices the government became more flexible. Thus, despite the radical leftist discourse of the Venezuelan government, it has been actively courting foreign investors.

Undoubtedly, the most important new development in the region's oil industry is the opening of the Mexican hydrocarbon sector to foreign investment. After more than seven decades of state monopoly, the administration of President Enrique Peña Nieto – leader of the PRI, the party that nationalized the sector in 1938 – promoted a path-breaking constitutional reform to make this opening possible. Thus, the last stronghold of state ownership in the region moved to allow the private sector to play a significant role in the exploitation of oil and gas resources. In the summer of 2015, the first exploration and production blocks were awarded to private operators (Flores-Macías 2016). Since then, there have been four very successful bidding rounds with participation from companies from around the world.

Even Argentina, after it renationalized in 2012, quickly announced that it wanted to attract foreign investors to develop its recently discovered nonconventional shale resources in the Vaca Muerta basin. The country signed a joint-venture agreement with Chevron to develop these sites and reached a settlement with Repsol, the expropriated shareholder of YPF (Vásquez 2016). Argentina also passed a new, much more liberal oil and gas law in 2014, reducing the government-take in oil and gas projects and offering higher domestic prices. Similarly, after the expropriation of oil contracts, Ecuador has recently announced new profit-sharing contracts. Bolivia has also announced reduced royalties for new projects to attract foreign partners in natural gas exploitation. Meanwhile, Brazil, Colombia, Peru, and Guatemala keep regularly auctioning oil blocks for exploration. In fact, this is arguably one of the most liberal periods in the history of the oil industry in the region, particularly measured by the amount of reserves accessible to foreign operators. So, is resource nationalism fading? It is important to note that oil liberalization does not always imply tax reductions, nor do tax increases always imply nationalization or expropriation, but they tend to go hand in hand.

One might be tempted to attribute the previous wave of resource nationalism largely to the more general phenomenon of the resurgence of the left in Latin America. After all, the nationalizers – Hugo Chávez of Venezuela, Evo Morales of Bolivia, Rafael Correa of Ecuador, and Cristina Fernández de Kirchner of Argentina – were leaders of the more radical variety of the left-wing movement in the region (Weyland et al. 2010). In contrast, countries that did not expropriate or moved in the opposite direction – such as Brazil, Colombia, and Peru, or more recently Mexico – have had either moderate left or center-right governments in power. However, to understand the dynamic of resource nationalism it is important to focus on the deeper determinants of the historical cycles of private opening and expropriation. These are the incentives faced by political leaders under different scenarios of international prices, stages of the investment cycle, production and reserve tendencies, and size of net exports (imports).

Expropriation in its different forms, including significant tax increases, tends to occur when prices rise substantially – that is, when its benefits increase significantly for the government. This has been the tendency throughout the developing world. Expropriation is also more likely to occur in an environment of high and increasing reserves and production, and when the country becomes a large net exporter. Thus, after a cycle of significant and successful private investment, the probability of expropriation paradoxically increases. Given the amounts of the oil rents, which can be as high as 90% of revenues, the fiscal benefits can be politically irresistible. Most relevant petroleum exporters are fiscally reliant on oil. Oil revenues represent more than 30% of total government revenue. Generally in oil projects, companies have to invest a lot of money in exploratory wells and field development infrastructure, and that infrastructure can generate revenues for a long period of time, while the costs of operation are a minor part of the investment. Thus, in this so-called high-sunk-cost sector, the effects of a decline in investment can take years to lead to the consequent decline in production. Therefore, government leaders with short-term horizons may be tempted to obtain high current benefits while deferring costs, leaving future leaders to bear the political consequences of declining production and revenues (Flores-Macías 2010; 2012).

This chapter proceeds as follows. Section 2 develops a theoretical framework to understand the key characteristics of the oil sector that influence its peculiar political economy, and briefly describes how rents are captured by states and its political-economy implications. Section 3 offers a general discussion of the evolution of oil taxation in Latin America and some more detailed case studies. Section 4 provides concluding remarks.

A PRIMER ON THE POLITICAL ECONOMY OF OIL TAXATION

Understanding the political economy of oil taxation in a specific country case requires analyzing: the particular characteristics of the oil industry that influence the way it is taxed and controlled by the state; the basic economics of the oil sector (the oil market environment, the investment risks, the stage in the investment cycle, and the oil fiscal dependency among other key variables); the geological endowment of the country, and its potential resources, reserves, production, and exporting capacity in relation to its economy and population; and the institutional framework of the country and the sector, specifically the organization of the sector and the fiscal and contractual regime to capture the rents. The focus of this chapter is on the intrinsic characteristics of the oil sector that promote cycles of tax liberalization and hardening in the context of Latin America and the oil market evolution during the last two decades.

Oil Sector Characteristics, Resource Nationalism, and Taxation

The oil sector has some peculiar characteristics that in some circumstances generate powerful incentives for resource nationalism and particularly for increasing the government-take, reneging on the fiscal "deal" made with investors (Klein et al. 1978; Williamson 1996). I define resource nationalism broadly as the drive to increase the "state-take" on oil revenues and to obtain more state control over the sector. I focus here on the first part of the definition, but this is often difficult to separate from the second part. One crucial aspect of resource nationalism is investment expropriation, meaning any significant change in the operator's deal that does not allow them to recover their investments. This definition includes discriminatory changes in taxation and regulations that severely affect the cash flow kept by the investor (e.g., local content rules and domestic energy subsidies).

The key characteristics of the oil sector that impact resource nationalism are: 1) the significant rents in oil extraction which are variable and volatile; 2) the high proportion of sunk costs in most oil investments; 3) the significant variation in risk across projects and stages of investment; 4) the concentration of significant oil reserves in developing countries with weak institutions and ineffective taxation regimes; and 5) the widespread consumption of oil products that represent a relevant part of a household's expenditures.

Oil extraction is different from other industries in that it generates very significant ***rents***, i.e. profits in excess of those which make it attractive to invest in the long run – in other words, returns above the opportunity cost of the labor and capital invested. Thus, by definition the state can capture all rents and an investor would still be attracted to invest in the long run. As an example, many oil fields in Latin America and elsewhere have costs of production lower than $20 per barrel, while the price of a barrel of oil was well above $100 until 2014. However, rents are very volatile, largely because the price of oil is highly volatile with a coefficient of variation of more than 0.8, and production costs can also change significantly. In addition, rents can vary considerably between projects depending on the characteristics of the reservoir, its location, the quality of oil, etc. There are projects which have break-evens below $10 (e.g., in Kuwait and Saudi Arabia) and projects in which they are above $100 (e.g., in Kazakhstan and Canada) currently in production. The volatility and variability of rents pose a challenge for the government to capture them in different price and profitability scenarios.

Oil extraction projects are generally characterized by ***high sunk costs***, meaning assets that once deployed cannot be used for a different purpose or have very low value outside of the project. So the opportunity cost ex-post, after investment is immobilized, is significantly lower than ex-ante, when there were many uses for the capital. The implication is that once these assets are deployed, the government can change the deal and the investor will have incentives to continue operating as long as it covers operational costs and nonsunk investments, even though it may never recover the sunken assets. As an example, the field of Kashagan in Kazakhstan has required more than $55 billion in initial investments, mostly sunk, for a planned production of about 400,000 barrels per day in the first phase. This implies a break-even cost of more than $100, but the estimated operational cost would be $8 per barrel, so if the government lets the operator keep $15 per barrel it would have incentives to operate, even though it is incurring in massive losses over the initial investment. Governments thus have incentives to offer attractive deals to get the investments, but once the investment is in place, they have incentives to renege on the deal and expropriate the project. This is particularly problematic since oil projects often take many years to develop, and decades to recover the investment.

The ***geological and economic risk*** of oil and gas projects differs significantly among projects and between the different stages of the project's life. In highly prospective areas with well-known geology and well-developed infrastructure, the risks are much lower than in unexplored areas with access difficulties. Uncertainty is high in the exploration phase; in some areas, more than seven in ten exploratory wells do not find commercial hydrocarbons. Once discovered, the development phase in a new area could also entail risking large capital investments with some significant uncertainty. However, during the exploitation phase of an already well-known field, the risks decline dramatically. Again, the evolving risk generates incentives for contract renegotiation and expropriation. Governments have incentives to offer very attractive conditions for exploration to compensate the risk, but once there is a major discovery there are powerful incentives to renegotiate. The difference in value of the project before winning the geological lottery and after can be very large: a lottery ticket has very little value before it wins and zero value if it does not win anything, but if it got the prize it is a different story.

In addition to geological and price risk, oil exploitation often has significant fiscal, regulatory, and political risks. A significant proportion of oil resources are located in developing countries with weak institutions.

Therefore, domestic institutions are often not strong enough to protect the property rights of investors when the rulers have strong incentives to renege on deals, as is often the case in the oil industry for the reasons mentioned above. In fact, historically, foreign investment in oil was protected largely by external mechanisms rather than domestic courts.

Finally, oil products are politically salient because they are needed for transportation, heating, and cooking, representing a relevant share of household consumption. As a result, there are incentives for governments to force producers to sell in the domestic market below the international price. This could constitute a form of revenue expropriation that is different from tax increases.

The Cycles of Investment and Expropriation: Structural and Institutional Sources

The aforementioned characteristics of the oil sector generate the tendency for "fiscal expropriation cycles." Governments have incentives to attract investments in oil and gas, particularly in order to reap the future fiscal benefits, but once investments are sunk, they have incentives to renege on the original agreement and capture a larger share of the revenues. The short-term benefits of expropriation can be high, while its costs, in terms of production decline and foregone revenues, are often paid in the distant future. The mismatch between the political incentives, with short-term horizons, and the investment incentives, with long-term horizons, is a source of significant conflict (Manzano and Monaldi 2008).

The timing of expropriation is highly influenced by the evolution of incentives. When an oil basin has not been developed, and the geology is unknown, expropriation is unlikely. However, after a significant cycle of investment has been completed, adding substantial reserves and production, and the risks have significantly declined, the conditions are ripe for expropriation. Similarly, when oil prices go significantly up, and the fiscal and contractual regimes are not able to sufficiently capture the additional rents, there are strong incentives to expropriate. The history of the oil industry in Latin America, other developing regions, and even in some advanced economies, is full of examples during price booms (Parra 2004). As will be shown in Table 2.2, insufficiently progressive regimes are major sources of oil taxation volatility.

The likelihood of expropriation also varies with other structural characteristics. Countries that are significant net exporters, and hence more fiscally dependent on oil, tend to view the oil sector largely as a source of fiscal rents and are thus more likely to be resource nationalists. Depending on the time horizon of rulers, rent maximization could be short sighted or have a more long-term perspective. Net importers are usually more focused on incentivizing production and getting to oil self-sufficiency, and therefore are less likely to be resource nationalists. The size and trend of the resource endowment, as well as its type, also matters. Countries with increasing production and reserves are less likely to care about the costs of expropriation, but countries with small or rapidly depleting reserves are compelled to be less resource nationalist. Similarly, if the country is endowed with easy-to-extract, low-cost, and low-risk oil reserves, it can afford to be more resource nationalist. However, if developing its reserves requires taking great risks and utilizing sophisticated technology, it is likely to be more pragmatic.

The likelihood of expropriation is also highly contingent on the institutional setting of the oil sector and on the wider political regime. In particular, two aspects are especially important: 1) the progressivity of the fiscal and contractual framework; and 2) the political constraints to contractual reneging. A progressive system is one in which the government-take increases as the profits from oil extraction increase. The fiscal and contractual regimes in Latin America and many other developing countries have tended to be regressive or mildly progressive. As a result, when prices go up the government-take does not increase proportionally and governments become dissatisfied with their share of profits.

The wider institutional setting is clearly also relevant. How easy is it for the executive to unilaterally change the government-take? And if it does, which costs does it have to face? If the institutional framework generates checks and balances to constrain the executive, expropriation is probably less likely. For example, countries such as Brazil, Colombia, and, recently, Mexico, created autonomous regulatory agencies to govern the sector. As Mahon points out in Chapter 8 on liberalism, having an independent judiciary that generally upholds the rule of law is clearly a significant source of credibility. However, as mentioned earlier, in weak institutional environments with few political constraints, external enforcement is typically what provides credibility.

The Role of National Oil Companies

State-owned enterprises, usually labeled national oil companies (NOCs), are a dominant force in the oil sector. There are few other sectors in the economy, especially tradable sectors, in which the state companies have such a large share of production. With the notable exception of the Anglo-Saxon producers, USA, Canada, the UK, and Australia, all the major oil producers (particularly exporters) in the world are dominated by NOCs, concentrating their production and, even more so, their oil reserves (Victor 2013). More than 80% of the world's oil proved reserves are controlled by NOCs. In the 1960s more than 80% of the world reserves were in the hands of private companies. In the 1970s, most of the reserves were nationalized. In Latin America, NOCs dominate in Argentina, Brazil, Bolivia, Colombia, Ecuador, Mexico, and Venezuela: all the relevant oil producers.

NOCs tend to dominate particularly in low-risk projects with high rents. Governments see no reason to share ownership in those projects. Rents are easier to capture, and inefficiencies are easily obscured by the naturally high profits. So they prevail in easy-to-produce areas with proved reserves that are geologically well known. In contrast, governments are less willing to go into frontier developments, such as unexplored areas, with high geological uncertainties and which require large investments, such as deep-offshore, unconventional, and depleted fields needing tertiary recovery techniques. Most of the oil reserves in the world were originally discovered by private firms and later handed to NOCs through nationalization, contract expiration, or cancelation. In the life of an oil basin, private companies dominate the early stages of discovery and development, are displaced in the stage of extraction of proved reserves, and comeback with depletion to apply secondary and tertiary recovery techniques. Private companies also dominate the operation in less-developed countries that do not have the state capacity to manage an NOC (Victor 2013).

In the 1990s, while most other state-controlled sectors were privatized, the ownership swing in the oil sector was less pronounced (Manzano and Monaldi 2008). One possible explanation is that due to the size of the rents in oil extraction, NOCs rarely lost money, which made privatization less compelling. In addition, NOCs can be very attractive tools for politicians to appropriate and manage the oil rents. Nevertheless, the role of the private sector in deep-offshore and unconventional extraction has remained significant and, as a result, as oil exploitation has moved to riskier areas, the share of production operated by private companies has increased, even though in aggregate the proven reserves are still heavily dominated by NOCs.

NOCs are somehow counterintuitively the most common victims of "revenue expropriation" in the sense that governments have an easier time extracting rents from them and not allowing them to recover their sunken investment or fulfill their long-term investment plans (Monaldi 2005). The investment horizons of the oil industry are too long compared to the political cycle, and there are often other uses for financial resources that are more urgent or politically beneficial in the short term. As in the case of private operators, the likelihood of NOC expropriation is highly determined by the type of institutional framework in place – in particular, the financial and operational autonomy of the NOC, its governance, the fiscal stability of the country, and the capacity of the political institutions to deliver long-term intertemporal commitments. Countries which are highly dependent on oil revenues and lack effective stabilization mechanisms, in which the executive controls the finances of the NOC, that have few political constraints, and in which politicians have short-term horizons are more likely to expropriate the NOC. Contrary to private operators, NOCs are also very vulnerable when oil prices decline and governments are financially desperate (Victor 2013).

THE FISCAL AND CONTRACTUAL FRAMEWORK OF THE OIL INDUSTRY

To understand the political economy of the taxation of oil it is necessary to analyze not only the regular taxation, such as corporate income tax, value-added tax, or import tariffs, but also other taxes, contributions, and levies paid by the producer to the state that are specific to the sector, such as royalties, surface taxes, windfall taxes, and the contractually established profit and production shares. All of these taken together, along with other regulations, determine the government-take on profits, which is the relevant variable from the perspective of the producer. In fact, other policies that transfer rents from the producer to specific constituencies, such as local content policies and energy subsidies, can be as relevant as taxes to an understanding of the political economy of the oil sector.

Since in Latin America the subsoil minerals are the property of the state, in order to develop the resource the producer needs a contract establishing the rules of exploitation. The classic contractual mechanism was the concession, which gave the signer of the lease the right to extract minerals in a specific area for a period of time. Traditionally, the ownership of the resource was transferred to the producer for that period of time and he had to pay royalties on the mineral produced and other special taxes (e.g., surface taxes).

In the last few decades, traditional concessions have been less common and most contracts maintain ownership of the resources in the hands of the state until it is produced and transferred to the producer under specific rules. There are four basic types of oil exploration and extraction contracts typically used (Jennings 2008):

1) Production-sharing contracts, in which the state grants a producer the right to extract the oil and undertake production to recover its costs. After cost recovery, the "profit oil" is shared between the producer and the state. In some cases, the producer has to also pay regular royalties and taxes.
2) Profit-sharing contracts: in this case the state or national oil company has the right to all the oil produced, and it pays the producer the costs and a share of the profits.
3) Service contracts, in which the operator is paid a service fee per barrel produced as a contractor. In its pure version, the operator does not share the risks or profits with the state; thus, all the upside of any price windfall is kept by the state.
4) Oil joint-ventures are contracts assigned to a mixed enterprise formed by the state and a partner-operator.

   In addition to these basic types, there are variations of them that often are a mix of two basic types. One important aspect of these contracts is if the government-take on profits or revenues varies with a measure of profitability. Increasingly, contracts have a scale according to which the government-take increases with a proxy of profits.

In addition to the contractual profit split, the fiscal regime typically includes other taxes and levies:

1) The royalties are the more traditional of these, i.e. a share of the production or of the gross revenues, which could be a set percentage rate or vary with a scale.
2) Commonly, oil producers have to also pay regular corporate taxes or have a special tax rate for oil activities, or a separate type of income tax. Note that in this case the levy is on net-profits, after costs, and generally royalties, and contractual government-shares have been deducted.
3) In many cases producers have to pay a signing bonus to obtain the contract, and often the magnitude of such a bonus is one of the bidding parameters of an auction in which the oil-producing areas are assigned.

4) Windfall taxes are special levies that apply only when the price of oil goes above a certain level. They vary significantly in terms of their structure, but all have the objective of allowing the state to capture the extraordinary rents from an oil price boom.
5) Resource rent taxes are taxes that are specifically designed to capture the rents, allowing the investor to recover the investment plus a rate of return, and then capturing an increasing share of any additional profits.

EVALUATING THE OIL FISCAL FRAMEWORK

In order to evaluate the fiscal framework, some key criteria are:

1) Neutral: a fiscal framework is neutral if it does not make unattractive any project with pretax positive social returns. An alternative definition is that it generates fewer distortions and does not alter the relative return of projects before and after taxes. Bidding bonuses and resource taxes are more neutral, income taxes are less so, and royalties are the least neutral, making projects uneconomic and inducing producers to leave oil in the ground and shift production in time.
2) Progressive: this means that the fiscal framework allows the government to increase its share of profits as the rate of return increases across the life of the project. Resource taxes are progressive; windfall taxes can increase progressiveness. Income taxes are less progressive, and royalties and bonuses are the least progressive.[1]
3) Fiscal revenue stability: some frameworks generate more stable streams of revenue than others. Royalties are the most stable since they do not depend on profits, but on gross revenues. Income taxes are less stable because they vary with profits.
4) Competitiveness: a regime is competitive if it allows the government to attract investment in different market scenarios.
5) Evasion: a more complex and sophisticated regime that requires detailed knowledge of costs and investments is easier to evade. Bonuses and royalties are simple, transparent, and very hard (or

[1] Royalties with a sliding scale based on profitability variables can be made more progressive.

impossible) to evade. Income taxes are more complex and easier to evade. Resource taxes and other sophisticated contractual production and profit-sharing regimes are easiest to evade and require significant state monitoring capacities.

It is useful to compare the two most widely used instruments – royalties and profit taxes – using the above criteria. Royalties are easier to collect, can be collected every month, are hard to evade, are front-loaded in time (which politicians like), and generate a more stable fiscal revenue stream; but they are regressive (i.e., as prices go up, the state-take goes down), so they do not capture rents effectively. Royalties are also distortionary and non-neutral. Profit taxes, on the other hand, are more neutral, less distortionary, and more progressive, but are easier to evade and generate less stable revenues. Thus, there are significant trade-offs between fiscal instruments. Politicians in states with weak capacities and shorter horizons tend to prefer royalty-based regimes.

POLITICAL ECONOMY OF OIL TAXATION IN LATIN AMERICA

Latin America has had different taxation and contractual regimes for the oil industry, but they have generally been characterized by both regressivity and volatility (Monaldi 2014). Regressive implies that the share of government-take on profits declines when profitability increases. Typically, the taxation and contractual regimes had a decreasing marginal take, meaning that when the price of oil went up, the current share of government-take on profits declined. During the oil price boom cycle many countries incorporated windfall taxes that made marginal tax rates increase with prices at high price levels, but they generally do not decrease at lower price levels such as those prevailing in 2015–2016. The volatility feature refers to the significant changes that have been implemented in the fiscal and contractual regimes. In most cases, these changes have been applied retroactively to projects that started under a different regime, so there has been no taxation regime stability.

Table 2.1 presents the basic elements of the tax regimes in selected countries in the region for 2010–2012. The evolution of the regimes is discussed later in the chapter, but first I want to stress that, with the exception of the windfall taxes approved during the oil price boom in 2005–2014, the fiscal regimes in the region have been based on royalties,

TABLE 2.1 *Basic oil taxation regimes' components in 2012*

Country	Royalty	Income Tax in Excess to Corporate Rate	Special Income Tax	Other Taxes	State Equity Share
Argentina	12%	No	No	Export tax 25%	Yes
Bolivia	18–50%	No	12.5% for dividend repatriation; 20% for excess profits	20–32% for large fields	Yes
Colombia	20% old contracts; variable with production, 8–25% in new contracts	No	7%	Offshore gas pays 60% of regular royalty; gas 80%; heavy oil 75%. Profit sharing when WTI>$33/bl	Yes
Ecuador	Variable 12.5–18.5% depending on the oil field	100% for Petroecuador	25%	Windfall tax	Yes
México (PEMEX)	No	35%	7.7%	61% right to exploit oil	Yes
Venezuela	33%*	16%	Windfall tax 50–60% when prices above budgeted price	Surface tax	Yes, minimum 60%

* Can be reduced to 20% for lower profitability projects

Source: Wood MacKenzie, CERA (2008), and author

which are highly regressive, and the regular corporate income taxes, which are not progressive. A few had some additional taxes that were generally not progressive. In addition, the new windfall taxes are progressive only for high oil prices; the regimes are still regressive at lower price levels. Mexico since the reform in 2014 is an exception, with royalties that vary with the price.

The taxes and government-take had been significantly changed to increase rates during the previous decade. Argentina, Bolivia, Brazil, Ecuador, and Venezuela increased taxes. In the case of Brazil, the increase was not retroactive (i.e., it did not apply to existing contracts); instead, taxes for the new pre-salt projects were increased. In Venezuela, some projects suffered a royalty rate increase from 1% to 33%, and others from 16.6% to 33%; income taxes were increased from 34% to 50%; and a windfall tax was approved. In Argentina, a new export tax of 30% was levied. In Bolivia, the royalties were significantly increased from 18% to 50% and new special taxes were approved. In Ecuador, a 90% windfall tax was approved.

To illustrate the regressiveness of the tax regime in practice, Table 2.2 shows how the fiscal take per barrel did not go up as the price of oil went up, and often even went down (Manzano and Monaldi 2008). In a study by CERA (2008), an energy consultancy, it is clear that at a price of $80 per barrel, the government-take was generally lower than at $55, and at $25 the investor-take was negative in some countries and very low in some others (see Figure 2.1).

The lack of progressiveness of the tax regime appears as one important variable to explain the significant changes that were

TABLE 2.2 *Fiscal take per barrel (% of international price)*

Country	1996–1998	1999–2001	2002–2004
WTI (average, US$)	*19*	*25*	*33*
Argentina	–	20	24
Bolivia	37	24	15
Colombia	22	21	22
Ecuador	66	46	51
Mexico	42	38	52
Trinidad and Tobago	37	16	23
Venezuela	51	47	53

Source: Manzano and Monaldi (2008)

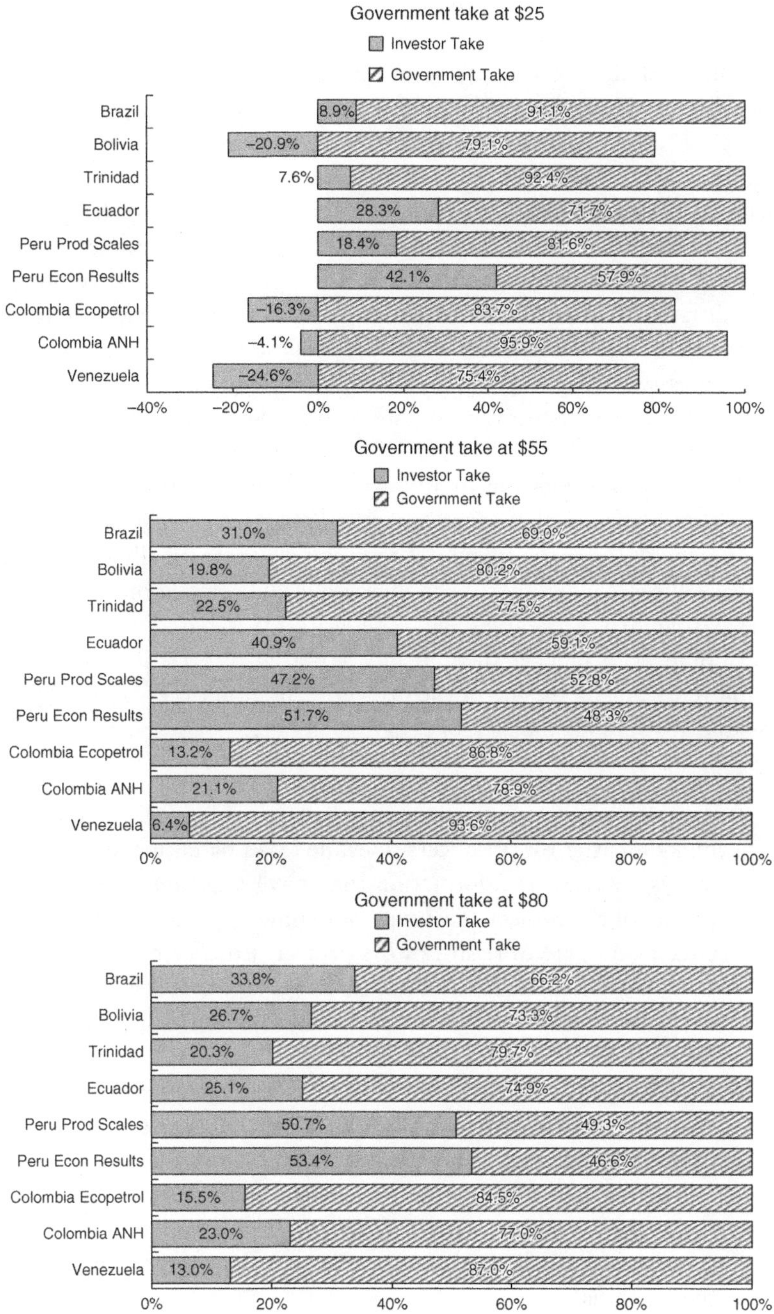

FIGURE 2.1 Government-take and investor-take at different oil prices
Government-take at $25
Government-take at $55
Government-take at $80
Source: Cambridge Energy Research Associates (2008)

implemented during the previous decade, particularly under the oil price boom. However, even some contracts that were quite progressive, such as the risk-service contracts in Venezuela and the Bolivian gas contracts, were forcefully renegotiated to increase the government-take. One possible explanation is that the contracts were progressive over the life of the contract, but the increases in government-take in the short term were insufficient for "impatient" governments. In addition, the opportunistic expropriation of projects was very tempting for the reasons explained in the previous section; therefore, the lack of progressivity might provide additional incentives, but it does not appear to be a necessary condition for expropriation and forced renegotiation.

One important question to address is: why are the fiscal regimes not more progressive in the region? A more progressive regime should be advantageous for governments. They would automatically capture the increase in rents when there is an increase in the price of oil or an otherwise particularly profitable field. There are taxes based on the rate of return of projects that can theoretically be extremely effective in capturing the oil rents during the life of the project. Why don't they prevail? Some possible answers for the lack of progressivity are:

1) Progressive regimes are more complex to manage, have higher monitoring costs, and require a more capable bureaucracy. They make it easier for producers to evade taxes by taking advantage of the asymmetry of information they have regarding the costs and profits of the project. This type of regime requires detailed knowledge of the rate of return of the project. Royalty-type regimes are easy to monitor and hard to evade, a feature that is very attractive for governments with low institutional capabilities like those in the region.
2) Governments typically prefer regimes that generate more stable revenue streams. Since royalties are a percentage of gross revenue or production, they generate a more stable revenue stream, guaranteeing a government-take even when there are no profits. Since the regions' governments are notoriously infective at managing revenue volatility, they could prefer royalty-type regimes despite their pitfalls.
3) The tax regimes are often designed during an opening of the oil sector during a low price cycle, sometimes to develop unexplored areas with high risks. Thus, the government is eager to offer

attractive terms to lure investors in. Later, when risks decline and prices go up, the political calculation changes and the lack of progressivity becomes a major issue, but initially it was not. This lack of foresight might seem hard to believe, but it has happened even in the USA and the UK.

4) The fiscal regimes more favored by economists, which are the most efficient and progressive based on the rate of return, tend to back-load the government-take to the end of a project, once the investor has recovered the costs. Therefore, impatient governments would be unhappy with those regimes. Moreover, when oil prices increase significantly and the government-take does not increase as rapidly in the short-term, the political pressures for a large take can rise, inside and outside the government. In fact, in the case of Bolivia it was the opposition who raised the issue.

THE RECENT EVOLUTION OF TAX REGIMES IN THE REGION

The evolution of oil taxation policy in the region during the last three decades can be captured in the following stylized facts. First, in the 1990s when oil prices were low and the countries in the region faced significant budgetary limitations, the oil sector was opened in most countries in the region (Martin 1999). Taxes were lowered, international oil companies were attracted to invest, and NOCs were partly or wholly privatized. Investment and production increased significantly in Argentina, Bolivia, Brazil, Ecuador, and Venezuela. Mexico was the major exception. Colombia was a partial exception since it did not make efforts to attract private investment, because production was going up in some recently discovered large fields.

Next, in the period between 2003 and 2013, a new wave of resource nationalism engulfed the region, with taxes increasing significantly, contracts forcefully renegotiated or canceled, and some projects and companies nationalized. The exceptions to this trend were Colombia, which performed an oil opening, and Peru, which continued its liberal oil policies.

Finally, since 2012 a new liberalization cycle appears to be brewing in the region. It started before the oil price collapse in 2014, and has become much stronger since. As can be seen in Table 2.3, countries have implemented tax reductions and other incentives for producers.

TABLE 2.3 *Major fiscal changes for oil companies in Latin America: 2014–2017*

Country	Change
Argentina	• Income tax reduced from 35% to 25% • Oil prices deregulated • Export tax on oil eliminated
Bolivia	• Liquids production incentives for new discoveries
Brazil	• Local content reduced • Frontier royalties reduced • Production sharing contracts with less government-take
Colombia	• General income tax increase. • Discount in royalty rates and income tax on exploration • Offshore tariff-free zones
Ecuador	• Production-sharing contacts with less government-take announced
Mexico	• Low minimum royalty and contractual takes • Caps to royalty bids
Venezuela	• Windfall tax not applied • Foreign exchange treatment improved

Source: Wood Mackenzie and author

As argued in this chapter, the endowment and phases of the investment cycle appear to have significant explanatory power for the different reactions during the oil price cycle of 2003–2014. Peru was an exception to the resource nationalism wave because it had been a net importer with relatively minor geological successes in oil (it did have success in natural gas, the Camisea field), thus it could not afford not to be open and attractive to investors during low or high prices. Colombia was late in its opening, but when production started to collapse in the early 2000s, and with the prospect of becoming a net importer, the country reacted promptly and significantly improved fiscal and contractual conditions. Mexico did not react until production started to collapse in the mid-2000s. All the net exporters with increasing exports and reserves increased taxes and became resource nationalists. Brazil, a net importer with dramatically increasing production and reserves, became resource nationalist, but did not alter the regime for existing projects.

NOCs have been significantly overtaxed, particularly in the large net exporting countries. Ecuador and Venezuela are the more extreme cases, wherein the oil companies are left with negative cash flow after the government-take. PEMEX in Mexico did not fare much better. Domestic energy subsidies have also been forced upon NOCs. In fact, the decline of the oil sector in these countries can be largely attributed to this issue. The following sections provide further detail for each country.

Venezuela

Venezuela is a major oil exporter. Oil represents more than half of fiscal revenue, and more than 90% of exports. The country has generally behaved as a short-horizon rent maximizer. In Venezuela, a successful opening to the private oil companies led to increased taxation and nationalization during the oil price boom, while the stagnation of that industry in turn has led to pragmatism in dealing with the problem.

In the 1990s, facing low oil prices, fiscal crises, and significant investment needs, Venezuela opened the oil sector to private investment in the more risky and less profitable projects. This was a major departure from the nationalization of 1975, which had made state-owned PDVSA the monopoly producer. The private projects had significantly lower taxes than PDVSA, largely because they had lower margins and/or higher risks. In particular, the extra-heavy oil ventures paid 34% income tax (PDVSA paid 67% at the time) and 1% royalty (PDVSA paid 16.6% at the time). The opening attracted significant investments by major international players, including Exxon, Shell, BP, Chevron, and Total, leading to a substantial increase in production of more than one million barrels per day (equivalent to more than a third of current production levels).

When Hugo Chávez (1999–2013) was elected president in 1998, oil prices bottomed out, but he did not change the existing oil deals until 2005, after all major investments had been made and prices had increased significantly. The protracted and confrontational expropriation process that ensued significantly increased the government-take on oil profits. The marginal government-fiscal-take in extra-heavy oil projects went up from 35% to 67%. Adding the additional equity, the total marginal state-take was as high as 93%. The government also approved windfall taxes on high prices. These measures significantly affected Venezuela's reputation, delaying all major new investments and creating very high opportunity-costs in terms of foregone future production (and thus fiscal revenues).

As production faltered and the high-spending regime became desperate for additional revenue, pragmatism led the government to offer investors better fiscal terms and guarantees. Although investors have continued to be cautious, the change in the Venezuelan government's attitude is palpable. This pragmatism – or desperation – has become more obvious since the price collapse because of the urgent need to increase investment and production. The government has waved the windfall tax and is offering a reduced royalty rate of 20% (from 33%) for new projects.

Thus, foreign investors were victims of the price boom and of their own success in increasing production and reserves. The cycle of investment and expropriation in Venezuela is similar to what happened in Argentina, Bolivia, and Ecuador. In all four countries an oil opening produced a large increase in privately operated production and reserves, followed by expropriation when conditions were ripe.

Bolivia

Bolivia is a major natural gas exporter, highly dependent on this export for fiscal revenues. In the late 1990s, the government implemented a privatization program that included the hydrocarbons sector. In addition, it offered attractive exploration and production gas contracts and was able to attract very significant investments: US$2.5 billion until 2003, representing about 40% of total foreign investment. Proven natural gas reserves increased sevenfold and exports more than fourfold. Before 1999, most of production went to the domestic market, so politically it was not attractive to maximize rents. However, exports to Brazil later became the main source of revenues and the political economy changed, so the government started behaving as an exporter.

The pressures to increase the government-take in natural gas were initiated by the political opposition to President Gonzalo Sánchez de Losada (1993–1997 and 2002–2003). He eventually resigned, and Evo Morales (2006–present) was elected president largely on a resource-nationalism platform. The combination of increased production and reserves with higher gas prices opened the door for a major forced renegotiation of taxes and the partial nationalization of the projects. Royalties were increased from 18% to 50%. Again, investors were victims of their own success. Interestingly, the contractual government-take was progressive in the life of the projects, but in the short-term the total government-take (largely based on the royalty) was regressive. Thus, both the public and the political leadership became impatient to receive the benefits. Recently, the government of Bolivia, worried about reserve and investment decline, has announced that is going to incentivize exploration activities by offering "flexible contractual terms," including faster capital recovery for the contractor.

Ecuador

Ecuador is also heavily dependent on oil. Oil revenues represent more than a third of the total fiscal revenues. Oil fiscal and contractual policies have been particularly, partly due to the significant political instability in the country. Petroecuador, the national oil company, has been the poster-case for an overtaxed enterprise, incapable of fulfilling its investment plans. In fact, due to the company's financial difficulties and the low oil prices of the 1990s, the oil sector was significantly opened; first in 1993, with the approval of production sharing contracts, and later in 1999, with the creation of joint ventures. The reforms were quite successful in attracting investment and increasing production.

In 2006, newly elected president Rafael Correa (2007–2017) began to cancel and renegotiate oil contracts. First, he approved a 50% windfall tax that he later increased to 90%. Additionally, he forced all contracts to be transformed into service contracts in which the government-take is 85–90%. Later, he signed new, more flexible contracts with Chinese NOCs, and announced more attractive terms for the service contracts to obtain investment in declining fields. In 2017, incoming president Lenín Moreno (2017–present) announced new production-sharing contracts to attract new investment.

Argentina

Argentina, like Ecuador, Bolivia, and Venezuela, had a very successful opening in the 1990s when it privatized YPF and reduced the government-take in oil projects. However, during the macroeconomic collapse of 2002, the government reneged on oil contracts approving a 30% export tax. The administrations of Néstor Kirchner (2003–2007) and Cristina Kirchner (2007–2015) continued a policy of regulating domestic prices that reduced the incentives for investors and led to a significant decline in production of oil and gas, and a worsening of the energy balance of payments, making Argentina a net importer. Eventually, this situation served as an argument to renationalize YPF in 2012.

Since nationalization, pragmatism has prevailed. The government appointed a well-respected oilman, Miguel Gallucio, to run the company, and he started new contracts with international oil companies, offering them more attractive terms (Vásquez 2016). Those terms were eventually enacted into a new oil law that gives YPF significant power and provides guarantees for the more attractive investor-take. Among the new elements of the law are: extended licenses, capped royalty rates, tax incentives, elimination of export tax for up to 20% of production, and a higher domestic price for gas. In the administration of President Mauricio Macri (2015–present), the government has continued to improve investor's conditions via domestic price incentives for gas.

Mexico

Mexico was an exception to the liberalizing trend of the 1990s. Historical and ideological reasons can help explain this exceptionalism, but the major factor behind the lack of reform is that Mexico's production kept increasing without significant new investments. The giant oil field of Cantarell, which produced more than two million barrels a day at its peak (or close to two-thirds of the country's production), allowed the government to over-tax, and to conceal the significant inefficiencies of the national oil monopoly, PEMEX. As Ondetti points out (Chapter 4 in this volume), the future costs of the lack of investment were not anticipated by the political leadership, and even less so by the general public, so there was no rush for reform.

Once Cantarell's production started to collapse in 2005, the need for reform became clearer but high oil prices made it initially less urgent. However, as PEMEX capital expenditures dramatically increased but barely slowed declining output, the case for reform became much stronger. Cantarell's production has declined more than 80% from its peak. With the election of President Enrique Peña Nieto (2012–2018), institutional gridlock eased and reform was finally passed. Mexico, like Venezuela in the past, began to open the riskier, less-profitable projects that require large investments and complex technology. In contrast to Venezuela, it is building a much more robust institutional framework to support reform. This might provide a longer life to the investment cycle. However, if the incentives for expropriation appear in the future, one cannot discard the possibility of a partial reversion of reform, especially given the enduring strength of nationalistic ideology in Mexico.

Mexico's new framework includes low minimum royalty rates, which contrast with the very high levies paid by PEMEX, and progressive contractual terms, in which the government-take rises with profits. In addition, the government-takes offered in the bidding rounds have been generally high. The progressive framework and contractual high government-take might dampen incentives for expropriation, but if politicians are impatient they still might have incentives to extract revenues earlier than scheduled.

Brazil

Even though Brazil is still a net importer of oil, it has increased its production more than fourfold over the last two decades, surpassing Mexico and Venezuela. As discussed by Schneider (Chapter 5 in this volume), that success is in large part the result of the liberalization of the oil industry in the 1990s, when Petrobras, the national oil company, was partially privatized and the petroleum sector opened to foreign investment. As a net importer, the country was eager to maximize its production and, until recently, did not focus on extracting fiscal rents. However, the discovery of massive deep-offshore reserves began to change governmental incentives. In contrast to its South American counterparts, Brazil did not nationalize or force contract renegotiations. However, it did increase the government-take for future offshore projects. It required Petrobras to be the operator and own at least 30% of the equity, established an ambitious policy of increasing the local content of investments, and increasingly subsidized the domestic gasoline market. Moreover, the participation of private shareholders of Petrobras was diluted when the government exchanged oil reserves for equity in the company – a move that many analysts considered a form of expropriation.

Thus, even though Brazil had been considered a model of oil regulatory policy in the region, the effects of its success and the prospect of becoming a net exporter also induced a milder version of resource nationalism. This behavior had negative implications for investment and production, which have not reached their targets during the last few years. The corruption scandal involving Petrobras' dealings with its local content contractors was a big blow for the company.

During the administration of President Michel Temer (2016–2018), most of the resource nationalist policies have been partially reversed. Petrobras does not have to be the operator, local content requirements have been made more flexible, royalties in frontier projects have been reduced, and minimum government-takes have been reduced.

Colombia

Along with Brazil, Colombia is the only other country that took advantage of the high oil prices to increase investment and production. It was the result of a major policy change aimed at attracting private investment, by the administration of president Álvaro Uribe (2002–2010). The country is highly dependent on oil revenues, which have reached more than 25% of the total fiscal revenues, but oil reserves are limited.

The case of Colombia has some parallels with those of Brazil and Mexico, for different reasons. Like Mexico, when facing a collapse in production Colombia copied the Brazilian liberalization model and achieved high production growth (close to a twofold increase in less than 5 years), but has not yet had geological luck in finding relevant new reserves. In contrast to Brazil, this situation provided strong incentives for the government to keep providing attractive conditions for investment. In fact, to offset the continued depletion of reserves in the low-price environment, the Colombian government has announced that terms would be further improved.

CONCLUSION

The incentives provided by price cycles, investment cycles, endowments, and institutions are key to understanding the waves of resource nationalism and liberalization and their consequences for taxation. The region has been more prone to this type of policy volatility than other regions in the world, possibly due to the combination of factional democracies, weak rule of law, and rampant inequality.

Given propitious circumstances, resource-nationalistic ideologies could flourish again. After a cycle of significant investment that adds substantial production and reserves, changing the rules may become tempting in the future, particularly if combined with oil price booms. Institutions that encourage governments to take more long-term approaches that limit their ability to opportunistically renege on deals could moderate the effects of such volatile incentives. Independent regulatory agencies, as well as progressive and effective fiscal and contractual regimes that properly tax the windfall profits, would be helpful.

Conversely, changing incentives, like those prompted by a prolonged period of low oil prices, could induce further pragmatism and liberalization. In general, net importers or countries that have both declining production or reserves and a portfolio of high-risk projects would be pressed to be more open and to offer better fiscal conditions.

From the country perspective, resource nationalism is only a problem if it hinders the development of the oil sector and has negative long-term welfare implications. A pragmatic version of nationalism, one that maximizes enduring benefits for the nation without volatile policy cycles, is highly desirable, if all too rare in Latin America. Understanding the challenges explored here and creating institutions to mitigate them should be one of the main long-term goals of policy reform in the region.

References

Cambridge Energy Research Associates [CERA]. 2008. "Fiscal Conditions in a Changing Oil Market." Briefing.

Flores-Macías, Gustavo. 2010. "Statist vs Pro-Market: Explaining Leftist Governments Economic Policies in Latin America," *Comparative Politics* 42 (4): 413–433.

2012. *After Neoliberalism? The Left and Economic Reforms in Latin America.* New York: Oxford University Press.

2016. "Latin America's New Turbulence: Mexico's Stalled Reforms," *Journal of Democracy* 27 (2): 66–78.

Jennings, Anthony. 2008. *Oil and Gas Exploration Contracts.* London: Sweet and Maxwell.

Klein, B., R. Crawford, and A. Alchian. 1978. "Vertical Integration, Appropriable Rents, and the Competitive Contracting Process," *Journal of Law and Economics* 21 (2): 297–326.

Manzano, Osmel and Francisco Monaldi. 2008. "The Political Economy of Oil Production in Latin America," *Economía* 9 (1): 59–103.

Martin, Jay. 1999. "Privatization of Latin American Energy," *Natural Resources and Environment* 14 (2): 103–110.

Monaldi, Francisco. 2005. "Inversiones Inmovilizadas, Instituciones y Compromiso Gubernamental: Implicaciones sobre la Evolución de la Inversión en la Industria Petrolera Venezolana," in José Pineda and Francisco Sáez (eds.), *Crecimiento Económico en Venezuela: Bajo el Signo del Petróleo*, Venezuela: Banco Central de Venezuela, 187–206.

2008. "Análisis institucional de la gobernabilidad y contratación en el sector petrolero: casos de la región andina," in Miguel Castilla, Ramón Espinasa, Peter Kalil, and Osmel Manzano (eds.), *Hacia la Integración Energética Hemisférica: Retos y Oportunidades.* Caracas: CAF – BID: 117–178.

2014. "The Mining Boom in Latin America," *Revista: Harvard Review of Latin America*, Winter, 13 (20): 6–8.

Parra, Francisco. 2004. *Oil Politics: A Modern History of Petroleum.* London: Tauris.

Sinnott, Emily, John Nash, and Augusto De la Torre. 2010. *Natural Resources in Latin America and the Caribbean: Beyond Booms and Busts?* Washington, DC: World Bank.

Vásquez, Patricia. 2016. *Argentina's Oil and Gas Sector.* Washington, DC: Woodrow Wilson Center for International Scholars.

Victor, David. 2013. "National Oil Companies and the Future of the Oil Industry," *Annual Review of Resource Economics* 5: 445–462.

Vivoda, Vlado. 2008. *The Return of the Obsolescing Bargain and the Decline of Big Oil: A Study of Bargaining in the Contemporary Oil Industry*. Saarbrücken: VDM Verlag.

Weyland, Kurt, Raúl Madrid, and Wendy Hunter (eds.). 2010. *Leftist Governments in Latin America: Successes and Shortcomings*. New York: Cambridge University Press.

Williamson, Oliver. 1996. *The Mechanisms of Governance*. New York: Oxford University Press.

Wood MacKenzie. n.d. Briefing by Wood Mackenzie Upstream and Fiscal Services.

3

Economic Growth and Tax Compliance in Latin America

Did the "Good Times" Help to Reduce Tax Evasion?[*]

Marcelo Bergman

1 TAX REVENUES AND TAX COMPLIANCE IN LATIN AMERICA

Over the last decade, countries in Latin America have enjoyed economic growth that has translated into higher tax revenues. Despite differences in tax structures, most countries had impressive increases in the tax collection as a share of the GDP. Table 3.1 shows the overall performance by country over the last twenty-five years.

The large increase in fiscal revenues occurred in most countries during the 1990s and the beginning of the twenty-first century.[1] In several countries, the last six or seven years show a stable pattern. Yet, as shown in the last two columns of Table 3.1, over the "commodity boom" period from 2000–2004 to 2011–2015, most countries of the region not only had larger GDPs, they also collected more taxes from these already larger GDPs.

Despite this unparalleled growth, it remains unclear whether tax compliance has risen in the region. In this first part, I present several indirect estimations of tax compliance for different taxes. I suggest that the data does not indicate any significant gains in the reduction of tax evasion in Latin America. Section 2 of this paper examines several explanations for such under-performance. Section 3 elaborates on a political explanation.

* I want to express my gratitude for very constructive support from the editor of this book, Gustavo Flores-Macías; and to Robert Kaufman, Ben Ross Schneider, and two anonymous reviewers for their constructive comments. I believe they have contributed to sharpening the arguments and making the chapter clearer.

1 On average, the region had a net increase of 3% of GDP in tax revenue (excluding social security and other nontax revenues) from the 1991–1993 to the 2006–2008 period (See IADB 2013 study in Corbacho et al. 2013).

TABLE 3.1 *Evolution of tax revenues (including social security contributions) as share of GDP*

	1990–94	1995–99	2000–04	2005	2007	2009	2010	2011	2012	2013	2014	2015	2016	2014–16	Dif* 2004–09	Dif* 1995–99
Argentina	17.4	19.0	20.7	24.5	26.4	28.9	29.1	29.3	30.6	31.2	31.1	32.0	31.3	31.5	52.1	65.9
Bolivia	10.5	14.5	17.2	20.0	19.8	21.7	20.3	22.1	24.4	25.3	26.2	27.6	26.0	26.6	54.2	83.2
Brazil	23.6	26.8	30.9	32.8	35.1	32.1	32.4	33.2	32.5	32.4	31.8	32.0	32.2	32.0	3.5	19.3
Chile	18.0	18.8	19.0	20.7	22.7	17.3	19.6	21.1	21.3	19.9	19.6	20.5	20.4	20.2	6.2	7.4
Colombia	12.9	15.5	16.3	18.1	19.1	18.6	18.0	18.8	19.7	20.1	20.4	20.8	19.8	20.3	24.7	31.1
Costa Rica	18.4	18.1	19.4	20.0	21.9	21.0	20.7	21.2	21.2	21.9	21.9	22.6	22.2	22.2	14.8	22.7
Dom Rep.	9.0	10.5	11.3	11.9	15.0	12.7	12.3	12.3	13.1	13.7	13.8	13.5	13.7	13.7	21.1	29.5
Ecuador	7.4	8.4	11.7	12.1	13.2	15.2	16.6	17.7	19.8	19.6	19.2	21.1	20.5	20.3	73.5	141.1
El Salvador	11.3	12.3	12.8	14.2	15.4	14.6	15.4	15.6	16.4	17.3	16.9	17.2	17.9	17.3	35.6	41.0
Guatemala	9.6	11.4	13.2	13.1	13.9	12.2	12.4	12.8	12.9	13.0	12.7	12.4	12.6	12.5	−4.8	10.2
Honduras	16.9	17.8	15.9	16.9	19.0	17.1	17.3	16.9	17.8	18.4	19.6	20.4	21.4	20.4	28.4	15.1
Mexico	13.0	11.9	13.4	12.1	12.6	13.0	13.4	13.3	13.1	13.8	14.2	16.2	17.2	15.9	18.9	33.6
Nicaragua	10.6	12.1	13.8	16.1	17.4	17.1	19.4	20.3	20.9	21.2	21.8	22.3	22.6	22.2	61.3	84.2
Panama	16.7	16.6	14.6	13.8	15.7	15.8	16.7	16.5	16.8	17.1	15.7	15.9	16.6	16.1	9.9	−3.0
Paraguay	7.3	11.7	12.0	13.8	13.9	16.1	16.5	16.9	17.7	16.4	17.8	17.9	17.5	17.7	47.7	52.1
Peru	14.0	16.0	15.2	16.4	18.4	16.9	17.8	18.6	19.3	19.2	19.0	17.2	16.1	17.4	14.7	8.7
Uruguay	20.6	21.6	21.7	23.9	25.1	25.9	26.2	26.6	26.9	27.5	27.3	27.0	27.9	27.4	26.0	27.2
Venezuela	15.7	14.2	12.4	15.9	17.0	14.2	11.8	13.4	14.1	14.4	18.9	20.8	14.4	18.0	45.0	27.1
L.A & Carib.	16.5	18.0	19.8	20.9	21.3	20.9	21.4	21.9	21.9	22.4	23.1	22.7	22.7	23.5	30.0	22.0
OECD – Avg	32.6	33.6	33.3	33.5	33.7	32.3	32.5	32.8	33.3	33.6	33.9	34.0	34.3	34.0	2.2	1.4

Dif (*) : % Difference between the average rate for the 2014–2016 period, compared to two other yearly average periods (1994–1999 and 2004–2009).
Source: Own elaboration based on OECD. Stat Revenue Statistics Latin America Countries: Comparative Tables at http://stats.oecd.org/index.aspx?DataSetCode=RSLACT

INDIRECT MEASURES FOR TAX COMPLIANCE

Tax compliance measures the level of actual collections compared to the expected total tax revenues to be collected had all taxpayers fulfilled their tax legal obligation in due time and accurately. There are several forms of noncompliance, from tax arrears or tax avoidance, to the most widespread: tax evasion. Each tax has its own compliance rate. It is well known that income taxes have higher rates of noncompliance than the VAT. Several variables play different roles in explaining tax evasion, and they will be examined in Section 2. In this section I estimate noncompliance using three different approaches.[2]

1.1 VAT Productivity

An in-depth examination of each country's efficacy in collecting taxes requires a finer analysis of levels of tax compliance based on the systematic comparison of the yields from a particular tax. A logical candidate for such analysis is the VAT.[3]

One way of using VAT to assess the extent of compliance in a given country is to analyze its productivity. This indicator (PVAT) measures the yield of each percentage point of the VAT as a share of GDP – i.e., the share of GDP collected by each percentage point of the VAT rate ([VAT/GDP]/tax rate). For example, in 2003 Argentina had a PVAT of 0.3, meaning that every VAT percentage point raised 0.3% of the GDP. Given that in this country the VAT rate was 21% and the total tax

[2] There are two methods to estimate tax compliance. One is based on a large representative sample of tax returns to determine levels of individual and corporate noncompliance. The other is to estimate the potential tax revenues of a given tax and compare it to the actual tax receipts. The first method is largely underused because it requires a very large sample and many auditors to collect the data. It makes it virtually impossible to run it effectively in most countries of the region. The most common approach, based on figures from national accounts, is to analyze potential revenues compared to actual revenues. Such a "gap" is the noncompliance rate.

[3] Several studies measure VAT compliance by constructing a *compliance coefficient* index that compares the gap between expected and actual tax revenue. It estimates potential tax revenue by using national accounts to calculate the total tax base. Once the base is estimated, it is multiplied by the tax rates. This produces the potential, or "expected," VAT revenue. The difference between the potential and the actual revenues generates the tax gap. The tax compliance coefficient must be accepted with certain reservations, because the tax base is calculated using national accounts, which at times are not entirely accurate (Bird 1992b) or are out of date (Friedman 1991; Serra 1991). Therefore, any tax compliance coefficient represents *an approximation* of the differences between potential and actual revenue.

revenues were 6.3% of the GDP, for every VAT point it raised 0.3% of the GDP. Since tax rates between countries are different, the PVAT rather than the VAT as a share GDP provides a better magnitude of tax compliance. In short, all things being equal, the higher the productivity rate, the lower the noncompliance.[4]

A major drawback for this simple methodology is that countries also have different tax bases, i.e., each country has several goods and services that are tax exempt, and their GDP has different weights (for instance, the share of investments, which of course are not taxed, can vary between countries). Since the tax base and the GDP structure directly affect the productivity level, for compliance purposes a comparison of PVAT between countries must be based on similar tax bases. Most, but not all Latin American countries have comparable tax bases of around 50% of their GDP (this means that approximately half of the GDP is taxable at a given VAT rate). However, this is an imperfect measure that provides orders of magnitudes for comparisons between countries.

Given that tax bases and GDP structures do not change significantly across short periods within each country, these measures provide very good assessments for the *evolution* of compliance in each country. Therefore, the data shown in Table 3.2 provides better longitudinal assessments of compliance within each country and less efficient estimation of compliance across countries.[5]

Table 3.2 shows a remarkable stability in productivity.[6] Seven of the eighteen countries indeed had double digit percentage growth in VAT productivity, but this is mostly due to larger tax bases (new goods and services taxed). Other countries have very modest increases in productivity despite the large revenue collected. This means that despite the large increase in total tax revenues shown in Table 3.1, most countries levied similar shares of value-added taxes. Several countries have higher VAT revenues over these years, but those increases stem from either larger tax bases, general economic improvements, or dubious national account

[4] Technically, lower rates improve productivity, but this effect is very small.

[5] For several countries, comparisons can be made easily, while for others comparisons should be made with care. For instance, Chile and Argentina have comparable tax bases and GDP structures. Therefore, the comparison of PVAT sheds light on the difference in tax evasion between those countries. However, the much lower rate of PVAT in Mexico also results from a smaller tax base. In Mexico, foods and medicines (as well as other goods) are VAT-exempt. Therefore, naturally, the VAT has lower productivity.

[6] A recent study by Díaz de Serralde (2017) using a new CIAT database has arrived at similar levels of VAT productivity for the year 2015. In short, the yield of VAT has not changed over recent years.

TABLE 3.2 *VAT yield*

Country	2003	2004	2005	2006	2007	2008	2009	2010	2011	2012	2003–05	2010–12	%Dif*
Argentina	0.30	0.36	0.36	0.37	0.39	0.41	0.42	0.43	0.46	0.49	0.34	0.46	35
Bolivia	0.62	0.65	0.69	0.68	0.71	0.74	0.67	0.68	0.75	n.d	0.65	0.72	9
Brasil	0.61	0.65	0.66	0.65	0.64	n.d	n.d.	n.d.	n.d.	n.d.	0.64	0.64	0
Chile	0.41	0.41	0.41	0.39	0.42	0.45	0.40	0.42	0.43	0.44	0.41	0.43	5
Colombia	0.34	0.35	0.37	0.40	0.39	0.40	0.37	0.38	0.40	0.39	0.35	0.39	9
Costa Rica	0.41	0.42	0.43	0.45	0.48	0.49	0.41	0.40	0.40	0.40	0.42	0.40	−5
Ecuador	0.41	0.39	0.40	n.d.	n.d.	n.d.	n.d.	n.d.	n.d.	n.d.	0.40	n.d.	n.d.
El Salvador	0.47	0.46	0.50	0.54	0.53	0.52	0.47	0.51	0.52	0.54	0.48	0.52	9
Guatemala	0.44	0.46	0.43	0.45	0.49	0.46	0.41	0.42	0.44	0.44	0.44	0.43	−2
Honduras	0.42	0.43	0.43	0.47	0.51	0.52	0.44	0.45	0.47	0.46	0.43	0.46	8
Mexico	0.22	0.22	0.23	0.24	0.24	0.25	0.23	0.24	0.23	0.23	0.22	0.23	4
Nicaragua	0.32	0.33	0.35	0.38	0.39	0.36	0.35	0.36	0.39	0.40	0.33	0.38	15
Panama	0.28	0.30	0.31	0.35	0.40	0.42	0.43	0.38	0.45	0.45	0.30	0.43	44
Paraguay	0.37	0.41	0.45	0.47	0.51	0.56	0.56	0.62	0.65	0.63	0.41	0.63	54
Peru	0.30	0.30	0.30	0.31	0.32	0.37	0.32	0.35	0.34	0.37	0.30	0.35	18
Dominican Republic	0.24	0.26	0.24	0.27	0.29	0.28	0.25	0.26	0.25	0.24	0.25	0.25	1
Uruguay	0.34	0.34	0.35	0.39	0.41	0.42	0.41	0.41	0.40	0.40	0.34	0.40	17
Venezuela	0.30	0.39	0.43	0.46	0.40	0.51	0.49	0.46	0.51	0.55	0.37	0.51	36

Dif* represents the difference in productivity from the average of years 2003–2005 and the average productivity for years 2010–2012, or with data for the last year available (e.g. Brazil).

Notes: Several countries had VAT reforms to include new goods and services during this decade. This was the case for Panama and Paraguay in the first half of the decade. Data for Argentina and Venezuela over the last five years should be analyzed with care given the manipulations in official inflation and therefore GDP statistics. For Uruguay, there was a reform in 2006 that expanded the tax base.

Source: Own elaboration based on data from CEPALSTAT (2015) and CIAT (2015)

estimations. In addition, for technical reasons, larger foreign trade improves VAT compliance.[7]

Although the PVAT comparison across countries can be misleading because differences in tax bases can bias the yield, some comparisons between countries with similar tax-base structures can be made. This is the case for Argentina and Chile, which have similar tax bases (Argentina's is slightly higher), and where Chile's higher PVAT indicates a higher compliance rate. Similarly, at a much lower tax base, Costa Rica and Mexico have comparable tax bases, and the former has higher compliance than the latter.

Since 2000, there were very few changes in the VAT, and tax rates remain constant in most countries, while the changes in tax rates that were introduced were of just 1% or 2%.[8] Tax bases do indeed affect productivity as more goods and services increase the tax revenues and therefore raise productivity. In terms of tax bases, the major increases for most countries occurred in the 1990s, although several countries (Argentina, Bolivia, Panama, Paraguay, and Uruguay) have broadened their tax base since then. Overall, this data shows that productivity has been stable, and no significant reduction in noncompliance can be observed in most countries. Instead, countries that increase PVAT are also those that added new goods and services to the tax base.

1.2 Informality

Informality is very high in Latin America. Using data from national surveys compiled by the International Labor Organization (ILO), Table 3.3 presents the share of employment in the informal sector.[9]

With the exception of Ecuador, Paraguay, and Uruguay, no other country reported a significant and steady reduction in labor informality over this expanding employment period. In short, the share of workers

[7] Exports and imports that grew significantly over the last decade have higher compliance rates because importers and exporters are taxed at the ports of entry or exit. Generally, high VAT withholding systems force customers or suppliers to also comply. In short, as the share of foreign trade rises, the VAT compliance naturally increases as well.

[8] The PVAT rates of Table 3.2 already adjust for the changing rates.

[9] There are different measures of informal employment. The ILO has other measures based on a more restricted definition, whereby rates are 1/3 of those presented here, but information is much less complete. However, the trend through the years for each country remains the same.

TABLE 3.3 *Share of informal employment (nonagricultural sector) as % of total*[10]

Country	2008	2009	2010	2011	2012	2013	2014	2015
Argentina	49.8	49.7	46.7	46.9	47.5	46	46.8	n.a.
Bolivia	79.6	77.8	n.a.	76.6	75.6	72.7	78.8	78.2
Brazil	n.a.	42.2	n.a.	38.4	38.2	37.1	37.8	38.3
Chile	n.a.	n.a.	41.8	40.9	38.7	37.8	38.9	38.9
Colombia	56.2	57.4	59.6	64.4	64.6	63.7	n.a.	n.a.
Costa Rica	n.a.	n.a.	33.8	32.8	35.3	37.3	36.9	37.4
Ecuador	63.7	60.9	56.4	52.9	52.3	49.2	48	51.0
El Salvador	63.6	66.4	65.8	65.6	66.1	65.4	62.9	62.9
Guatemala	n.a.	n.a.	75.1	74.6	76.8	74.4	74.2	72.8
Honduras	71.6	73.9	76.4	70.7	72.8	73.4	74.2	73.8
Mexico	52.5	53.7	54.2	54.2	54.6	53.9	n.a.	n.a.
Nicaragua	65.7	n.a.	75	n.a.	n.a.	n.a.	n.a.	n.a.
Panama	n.a.	43.8	n.a.	n.a.	39.5	40.4	n.a.	n.a.
Paraguay	72.9	70.7	70.3	65.8	66.5	64.4	n.a.	n.a.
Peru	71.9	69.9	70.3	67.5	67.1	68.8	n.a.	n.a.
Dom. Rep.	51.6	48.5	50.6	51.6	53.2	53.0	51.7	50.7
Uruguay	40.3	39.8	37.8	35.5	34.1	33.2	23.5	24.1
Venezuela	n.a.	47.5	n.a.	n.a.	n.a.	n.a.	n.a.	n.a.

Notes: n.a. means that the information is unavailable from this source. Many countries have incomplete reporting. Sources for each country vary. I use a similar criterion when the information was available: national surveys for employment. Data for Argentina is for urban centers.
Source: Own estimation based on ILO (2018)

that do not contribute to social security or pension systems and that do not pay direct taxes in the region remains very high.[11]

[10] Informal employed is defined by the ILO as "persons who in their main or secondary jobs were: Own-account workers, employers and members of producers; cooperatives employed in their own informal sector enterprises ... These workers usually do not have explicit, written contracts of employment, and usually their employment is not subject to labor legislation, social security regulations, collective agreements, etc.; employees holding informal jobs, whether employed by formal sector enterprises, informal sector enterprises, or as paid domestic workers by households" (Hussmanns 2003).

[11] Although some countries have scattered exceptions, from a legal standpoint, all workers in the regions must be registered and are due to pay taxes and contributions to social security and public retirement funds, which are compulsory in most countries of the region.

Informality, of course, does not constitute a direct measure of tax compliance. However, significant reductions in income tax evasion could be gained not only by raising the tax burden of regular contributors, but also by augmenting the number of taxpayers. This of course has important political consequences, and governments usually sidestepped strong enforcement in order to avoid putting many informal workers and enterprises out of business, a subject to be discussed in Section 2.[12] The overall argument is that since this informal sector has not decreased over the last two decades, it has not impacted in the reduction of noncompliance.

The only significant gains in personal income tax compliance in the region were achieved through the increase in collection among "captive employees" in the formal sector. Tax thresholds were lowered, and therefore taxes as a share of their income have risen. The most significant goal of broadening the tax base to increase the number of compliers appeared to have failed. Governments taxed employees in the formal sectors and let informality flourish. In Sections 2 and 3 of this chapter I will describe the important distributive and political consequences of these policies.

1.3 Income Tax Compliance

In terms of personal income taxes, as mentioned, there are no studies that measure noncompliance to study the problem over time. However, revenues are very low. In terms of compliance, scattered estimations for nine Latin American countries conducted over the last decade show tax noncompliance rates for income taxes ranging from 40% to 70%.[13]

Figure 3.1 shows personal income tax collection as a share of GDP over time.[14] With the exception of a few countries that show modest increases (Brazil, Peru), most have stagnated rates of revenue as a share of GDP.

[12] I am not by any means taking a stand on the issue. In this chapter I just want to bring to the reader's attention that a good share of the GDP is located in the informal and even illegal economies of most countries in the region, and that this explains in part why tax revenue as a share of GDP is relatively low. Governments cannot tax large segments of markets simply because they are informal and hard to tax. Since the informal economy is large (as opposed to most OECD countries), tax revenues as a share of GDP will be lower.

[13] These countries are: Peru, El Salvador, Mexico, Costa Rica, Chile, Argentina, Rep. Dominicana, Ecuador and Guatemala, as reported by Corbacho et al. (2013, 23).

[14] As mentioned, compliance indicators for the income tax require data and tax-return audit analysis that does not exist in the region. Other indirect estimations of tax bases provide indirect assessments but they do not exist for most countries, or for every year. I use this indicator as a proxy.

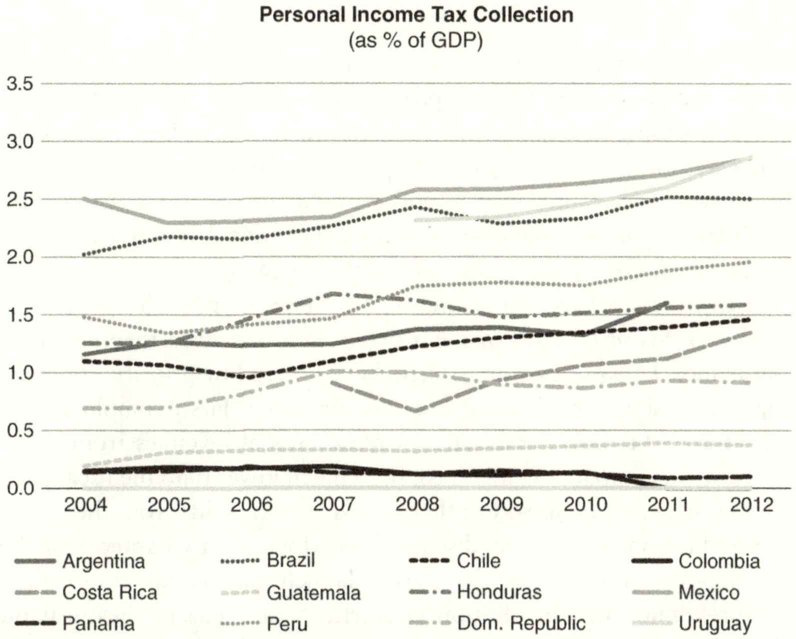

FIGURE 3.1 Personal income tax collection (as % of GDP)
Source: Own elaboration based on CEPALSTAT (2015) (Ingresos Tributarios por Tipo de Ingreso en porcentajes del PIB)

The latest data for 2015 shows that only three countries in the region collected more than 3 % of GDP in personal income tax, and another three countries slightly above 2%.[15] As Flores-Macías points out in the Introduction to this volume, this has been one of the most prosperous decades of the last century, yet personal income tax collection that is procyclical and directly affected by levels of prosperity does not appear to have improved. In short, despite differences among countries, the evolution of these three indirect indicators failed to show any important gains in tax compliance for the vast majority of countries in the region.

[15] These are: Argentina 3.22%, Mexico 3.53%, and Uruguay 3.50%; and Chile 2.06%, Brazil 2.68%, and El Salvador 2.01%. The rest collected less than 2% in Personal Income Tax revenues. See www.iadb.org/es/sectores/reforma-modernizacion-del-estado/presion-fiscal/inicio. OECD countries collect on average more than 10% of GDP; see https://data.oecd.org/tax/tax-on-personal-income.htm#indicator-chart

2 ACCOUNTING FOR TAX NONCOMPLIANCE

Tax compliance is procyclical, so times of prosperity are the most conducive to reducing tax evasion because profits are larger and therefore taxpayers are more willing to comply with tax laws (IMF 2015). Given that Latin America enjoyed one of the most prosperous decades since the postwar era, theory would have predicted important reductions in tax evasion. Why hasn't tax compliance significantly improved in Latin America over the last decade, when taxpayers were at least slightly better off?

In this section I examine several hypotheses to partially provide an answer to this puzzle. All of them derive from standard theories of tax compliance. I also suggest that rulers have placed low priorities on reducing tax evasion. Three hypotheses are advanced. First, compliance did not improve because the extraction of additional revenues from a tax-enforcement campaign would have been much lower than the fiscal gains from taxing commodities. In other words, as tax yields from the export commodities increased – as discussed by Monaldi in Chapter 2 of this volume – the appeal for authorities to launch massive tax-enforcement measures diminished. In addition, countries' fiscal needs, on the one hand, and the international economic environment, on the other, did not make the reduction of tax evasion a priority. The high international liquidity, the low cost of money, and countries' better macroeconomic performance reduced the incentives for governments to engage in tax compliance campaigns.

Second, compliance with taxes stagnated because, as Mahon underscores in Chapter 8, the tax structure in the region still builds on indirect taxes (VAT, international trade, and so on), and thus the influence of direct taxes on income and property remain small, lowering the ceiling for compliance growth. In other words, given the tax structure of most Latin American countries, as the threshold for compliance is high, there are diminishing returns for improvements. As opposed to the stressed public fiscal sector of the 1990s, in the 2000s there was lower pressure to launch policies of fiscal extraction via strong tax enforcement.

Third, following standard theories of tax compliance, people pay their due taxes as a result of a combination of "state coercive power" and "state persuasive power." As long as taxpayers feel that they may get caught cheating, and that the state delivers meaningful goods and service in exchange for their taxes, people will be more willing to comply. In short, deterrence and trust play important roles. Tax evasion in Latin America could be explained by the fact that these two components of compliance (state capacities to enforce the tax laws, and the trust people have on authorities to deliver public goods) have not really changed during recent decades.

In Section 3, I explore a tentative political-electoral proposition. I argue that reductions in tax evasion would have fallen precisely on those taxpayers that are the larger constituents of populist governments. The harm could have been produced in two different ways: First, broadening the tax base implies taxing very small entrepreneurs and the informal economy. Second, hitting the informal market hard would have raised consumer prices in marketplaces where significant levels of consumption of low-income segments are happening. Therefore, strong tax enforcement might have produced economic concentration, higher consumer prices, and therefore reduced consumption among low-income segments. In summary, tax evasion indirectly became a form of subsidy from concentrated businesses (those who do pay taxes) to the thousands of sole proprietors, small enterprises, and consumers who have avoided taxes. As seen in the markets of stolen and pirated goods (Bergman 2018), tax evasion actually has served potential constituents.

In the remainder of this chapter, I will lend initial descriptive support to these propositions.

The Commodity Trap

The commodity boom has been the hallmark of taxation in Latin America over the last decade. As the Introduction to this volume shows, governments have raised a significant amount of resources in different ways: by directly taxing different goods at different rates (mining, oil, agricultural goods, and many others), and indirectly through income and property taxes as well as higher revenues from VAT. Governments benefited from high prices and profits from the commodity export industries – see Monaldi, Chapter 2 in this volume, for a discussion. In the early 1990s, revenues for Latin American countries totaled 18.6% of GDP, while in the late 2000s they were 23.2% of even larger GDPs (Corbacho et al. 2013, 11). Most of these net increases are associated with the commodity boom. Every country applied its own scheme based on the type of commodity it exports (oil in Venezuela and Ecuador, mining in Chile and Peru, agricultural goods in Argentina and Brazil).

An IADB study (Corbacho et al, 2013, ch. 10) concludes that for a group of eight countries, the revenues for nonrenewable commodities doubled from 3.9% of GDP in the early 1990s to 7.9% in the mid 2000s.

Other renewable commodities (agricultural goods) are more difficult to estimate because they are mostly reflected in corporate income tax revenues that for the entire region went from 1.9% to 3.4%, and other taxes. The revenues that originated just from the commodity boom were several percentage points of GDP. In contrast, good tax-compliance campaign efforts would have raised less than 2% of GDP. There are no precedents in the last twenty years in the region where measures to reduce tax evasion have raised additional revenues exceeding 1% of GDP over a two- to three-year span (CIAT 2018).

In terms of compliance, commodity taxes are highly efficient. Authorities need to effectively control the ports of exits, i.e., to have moderately efficient custom agencies that can control the quantities of shipments, assess the true value of the exported goods, and exert inner controls to avoid serious corruption schemes.[16] Given that the value of commodities is well known (they are traded daily in different stock exchanges) it is hard to underestimate income and evade taxes at the port of exits. In short, custom agents need to effectively control twenty or thirty large exporting firms that ship overseas the reported quantities, and apply the accrued tax rate.

Tax evasion on commodity exports is still possible, and in fact has occurred in the region. The most well-known cause derives from differences in tax rates between neighboring countries. A similar commodity produced in two neighboring countries but taxed at different rates can create incentives for exporters to smuggle these goods from the high-tariff to the low-tariff country, to reduce the tax burden. For instance, there have been reports that oil was smuggled from Venezuela to Colombia, livestock from Argentina to Paraguay, and soybeans from Argentina to Uruguay and Paraguay. Nevertheless, the overall extent of tax evasion using these schemes would not represent a significant amount of the total taxes due.

In sum, the relative ease of controlling few export firms and the quantities shipped at very few ports of exits (5–10) has allowed authorities to run efficient departments to raise large revenues. This is a "dream come

[16] Some corruption by custom agents has been found almost in every country. They often serve private interests or indirectly benefit politicians to fund all sorts of political ventures. Not many cases have been successfully investigated in courts or administrative offices, although some cases have been prosecuted recently (e.g., the case of Petrobras in Brazil.) I claim, however, that the relative size of these corruption schemes represents a very small fraction of the total revenues raised in export tariffs, and other indirect taxes levied by custom agents.

true" for tax collection agencies. Exerting effective control over a few large taxpayers ensures wide compliance throughout the entire production chain, and if corruption schemes remain under control, the level of tax evasion will be very low.[17]

Good compliance on commodity taxes and fees also helped to improve compliance on direct taxes such as income and property taxes. The net increase of income tax revenues in Latin America comes from corporation profits rather than from individual net growth. The region's average income tax collection went from 2.1% of GDP for 1996–2000 to 3.4% for 2006–2010, whereas in individual income taxes it went from 1.7% to 2.0% of GDP for the same period (Corbacho et al. 2013, 10). Export taxes, which had been eliminated from most countries throughout the twentieth century, have resurfaced recently to capture a good share of profits from high prices of agricultural exports. In Argentina, for example, this tax represents 9% of total tax revenues or 3% of GDP (Corbacho et al. 2013, 338).[18] The appeal of export revenues is the ease of taxing them. Once central authorities have almost complete information regarding production and transactions of key trades, they can assess the values of profits and land, and tax them accordingly.

In short, the commodity boom has allowed tax administrations to gather information on producers and other taxpayers in order to estimate presumed income and property taxes.[19] Despite these important gains, compliance in these two taxes has been lower because surveillance and control, especially for the income and property tax of thousands of taxpayers, requires stronger supervision by the tax agencies, as Mahon (Chapter 8) points out. This is the area where voluntary compliance has an effect, and, as will be shown, this has not risen.

Finally, an important consequence of a friendly international environment should not be overlooked. The low cost of money has directly

[17] Taxing at the ports of exits for the quantities and current values of a given good forces the exporter to withhold the given rates from the producer of these goods, and they in turn from its suppliers. In other words, effective control of export taxes guarantees automatic cascade compliance of the different economic actors throughout the entire production chain.

[18] Export taxes create many distortions on the long run affecting the allocation of investments and sector profitability. Argentina has experienced many of these externalities in the past (Díaz Alejandro 1975). These are imperfect substitutes for income tax. They are levied precisely because tax compliance rates are low and they are much easier to collect under high-tax-evasion environments.

[19] In most countries, income taxes are usually levied by central government and property taxes by subnational authorities.

contributed to higher commodity prices and more revenue. Yet several international variables also had an indirect effect on governments' lower incentives to improve tax enforcement and compliance. First, over the last decade most countries in the region enjoyed fiscal balances and were not pressed to narrow gap deficits, as Flores-Macías notes in the Introduction. Thus, compared to the 1980s and 1990s, the reduction of tax evasion in order to raise additional tax revenues was less urgent. Second, the role of international lender organizations had decreased. Most countries did not request stabilization program support and, therefore, the IMF and other organizations had a diminishing role in framing tax policies and enforcement. Third, given the remarkably low international interest rates and large liquidity, the low cost of money enabled countries to borrow on the open markets at very favorable terms. In short, countries issued debt in the bond markets at very low rates when they wanted to raise funds, particularly those that posted sound macroeconomic indicators.

In summary, the commodity boom had at least two important effects. First, it rapidly raised significant revenues that governments could spend on different programs without incurring serious fiscal deficits like they had in previous decades. Levying even a fraction of these revenues through the reduction of tax evasion in VAT or income taxes would have been impossible, or at least would have taken many years. Second, given the structure of commodities exports, these are goods that are hard to evade. Tax administrations were thus able to collect a very large share of commodity taxes.

Expanding the Tax Base

From the late 1980s into the early 2000s, tax compliance in Latin America improved through several measures. The two most important measures were turning the VAT into the workhorse of tax collection and strengthening the tax administration. VAT is a "compliance friendly" tax for several well-known reasons beyond this chapter (see Bird 1992a; Gillis et al. 1990). In terms of tax administrations, two important initiatives yielded the highest compliance returns. The first is the establishment in each tax administration of "large taxpayers" departments, which monitor daily approximately 2,000 large firms and contribute to a cascade effect on compliance for mid-level suppliers. Second, compliance improved due to the large investment in information technology that allowed tax administrations to monitor large transactions and process third-party information from financial institutions.

This strategy appears to have reached a ceiling. The speed of reducing VAT evasion from, say, 60% to 30% was faster through these administrative measures. However, to reduce tax evasion from 30% to 15% requires significant increases in the voluntary compliance of hundreds of thousands of taxpayers. In other words, since the early 2000s, gains in VAT compliance could be obtained by a significant expansion of compliance among a larger tax base. As shown in Table 3.2, PVAT had either modest increases or remained stagnant during the last decade, in spite of the good economic times. This suggests that the share of the tax base that remains unreachable for the tax agencies continues to be large.

Conversely, there has been room for gains in the personal income and property taxes, yet no major improvements in compliance with these taxes have been observed.[20] The structure of the income tax in Latin America has two important features: in most countries capital gains are tax exempt, and a significant share of income is produced in the informal market. In most countries, personal income taxes are paid by employees in the public sector and high-income employees in the formal market. As Tanzi (2013) and others have highlighted, this structure makes the tax base relatively small. Rather than a true income tax, this is largely a tax on wages and salaries (and sometimes dividends) covering just a small share of moderate- and high-income employees.[21]

On the other hand, property taxes are levied by typically weak local authorities that are unwilling to tax their own constituents, opting instead to be funded by the central governments in exchange for political alignment and support. As Mahon highlights in Chapter 8, in a large country such as Mexico, for example, local tax administrations collect less than 1% of GDP in subnational taxes (including the "impuesto predial"). Local revenues for most Latin American countries in 2015 did not exceed 2% of GDP. Conversely, tax evasion for the most part is very high. Thus, the contribution of subnational authorities to central tax administration is in most cases very poor. There are a few exception that have made gains in

[20] A recent comprehensive publication by the IADB estimates the income "tax gap" of countries and regions by measuring the tax collection (as a GDP share) as compared to the expected revenues to be collected for each country given different variables and the performance of other countries of similar development. All countries in Latin America underperform by several GDP percentage points. See Corbacho et al. (2013, 6).

[21] For most countries in the region, the number of taxpayers for the personal income tax is less than 10% of the population (Corbacho et al. 2013, 181). A recent study of the OECD (2016) estimates that overall cost of taxes in salaries and wages for Latin America is 21.7%, while in OECD countries it is 35.9%. This is because in Latin America the tax brackets are lower and informality is much larger.

developing tax local capacities over the last decades, such Brazil (subnational revenues in 2015 were 9.81% of GDP), Argentina (6.53%), and Colombia (3.53%).[22]

The evidence from Figure 3.1 suggests that there were no major gains in income tax compliance, whereas Table 3.3 indirectly shows that the tax base probably remains small, while informality continues to be high. Although the informal sector has historically accounted for a significant share of GDP in most Latin American countries, the recent economic growth has not reduced this share; in fact, it may have increased it. Governments have not only tolerated traditional informality, they have allowed it to grow, and, consequently, no significant new income taxes were collected.

In short, given the current income tax structure, a true dent in direct income and property tax compliance would have been possible with the broadening of the tax base, i.e., expanding the number of taxpayers, which implies a drastic reduction of informality and a tax administration's firm commitment to tax middle- and low-income taxpayers. This, in addition, entails a high-stake political cost. Section 3 examines this political dimension.

Finally, I claim that under a favorable international environment, as opposed to the 1990s, governments have not launched major tax-enforcement initiatives, nor have tax administrations' capacities increased significantly. Administrative measures were much easier to pass (less resisted), and therefore tax administration increased the reporting burden and the withholding of taxes for large taxpayers (financial, communications, energy, and foreign trade sectors), while modest gains were made for tax compliance. I speculate that since there was no perceived urgency to raise significant revenues, the gains in compliance through better tax enforcement were perceived as too high.

In summary, general compliance with VAT reached relatively high rates by Latin American standards, and any additional gain would require stronger efforts for comparatively diminishing returns. Similarly, given the structure of the personal income tax – basically a tax on wage and salaries – potential additional revenues have a low ceiling. Naturally, tax authorities will look for other venues to increase tax revenues.[23] For

[22] See www.iadb.org/es/sectores/reforma-modernizacion-del-estado/presion-fiscal/inicio</i>

[23] A true income tax requires a tax reform that would tax capital gains, yet this is a terrain this chapter does not analyze (see Mahon et al. 2014). Income tax reform, of course, remains a highly political contested issue in the region.

reasons to be discussed below (see "Tax Morale and Equity in Taxation"), expanding the tax base (i.e., taxing more taxpayers) is politically costly for the low returns they can yield, and, therefore, I speculate that governments refrain from aggressively pursuing such a strategy.[24]

Tax Morale and Equity in Taxation

Theories of tax compliance are based on the strategic cooperation paradigm. People will cooperate (pay their tax dues) as long as the state deliver meaningful goods for their compliance (vertical cooperation) and other taxpayers do not cheat (horizontal cooperation). Taxpayers become contingent compliers to the extent that these two conditions are met (Levi 1988; Scholz and Pinney 1995; Torgler 2007; Bergman 2009).

These two principles – exchange (vertical) equity and horizontal fairness – have received differing attention. Most studies on tax compliance have focused on how rulers can create the right institutions to enhance vertical equity and trust, but, surprisingly, much less attention has been directed to understanding how rulers can guarantee that cooperators are not being exploited (horizontal fairness). Better compliance can be ensured if states succeed in deterring passive cooperators from defecting in the tax game (Lederman 2003; Scholz 2003; Bergman 2009; Steinmo 2018). Tax evasion depends more on the ecology of taxation than on the optimality of enforcement.

The perverse noncompliance equilibrium, where relatively few taxpayers carry the burden while many others cheat on their taxes, has not changed in Latin America over the last decade. In effect, despite broadening the tax base in the 1990s, no major improvements were made in the last few years. This uneven burden deepens the sense of unfairness, because taxpayers perceive that rulers do not fulfill the second principle of the tax compliance contract: ensure that everybody (or at least most people) pays their fair share. Such violation conspires against efforts to reduce tax evasion. Under this equilibrium, taxpayers' initial strategy is always defection from cooperation. Latin American taxpayers' initial thought is how they can escape cooperation (evade taxes), rather than assume initially that taxes are part of the costs of any transaction. As long as taxpayers perceive that others cheat, they will try hard to cheat.[25]

[24] Unless there was a political motivation, such as prosecuting political opponents.

[25] This is not to say that they will not comply. If they feel that they are monitored by the tax authority, or a third party withholds their tax dues, they of course will comply. However,

Countries that attempt to reduce tax evasion rely on two different (and often complementary) strategies: one is tax reforms that seek to introduce compliance-friendly taxes and schemes, such as the reduction of loopholes and exemptions. Another is tax enforcement and administration, such as creating withholding systems, multiple reporting schemes, and audit policies. In the last decade, most countries have not raised the enforcement capacities of tax administrations. Indeed, they have made little effort to build horizontal fairness. Consequently, very few cases of tax fraud were prosecuted; the number of audits remains constant in countries such as Chile, Brazil, Mexico, and Argentina (CIAT 2015); and withholding and reporting schemes were expanded for "captive taxpayers." Yet, their effect has been marginal.

Rulers in Latin America have done very little over the past fifteen years to alter this equilibrium (Chile and Uruguay are the exception). They have even stopped talking about tax evasion as indirectly providing legitimacy to this perverse equilibrium. Tax-enforcement strategies have followed the "ease of collection" principle – i.e., they have focused on monitoring those large taxpayers that help to collect the larger amount of revenues.[26] Under noncompliance ecologies, enforcement must first generate the basic conditions of cooperation, yet no significant initiatives were observed in that direction. The steady rates of informality are a clear sign of such equilibrium. As Mahon discusses (see Chapter 8), voluntary compliance, or the initial cooperative steps of taxpayers that ensure large collections and low tax evasion, are still very difficult to achieve in most countries in the region.[27]

The failure to reduce tax noncompliance in the region is partly the result of an adverse equilibrium wherein a large number of potential taxpayers and a good portion of the GDP remain outside the reach of

under this equilibrium most taxpayers in the region are considered "contribuyentes cautivos" – that is, those who cannot escape from the tax authority. Given such an opportunity, they will most likely evade their taxes.

[26] In several countries there is a saying about tax auditors: "Salen a cazar dentro del zoológico" (they hunt within the zoo). It means that they rely heavily on "captive" taxpayers but do not "hunt" outside the known tax registry. However, it is the hard-to-tax who account for a large share of tax evasion.

[27] As this book goes to production, an exciting collection of papers coordinated by Sven Steinmo (2018) study the historical conditions that elicited a "leap of faith" and successful tax compliance regimes in Sweden, Britain, and the United States, and failed ones in Italy and Romania. Legacies of effective states and critical junctures in the former countries created an environment where taxpayers comply, because they have faith that the regime is fair and others comply as well. Very few countries in Latin America have fostered such virtuous circles.

tax authorities. This has created incentives for taxpayers that are under the "watching eyes" of the tax authorities to aggressively look for evasion tactics. Industries for illegal tax IDs, fake invoices, bogus transactions, and blatant fraudulent schemes (including kickbacks and other corruption mechanisms) have proliferated in the region. However, no Latin America country had more than ten taxpayers criminally convicted since 2007 (CIAT 2018).

In sum, in addition to the noncompliance of nonregistered taxpayers, most tax evasion probably comes from taxpayers who aggressively look to avoid taxation given their perception that others will do the same, and therefore tax evasion becomes a strategy to remain competitive. When rulers fail to guarantee the terms of horizontal fairness, conditional cooperators' best strategy is defection. Nothing has really changed in this regard in Latin America since the turn of the century.

3 A POLITICAL DIMENSION OF TAX AVOIDANCE

When do governments decide to enforce their tax laws? Why do they sometimes tolerate tax evasion, or at least significant tax avoidance? How do they decide to pursue and heavily tax certain taxpayers and not others? These are critical questions not yet answered in the Latin American context. This political dimension might also explain to a large degree the levels of noncompliance in the region.

The burden of taxation in Latin America falls heavily on the formal and more dynamic economy. Taxes have important distributive consequences. To the extent that economic sectors are not taxed, this affects the distribution of income and wealth. In this part, I speculate with an alternative hypothesis that needs further elaboration and support, yet logically merits some consideration. I suggest that for political-electoral reasons, popular rulers in Latin America opted to avoid broadening the tax base in order to fight tax evasion, because such a strategy could have hurt their voters. I raise this proposition as speculation because no firm data has been collected to prove it.

Success in the reduction of tax evasion might produce two externalities: First, it can eliminate thousands of sole proprietors and small firms because they use tax avoidance to remain competitive. Shop owners, small growers, individual suppliers, and the like would most likely go bankrupt if they had to report taxes accurately. Small-scale producers and firms with only a few employees are not able to compete in true open markets. Taxation, particularly the high tax rates given the small tax bases, could become a heavy burden for the hundreds of thousands (millions, even) of individuals who work in this sector.

Second, improvements in tax compliance may imply less access to goods and services by low-income sectors. In effect, tax evasion by firms in the informal markets is used to provide goods and services at low prices. Growers, producers, and shop owners evade taxes to reduce operating costs. They supply goods and services in the informal market, where a significant proportion of consumers shop daily. Every city in Latin America has several makeshift marketplaces where a significant number of commercial transactions are conducted daily at very low prices.[28] The tax evaded in these transactions indirectly becomes a state subsidy to these consumers, which has a net effect in raising the level of consumption because customers can stretch their income to increase their level of purchases. In short, tax evasion indirectly enhances consumption among low-income segments that shop in informal marketplaces.

According to ECLAC (2017), between 2001 and 2010 the percentage of change in household expenditure per capita grew by more than 20% on average,[29] the most significant regional increase over the last five decades. Although there is no breakdown of consumption by deciles of income, low-income segments have benefited the most. The relative growth of the first three deciles over the period has been impressive in all eighteen Latin American countries. For example, the growth rate in income for the first (poorest) and tenth deciles between 2001 and 2012 has been in Argentina at 125% and 9% respectively, in Brazil at 159% and 26%, in Chile at 59% and 16%, in Mexico at 56% and 1%, and in Peru at 122% and 46%. The second and third deciles have also performed very well. In short, the rate of growth in personal income has been proportionally higher among low-income deciles. Since the first three deciles allocate almost their entire income to consumption, it is safe to assume that the rate of consumption by low-income segments has grown impressively over this period.

Most low-income segments in Latin America shop in the informal economy. From mom-and-pop stores to fairs and makeshift marketplaces, the first three deciles acquire their goods mostly in a wide supply of venues that rarely report taxes. Moreover, the establishment of these outlets has allowed other mid-level income groups to also shop in these venues. In sum, a large share of the growth in income was channeled to the

[28] Goods sold in these markets are mostly piracy, but stolen goods are also traded and sold.

[29] Argentina 14%, Brazil 30%, Chile 43%, Mexico 12% Paraguay 27%, Peru 44%, Uruguay 30%.

informal economy. Why did authorities not try to significantly tax this increasing share of the GDP?

Holland (2016) has called for forbearance regarding this political reluctance to enforce the laws. This is a useful concept also applicable to tax laws.[30] As opposed to the 1990s, when modern tax agencies pursued an aggressive policy against tax evasion, during the last decade it appears that law enforcement was heavily targeted to political opponents or strategic actors. Rulers in the region avoided heavy pressure on the informal economy.[31]

These two effects – the proliferation of individual and small firms, and the rise in consumption among low-income and periphery city dwellers – could have been hit hard if stringent enforcement on these "hard to tax" individuals had taken place.[32] Over the last decade, rulers and tax administrators have known perfectly well where these undercoded production facilities and makeshift trading marketplaces were located, yet no enforcement to dismantle them was launched. The question remains: Why didn't rulers enforce the tax laws on these easy to detect tax noncompliers?[33]

The initial exploratory considerations put forth in this section suggest that since fiscal deficits have not exerted strong pressure, and as important revenues came from other sources, rulers felt less compelled to narrow the tax gap. The good times made it easier to tax the rich rather than those on a low income, particularly since they have provided healthy majorities at the polls. Rulers appeared to have learned the political lessons of the 1990s.

FINAL REMARKS

In this chapter, I assembled and examined initial descriptive data for most countries in Latin America to show that there is no strong evidence that tax compliance in the region has increased since the turn of the century. Only a few countries have improved levels of compliance in specific single

30 This idea is also developed (without that name) in Bergman (2009).

31 This unwillingness to crack down on illegal markets has also had unintended effects on the rise in crime in Latin America over the last two decades. I fully examine this subject in Bergman (2018). The overall argument is similar: "inaction" in eliminating illegal markets may have short-term benefits for incumbents, but also strong unintended consequences.

32 This happened to a degree in the 1990s, eliciting strong resistance from leaders and popular sectors.

33 Police and other authorities sometimes threaten small entrepreneurs in order to raise illegal revenues. This type of corruption has been very common in the region, and is a corrupt mechanism of extortion by officers.

taxes, particularly those countries that did not have such increases during the 1990s. The evidence shows that after reaching moderate rates of tax compliance, most countries have not further reduced tax evasion, despite the large improvements in tax administrations.

To account for this lack of progress I present several hypotheses. My central claim is that "the good times" of the commodity boom and the cheap cost of money have reduced the pressure on fiscal deficits, and therefore there was less need to look for alternative revenues. After the initial gains obtained by most nations during the 1990s, to further reduce tax evasion would imply a significant expansion of the tax base – e.g., taxing the informal economy. This has significant implications, and is difficult to achieve for several reasons. First, moving from a noncompliance to a compliance equilibrium where most people pay their dues requires time, persistence, and strong state capacities. Second, given the tax structures of most countries, the revenue gains from successful tax-evasion reduction are small compared to the gains obtained in the 1990s, and from new commodity taxes and revenues. And third, it appears that the lack of political will to close the tax-evasion gap might be tied to the adverse impact these policies could have on the rulers' own electoral base.

References

Bergman, Marcelo. 2009. *Tax Evasion and the Rule of Law in Latin America: The Political Economy of Cheating and Compliance in Argentina and Chile*. College Park: Penn State University Press.

2018. *More Money, More Crime: Prosperity and Rising Crime in Latin America*. New York: Oxford University Press.

Bird, Richard. 1992a. "Tax Reform in Latin America: A Review of Some Recent Experience," *Latin American Research Review* 27: 7–36.

1992b. *Tax Policy and Economic Development*. Baltimore: Johns Hopkins University Press.

CEPALSTAT. 2015. *Bases de Datos y Publicaciones Estadísticas*. CEPAL: http://estadisticas.cepal.org/cepalstat/WEB_CEPALSTAT/estadisticasIndicadores.asp?idioma=e

CIAT. 2015. Historical Rates of Value Added Taxes (VAT), at Tax Rates in Latin America: www.ciat.org/index.php/en/products-and-services/ciatdata/tax-rates.html

CIAT. 2018. Tax Performance: www.ciat.org/index.php/en/products-and-services/ciatdata/tax-performance.html

Corbacho, Ana, Vicente Fretes, and Eduardo Lora (eds.). 2013. *More than Revenue: Taxation as a Development Tool*. Washington, DC: IADB.

Díaz Alejandro, Carlos. 1975. *Ensayos sobre la historia económica Argentina*. Buenos Aires: Amorrortu.

Díaz de Sarralde, Santiago. 2017. "Value Added Tax: Revenue, Efficiency, Tax Expenditures and Inefficiencies in Latin America," *Documentos de Trabajo CIAT* (November), Centro Interamericano de Administraciones Tributarias.

ECLAC. 2017. Social Panorama of Latin America 2015. Santiago: Economic Commission for Latin America and the Caribbean.

Friedman, J. 1991. *Estudio de la Evasión en el IVA*. Santiago: Universidad de Chile.

Gillis, Malcolm, Carlo Shoup, and Gerardo Sicat. 1990. *Value-Added Taxation in Development Countries*. Washington, DC: World Bank.

Holland, Alisha. 2016. "Forbearance," *American Political Science Review* 110 (2): 232–246.

Hussmanns, Ralf. 2003. Defining and Measuring Formal Employment. Geneva: International Labor Organization: www.ilo.org/public/english/bureau/stat/download/papers/meas.pdf

ILO [International Labour Organization]. 2018. *Labor Statistics*: www.ilo.org/global/statistics-and-databases/lang–en/index.htm

IMF [International Monetary Fund]. 2015. *Current Challenges in Revenue Mobilization: Improving Tax Compliance*. Staff Report: www.imf.org/external/np/pp/eng/2015/020215a.pdf

Lederman, L. 2003. "The Interplay Between Norms and Enforcement in Tax Compliance," *Ohio State Law Journal* 64: 1453–1514.

Levi, Margaret. 1988. *On Rule and Revenue*. Berkeley: University of California Press.

Mahon, James, Marcelo Bergman, and Cynthia Arnson (eds.). 2014. *Progressive Tax Reform and Equality in Latin America*. Washington, DC: Woodrow Wilson Center for Scholars.

OECD. 2016. *Taxing Wages in Latin America and the Caribbean*. Paris: OECD: www.oecd.org/tax/taxing-wages-in-latin-america-and-the-caribbean-2016-9789264262607-en.htm.

2018. *Revenue Statistics in Latin America and the Caribbean, 2018*. Paris: OECD: www.oecd.org/tax/tax-policy/revenue-statistics-in-latin-america-and-the-caribbean-24104736.htm

Scholz, John. 2003. "Contractual Compliance and the Federal Income Tax System," *Washington University Journal of Law & Policy* 13: 139–203.

Scholz, John and Neil Pinney. 1995. "Duty, Fear, and Tax Compliance: The Heuristic Basis of Citizenship Behavior," *American Journal of Political Science* 39 (2): 490–512.

Serra, Pablo. 1991. "Estimación de la Evasión en el Impuesto al Valor Agregado," *Serie Documentos de Trabajo #5*. Santiago de Chile: Universidad de Chile.

Steinmo, Sven. 2018. *The Leap of Faith: The Fiscal Foundations of Successful Government in Europe and America*. New York: Oxford University Press.

Tanzi, Vito. 2013. *Tax Reform in Latin America: A Long Term Assessment*. Washington, DC: Woodrow Wilson International Center for Scholars, at www.wilsoncenter.org/publication/tax-reform-latin-america-long-term-assessment

Torgler, Benno. 2007. *Tax Compliance and Tax Morale: A Theoretical and Empirical Analysis*. Cheltenham: Edward Elgar Publishing.

4

Once Bitten, Twice Shy: Path Dependence, Power Resources, and the Magnitude of the Tax Burden in Latin America

Gabriel Ondetti

Although there is little agreement on what constitutes an ideal level of taxation, it is hard to dispute the idea that the magnitude of the tax burden is an important characteristic of national states, affecting the amount of resources available for both good uses and bad ones. Within Latin America, as Flores-Macías notes in the Introduction to this volume, there are striking differences on this variable. Countries such as Argentina, Brazil, and Uruguay have overall tax revenues equivalent to more than 28% of gross domestic product (GDP),[1] a level exceeding that of wealthy countries such as Australia, Japan, and the United States, which theory suggests should tend to have heavier taxation. Meanwhile, countries, such as Guatemala, Haiti, and Mexico subsist on substantially less than half that level.

In this chapter I explore the reasons behind these differences through a comparison of Brazil, Chile, and Mexico. This set of countries offers wide variance on the dependent variable. Over the past five years Brazil's tax revenues have averaged 34% of GDP, Chile's 19%, and Mexico's only 12% (CEPALSTAT n.d.). In addition, these countries are similar enough with regard to a number of standard explanations of taxation level, including economic development, regime type, and presidentialism (versus parliamentarism), to ease the problem of "too few cases, too many variables" potentially encountered in small-N research (Goggin 1986).

Students of Latin American political economy may well perceive that there is an obvious solution to this empirical puzzle: natural resource wealth. An extensive literature suggests that, since taxation is technically

[1] Including social security and subnational taxes.

and politically difficult – as discussed by Monaldi (Chapter 2 in this volume) – authorities with access to resource revenues tend to tax more lightly (Karl 1997; Ross 2001; Patrucchi and Grottola 2011). Furthermore, of this group of countries, Mexico has easily the largest nontax revenues from natural resources, followed by Chile and then Brazil: exactly the ordering we would expect if the tax burden is an inverse function of resource revenues.

While valid to some extent, this answer is nevertheless quite incomplete. It does explain much of the difference between the Mexican and Chilean tax burdens, but falls far short of accounting for the yawning gap between those two countries and Brazil. If Brazil's heavy taxation were simply a substitute for a smaller flow of resource revenues, then its total fiscal resources (including tax- and nontax sources) would be roughly in line with those of the other two countries. As explained later in the chapter, however, they are in fact vastly greater.

Therefore, to complement the natural-resource-based argument, I develop another account, one that melds two theoretical perspectives that are usually considered separate or (at least in stronger versions) even competing: power resources (Korpi 1978; Stephens 1979; Huber and Stephens 2012) and path dependence (North 1990; Mahoney 2000; Pierson 2004).

To begin with, I contend that a key variable explaining the huge difference in tax burdens between Mexico and Chile, on the one hand, and Brazil, on the other, is the relative influence of the political left and right, broadly defined to include both parties and actors in civil society. In the first two countries, the combination of a cohesive conservative bloc and a weak labor movement has helped keep tax revenues low despite the democratizing trends of recent decades. In Brazil, in contrast, a weakly organized right and a solid alliance of unions, popular movements, and left parties have supported the robust growth of spending and taxation.

Furthermore, I argue that, perhaps ironically, the superior force of the right in Chile and Mexico can be traced to the enduring impact of earlier episodes in which left-leaning governments implemented reforms that deeply threatened private property and employer control over the workforce. A crucial – if clearly unintended – legacy of these episodes was to galvanize the political mobilization and organization of economic elites and their conservative allies. "Once bitten," by state activism, Mexican and Chilean elites became "twice shy" about augmenting the state's resources. In contrast, Brazilian capitalists have never faced a government willing and politically able to implement profound redistributive reforms. As a result, they have remained relatively disorganized and lackadaisical in the face of public sector growth.

As these arguments suggest, this chapter portrays elite preferences regarding taxation, and state intervention in general, as being socially constructed, rather than fixed. While there may be an inherent tendency for business and the wealthy to more strenuously oppose direct taxes, due to their redistributive impact, both the intensity of this opposition and the disposition to accept other types of taxes vary as a function of historical experiences that impart enduring "lessons" about the character and reliability of the state.

COMPARING TAX SYSTEMS

Latin America has often been characterized as a low-tax region but, as Table 4.1 clearly demonstrates, tax burdens (including all levels of government, as well as contributions to public social security programs) vary quite widely across the region. The three countries examined here reflect this diversity. They include the country with the heaviest tax burden (Brazil), the one with the lightest tax burden (Mexico), and one that is very close to the regional average (Chile).

There are also substantial differences among these three countries with regard to the types of taxes they derive their revenue from, as can be seen in Table 4.2. As the Introduction to this volume points out, Latin

TABLE 4.1 *Average tax burden among Latin American countries, 2009–2013*

Country	Tax Revenues/ GDP (%)	Country	Tax Revenues/ GDP (%)
Brazil	**34.4**	*Panama	16.7
Uruguay	30.1	Honduras	16.6
Argentina	28.1	El Salvador	16.5
Costa Rica	21.9	Paraguay	14.1
Bolivia	21.8	Dominican Republic	13.9
Nicaragua	19.6	+Venezuela	13.4
Chile	**19.1**	Guatemala	12.6
Colombia	18.2	+Haiti	12.3
Peru	18.2	**Mexico**	**11.5**
Ecuador	17.8	Regional Average	18.8

Sources: CEPALSTAT (n.d.) and CIAT-IDB (n.d.)
* 2008–2012; + Central government only

TABLE 4.2 *Tax structures, tax burdens, and total fiscal revenues, 2009–2013*

	Type of Tax					Level of Collection			Tax Burden	Total Fiscal Revenues
Country/ Region	Direct	Indirect	Social Security	Other	Total	National	Subnational	Total	% GDP	% GDP
Brazil	29.5	44.1	25.5	0.9	100	68.9	31.1	100	34.4	34.8
Chile	38.2	53.4	7.3	1.0	100	92.7	7.3	100	19.1	20.9
Mexico	52.2	32.2	13.9	1.7	100	93.9	6.1	100	11.5	19.9
*Latin America	31.1	51.9	15.3	1.7	100	89.4	10.6	100	18.8	24.3

Sources: CEPALSTAT (n.d.) and CIAT-IDB (n.d.)
* Not including Haiti and Venezuela

American countries generally do not rely heavily on direct taxation. However, Mexico is an exception, since such taxes (most notably the income tax) account for more than half the country's tax revenues. Chile is also above the regional average for this variable.[2] Mexico is also exceptional in terms of its light use of indirect taxes, a category that includes value-added taxes, or VATs. Social security plays by far the largest role in Brazil, followed by Mexico. Brazil's tax system is also considerably more decentralized than the other two. It is hard to say which country's tax structure is most typical of Latin America, since each converges with the regional average in some ways and diverges in others, as Table 4.2 indicates.

The gaps in the magnitude of the tax burden between Brazil and the other two countries narrow substantially when only central government taxes are taken into consideration. However, Brazil's central government tax burden (23.7% of GDP for the most recent five years of data) is still more than a third heavier than Chile's (17.7%) and well over double Mexico's (10.8%). In any case, it makes little sense to ignore subnational governments. Such governments are crucial components of the overall public sector, especially in Brazil, where they provide public security, education, healthcare, sanitation, and other essential public services (Arretche 2012). In addition, in some policy areas (e.g., education and healthcare) there is a complex sharing of responsibility between different

[2] Nevertheless, given the magnitude of its tax burden, Brazil still has heavier direct taxation relative to GDP than either Chile or (by a wide margin) Mexico.

levels of government in Brazil, making any attempt to treat them as separate systems artificial. Some of that complexity also exists in Mexico (Díaz-Cayeros 2006).

Figure 4.1 shows that the contemporary variance in the tax burden among my cases is not a historical constant. In the 1960s and 1970s, Chile's tax burden was at least equal to Brazil's, and was possibly the heaviest in Latin America. Both countries had experienced rather consistent growth in their tax revenues since the 1920s, and in both of them the second half of the 1960s had brought a particularly robust expansion. However, reforms undertaken in Chile during the early 1980s, including privatization of the large social security system and reduced income taxation, led to a sharp decline in the tax burden. Largely as a result of this, Brazil's tax load clearly surpassed Chile's. The gap between these countries widened into a chasm over the next two decades, as Brazilian revenues grew in a sustained fashion under democracy while Chile's did not. Mexico, for its part, has seemingly always had a lighter tax burden, but the distance between it and Brazil and Chile widened after World War II, when Mexico's revenues began to stagnate relative to GDP, while those of the other countries grew. As emphasized later in the chapter (see "The Limits of Existing Explanations"), the divergence between Mexico and the other countries cannot be attributed to oil, which was not an important source of fiscal revenue during this period.

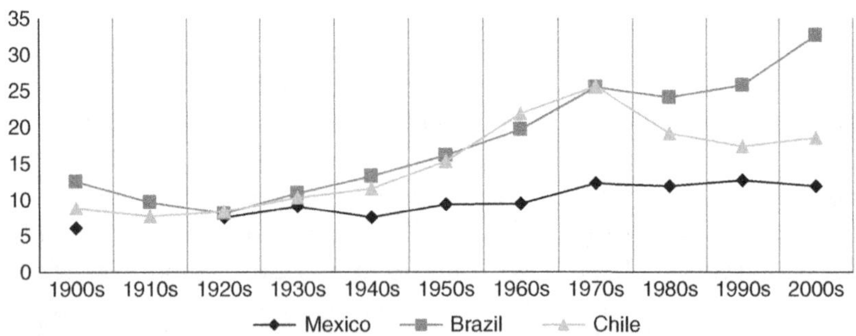

FIGURE 4.1 Evolution of the tax burden in Brazil, Chile, and Mexico, 1900–2009 (decadal averages)*

* Data for Chile do not include social security prior to 1950.

Sources: For 1980–2009, ECLAC (http://estadisticas.cepal.org/cepalstat/WEB_CEPALSTAT/estadisticasIndicadores.asp?idioma=i); for earlier decades: Brazil, IBGE (2006); Chile, Díaz et al. (2010) and World Bank (1961, 1966, 1970, 1984); Mexico, Díaz-Cayeros (2006, 36).

Data limitations prohibit a systematic comparison of the historical evolution of the tax structure among these cases. Nevertheless, the available data seem consistent with the contemporary association between light taxation and relatively heavy reliance on direct taxes. Figures from 1950, 1960, and 1970 indicate that direct taxes consistently made up a larger share of tax revenues in Mexico than in Brazil or Chile, where the overall tax burden was heavier (Fitzgerald 1978, 132).[3] With regard to centralization, Chile's tax system has traditionally been centralized and Brazil's (with some fluctuations) decentralized, but Mexico's has evolved over time (Aboites Aguilar 2003). In the 1920s and 1930s, Mexican subnational governments accounted for about a third of the total tax take (Díaz-Cayeros 2006, 36). Their share declined significantly in the 1940s, then plummeted in the 1980s with the introduction of the federal VAT, which replaced a number of subnational taxes.

THEORIES OF THE TAX BURDEN

Different types of taxes have different impacts on society and thus are shaped by distinct causal dynamics. Nevertheless, there are good reasons to treat the overall tax burden as a single dependent variable. With few exceptions, states impose taxes mainly to raise revenue for spending, and all taxes serve that purpose. To some extent, they are interchangeable. For example, while left-leaning actors favor direct taxes, since they are more redistributive, they are often willing to resort to other types to fund their desired programs if raising sufficient revenue through direct taxation is infeasible. Consequently, as discussed later in the chapter, larger public sectors tend to be funded mainly through regressive taxes. Second, as I discuss below, right-wing actors in the case study countries have typically opposed all types of taxation because they all distort the economy to some degree and facilitate state intervention.

The scholarship on taxation and public sector size offers a variety of potential strategies for explaining tax burden variance. They can be usefully parsed into four broad categories – economic, institutional, actor-centric, and path-dependent – based on the nature of the causal variable. A central theme of the literature is that the magnitude of the state reflects economic conditions. Economic development, in particular, is widely

[3] These data do not include social security, but since Mexico's social security revenues were modest (especially compared to Chile's) including them would only reinforce the comparatively larger role of direct taxes in the Mexican case.

viewed (albeit for varying reasons) as encouraging heavier taxation (Bird 1971; Cetrángolo and Gómez Sabaíni 2007). Some scholars have also argued that involvement in international trade promotes heavier taxation because external trade shocks foment demands for social insurance (Rodrik 1998). In contrast, the size of the farm sector is said to impede taxation because agriculture is hard to tax (Pessino and Fenochietto 2010). Natural resource wealth controlled by the state is also believed to engender low taxation by allowing authorities to rely on resource rents, which are politically easier to exploit than taxation and require less bureaucratic capacity (Pessino and Fenochietto 2010; Patrucchi and Grottola 2011).

Other theories depict the magnitude of the tax burden as a product of domestic political institutions. At a macro level, democracy is widely hypothesized to promote heavier taxation, either because it increases the ability of poorer people to advance demands for redistribution, or because it enhances the legitimacy of the state's own demands for revenue (Lindert 2004; Cárdenas 2010; Besley and Persson 2013). A variant of this theory is that democracy promotes state growth only in the presence of pronounced income inequality, because in more equitable settings the median voter views redistribution as less desirable (Meltzer and Richard 1981). Although this perspective has been influential, some scholars have made largely the opposite claim: that inequality tends to discourage redistribution and taxation (Cárdenas 2010; Huber and Stephens 2012).

Some other institutional arguments focus on the structure of specific democratic institutions. Scholars have argued that presidentialism discourages state growth by impeding rent extraction by politicians (Persson and Tabellini 2003). It has also been argued that federalism tends to keep the tax burden low, either by spurring subnational governments to compete for investment by lowering taxes or by enhancing accountability to citizens (Brennan and Buchanan 1980). However, one scholar has argued that in Latin America federalism tends to promote higher taxation, largely because it is characterized by "vertical fiscal imbalance," in which subnational authorities can spend heavily while relying on revenue transfers from the central government (Stein 1999). This finding was echoed by a broader, cross-regional study (Rodden 2003).

Actor-centric perspectives link the size of the tax burden to the influence of particular political actors. The most traditional emphasizes organizations, especially labor unions and leftist or populist parties, that represent the demands of nonelites for socioeconomic equality (Cameron 1978; Steinmo and Tolbert 1998; Stein and Caro 2013). Since meeting such demands requires revenues, a strong left tends to drive up the tax burden.

Though focusing on taxation, these works are congruent with the "power resources" school of welfare state development, which identifies labor/left party influence as a key determinant of social spending, at least under democracy (Korpi 1978; Stephens 1979; Huber and Stephens 2012).

A more recent actor-centric branch of research focuses not on labor, but on economic elites. These works, based mainly on the Latin American experience, emphasize intra-elite political cohesion and the strength of elite ties to the state, especially in the form of conservative parties and mechanisms of consultation with executive-branch officials. Ironically, however, they disagree about whether such conditions facilitate or impede revenue-raising tax reform.

On the one hand, Fairfield (Chapter 7 in this volume; see also 2010, 2015) argues that, since elites are inherently opposed to taxation (especially direct taxation), the more cohesive and politically connected the business class is, the harder it is to raise taxes. As she acknowledges, her thesis converges with the power-resources perspective in the sense that both emphasize the balance of class power, although they focus on different actors (Fairfield 2015, 21). On the other hand, in recent years a number of scholars have suggested that united and influential business elites can actually facilitate higher taxation, especially if pro-business parties control the government (Schneider 2012; Flores-Macías 2014). In such a setting, business elites may not resist higher taxation very strongly because they feel confident that the resulting revenues will be used for purposes consistent with their own interests.

The abovementioned theories emphasize the ongoing influence of certain variables on tax policy, or what Stinchcombe (1968) called "constant causation." However, there is another perspective, referred to as "path dependence," that stresses the enduring influence of past outcomes (North 1990; Mahoney 2000; Pierson 2000). There is considerable disagreement over what exactly path dependence means (Bennett and Elman 2006; Mahoney and Shensul 2006). However, there is also broad agreement that it refers to instances in which historical events give rise to rules, organizations, or informal understandings that are stubbornly resistant to subsequent changes in relevant contextual conditions. Whereas constant-cause explanations implicitly assume that variables respond to each other relatively fluidly, path dependence underscores the rigidity or "stickiness" of political arrangements once established (Thelen 2003).

To my knowledge, there is no study that explicitly applies this notion to explain variance in contemporary tax burdens, but at least two path-dependence-based analyses address closely related topics. One is Kato's (2003) study of the links between tax policy decisions and welfare spending. Focusing mainly on the developed world, Kato argues that countries that adopted a VAT prior to the early 1970s, when global economic growth began to slow, were able to maintain or expand welfare spending in subsequent decades because the VAT was an efficient revenue-raising tool. In contrast, countries that did not adopt a VAT during this period found themselves politically unable to transform it into a major component of their tax system in later years, due to rising resistance to taxation (as a result of slower growth) and greater consciousness of the VAT's regressivity. Consequently, their revenues stagnated, limiting the resources available for social spending. Kato's dependent variable is social spending, rather than the tax burden, but those two variables are closely related, since the ability to spend depends on taxation and in modern states social programs typically absorb a large proportion of revenue.

Also relevant is Kurtz's (2013) study of enduring differences in state capacity, or the ability to govern effectively, across Latin America. Although state capacity is broader than taxation, for Kurtz the magnitude of the tax burden is a crucial component of this variable. Based on case studies of Argentina, Chile, Peru, and Uruguay, Kurtz argues that variation in state capacity can be traced to the outcome of two historical "critical junctures": the transition to independence in the nineteenth century, and the political incorporation of nonelite groups during the first part of the twentieth century.

Strong states arose during the postindependence decades when two conditions were present: labor was not legally servile, and regional elites established a harmonious relationship at the national level. The results of the first juncture partly determined that of the second. Where the state was already weak (which was mainly in Peru), the emergence of new political actors only weakened it further. Where it was stronger, the impact of nonelite incorporation depended on sequencing. The concurrent incorporation of middle- and working-class groups in Chile and Uruguay reinforced state strength, while the earlier incorporation of the middle class into the oligarchic order in Argentina weakened it, essentially by making the subsequent incorporation of workers more conflictive and destabilizing.

THE LIMITS OF EXISTING EXPLANATIONS

Having laid out various theoretical tools, I now proceed to assess their utility for explaining variation in contemporary tax burdens among my three cases. I begin in this section by emphasizing the inability of most of the theories to clarify this puzzle. Then, in the two sections that follow this one, I lay out an empirical account that draws on key insights from both the actor-centric perspective (in particular, its power resources variant) and the concept of path dependency.

Most of the economic explanations of the tax burden are flatly contradicted by the cases examined here. Despite being similarly developed in terms of per capita GDP, Brazil and Mexico have radically different tax burdens. Meanwhile, Chile's somewhat higher development level would be expected to give it the heaviest taxation, but it actually has a much lighter tax burden than Brazil.[4] Similarly, the larger contribution of agriculture to Brazil's economy should tend to depress taxation relative to Chile and Mexico, but Brazil has easily the heaviest tax burden of the three.[5] Finally, both Mexico and Chile are much more integrated into global trade than Brazil, which theoretically should tend to result in higher taxation.[6] As we have seen, however, the reality is drastically at odds with this prediction.

The major exception to the inadequacy of economic explanations is the notion that nontax natural-resource revenues reduce taxation, which, as Flores-Macías notes in the Introduction to this volume, is quite relevant to Latin America. Mexico's extremely low tax burden can be explained in part by the fact that it is a major oil producer and roughly 40% of its fiscal revenues in recent years have come from the state oil company, Mexican Petroleum (*Petróleos Mexicanos* [PEMEX]). In Chile, a far smaller but still significant amount of nontax revenue also comes from natural resources, especially copper. Two-thirds of Chile's copper production comes from private firms, which contribute to fiscal revenues through taxes (Correa 2016, 29). However, the state-owned National Copper Corporation (*Corporación Nacional del Cobre*, CODELCO) is an important contributor of nontax revenue to public coffers. In contrast, as Monaldi points out (Chapter 2 in this volume), the Brazilian state's resource revenues are of negligible importance. Brazilian authorities thus have little choice but to rely on taxation to provide fiscal resources.

[4] In 2013, Brazil's per capita GDP (in current US dollars) was $11,961, Mexico's was $10,553, and Chile's was $15,718. Historically, Mexico has tended to be wealthier than Brazil but poorer than Chile (Astorga et al. 2005).

[5] Agriculture, forestry, and fishing comprise 4.5% of GDP in Brazil, compared to 3.1% in Chile and 3.2% in Mexico (CEPALSTAT).

[6] The share of exports and imports in Brazil's GDP is about half that of Chile and Mexico (CEPALSTAT n.d.).

Though compelling, resource wealth falls far short of offering a complete account of the differences in taxation among my cases. Part of the reason can be gleaned from Table 4.2, which also compares tax revenues and total fiscal revenues as a percentage of GDP. The table shows that the difference in tax burdens between Chile and Mexico can largely be explained as a function of Mexico's larger flow of nontax revenue, since the fiscal revenues of the two countries are similar. However, Brazil's total fiscal revenues are a whopping 65–75% greater.[7] Thus, after taking account of resource revenues, what we have left is essentially a two-sided comparison between, on the one hand, two countries with relatively compact public sectors (even compared to the regional average) and, on the other, a country that by the standards of the developing world possesses vast fiscal resources. In addition, a natural-resource-based account of Mexico's light taxation faces a major chronological problem: the fact that Mexico's status as a very low-tax country by regional standards became apparent roughly two decades before its oil boom of the late 1970s, which abruptly turned PEMEX into a central pillar of the fiscal system (Chávez M. 2005; Farfán Mares 2011).

Most of the institutional explanations also fall short, or are simply irrelevant. All three countries have presidential forms of government, so the influential presidentialism–parliamentarism account is not applicable here. With regard to federalism, the outcomes clearly contradict theoretical expectations. Brazil's decentralized federalism, in which state and local governments have considerable tax capacity, should depress taxation relative to Mexico and Chile, where taxation is currently much more centralized and there is, especially in the Mexican case, a far greater vertical fiscal imbalance (Corbacho et al. 2013, 83).

The macro-institution of democracy, often seen as encouraging heavier taxation, requires more careful consideration. All three countries are routinely viewed as electoral democracies today. Nevertheless, their contemporary regimes vary in age. Brazil emerged from military rule in 1985 and Chile in 1990. Mexico's democratic transition is harder to date, since the old regime was not an outright dictatorship but rather a hegemonic party system led by the Institutional Revolutionary Party (*Partido Revolucionario Institucional* [PRI]). However, most experts would probably view it as occurring mainly during the 1990s, when a series of electoral reforms set the stage for the PRI's loss of its legislative majority

[7] Even if legally mandated contributions to private social security accounts are counted as part of Chile's fiscal revenues, the Brazilian figure is still almost 40% greater.

in 1997 and eventual defeat in the 2000 presidential election. Given that the variance in the age of the current democratic regime parallels the variance in tax burdens, could the former help explain the latter?

I would argue against this interpretation. Unlike most other countries in the region, Mexico's tax burden has shown few signs of increasing significantly under democracy. Tax revenues as a percentage of GDP are lower today than in the early 1990s (CEPALSTAT n.d.). If authoritarianism were the key factor suppressing taxation, we should presumably have expected democratization to bring about a significant revenue boost. Chile's tax burden has also increased slowly since the democratic transition. A tax reform at the outset of democracy in 1990 raised tax revenues by about 2% of GDP, but the tax burden remained virtually stagnant for a quarter century thereafter. In Brazil, in comparison, tax revenues have increased by some 10% of GDP under democracy (CEPALSTAT n.d.). Thus, while it is quite possible that democracy, other things being equal, does encourage higher taxation, there is little evidence at this point that the differences in tax burden among these cases can be explained by the number of years that have passed since their respective democratic transitions.

An alternative approach to the regime-type variable might focus not on the current regime but on the number of years of democratic governance in a country's overall history. However, this approach fares no better. Although Mexico clearly has the least overall experience with competitive politics, most scholars would probably view Chile as having a longer democratic tradition than Brazil, since it adopted its first democratic regime more than a decade earlier and spent less time under military rule (Drake 2009, 6). However, Brazil has a much heavier tax burden than Chile. Taking into consideration the evolution of the suffrage does not help, either. Of the three countries, low-tax Mexico actually eliminated literacy requirements for voting earliest (1917) and high-tax Brazil latest (1988).[8] Brazil enfranchised women earliest (1932), but when Chile finally did so in 1970 (17 years after Mexico) it already had a tax burden fairly similar to Brazil's and much heavier than Mexico's.

The Meltzer–Richard variant of the democracy variable is on the surface more convincing. Given that Brazil has traditionally been the most inequitable of these countries, one might suspect that its taxation level has increased the most because the median Brazilian voter demands more redistribution. Yet, this interpretation faces important problems. To begin with, Chile's inequality spiked sharply upward during the military, so that by 1990 the

[8] Chile did so in 1970.

country's Gini coefficient for income was similar to Brazil's at the time of its own transition.[9] Of the three countries, only Mexico's inequality was significantly lower, though still high. In addition, the idea that poorer people tend to view redistribution more favorably is not clearly supported by public opinion data or voting patterns, as highlighted by Bogliaccini and Luna (Chapter 9 in this volume). For example, in Brazil studies have shown that people of higher social status are more likely to embrace redistribution than those of low social status (Ondetti 2015, 758). Moreover, it is only relatively recently, and mainly in presidential elections, that Brazilian leftist parties have made major headway among the truly poor.

With regard to the actor-centric perspective, the argument that clearly does not provide leverage in this particular set of cases is the one that associates economic elite cohesion with success in raising taxes (Schneider 2012; Flores-Macías 2014). As Schneider (2002, 2004) has argued, Mexico and Chile have among the most politically cohesive business sectors in the region, while Brazil's is notably fragmented. Nevertheless, Brazilian tax revenues have risen steadily for decades, while those of the other two countries have been relatively stagnant. Undoubtedly, there are contexts in which a tightly knit economic elite with strong ties to governing authorities can facilitate revenue-raising tax reform, but as an explanation of variation in tax burdens among the cases analyzed here, this perspective is unsatisfactory.

The available path-dependency-based explanations also seem inadequate, albeit for differing reasons. Kato's theory of welfare-state magnitude based on the timing of VAT adoption is superficially appealing, but ultimately unconvincing. My cases accord with her argument in the sense that Brazil, which has much higher tax revenues and social spending than the other two countries,[10] also introduced its VAT earlier. Brazil adopted a VAT in 1966, while Chile did so in 1974 and Mexico in 1980. However, contrary to Kato's expectation, the VAT has not been the dominant force behind Brazil's rising taxation in recent decades. Newer, indirect taxes called "social contributions" have been more important (Afonso 2013), and their role was particularly crucial during the 1990s, a period of sluggish growth overall. Moreover, direct taxes, though still less significant than indirect ones,

[9] Brazil's 1985 Gini was 0.552, while Chile's 1990 Gini was 0.572 (World Bank reports archive: http://documents.worldbank.org/curated/en/home).

[10] For example, in 2009, Brazil's total social expenditures equaled 26.2% of GDP, compared to 15.7% in Chile and 11.2% in Mexico (CEPALSTAT).

have actually increased their share of total tax revenue since the introduction of the VAT (Ondetti 2015, 755).

Kurtz's path-dependency account faces a major obstacle in the context of the present comparison: the fact that the country with easily the heaviest tax burden (Brazil) employed a system of explicitly servile labor until 1888 – longer than any other country in the Americas. By the logic of the argument, slavery should have impeded the creation of a strong, capable state. However, historical analyses suggest that the national state was already rather extensive and interventionist at the outset of the twentieth century (Topik 1987). An even more important objection, however, is that Kurtz's view of the tax burden as a reflection of broader state capacity does not ring true among this set of cases. In particular, Chile clearly ranks above Brazil on standard measures of state capacity, such as corruption, but has a far lighter tax burden.

A POWER-RESOURCES INTERPRETATION

As discussed, a number of scholars have traced differences in taxation, as well as in spending, to the relative power of left parties, labor unions, and other groups representing nonelites (Stephens 1979; Cameron 1978; Huber and Stephens 2012; Stein and Caro 2013). Fairfield (2010, 2015) has essentially extended this "power resources" argument by emphasizing the effects of variation in the political resources of elites – see Fairfield, Chapter 7 in this volume. This overall perspective, I argue, rings true for the cases examined here.

The contrast among the cases is sharpest with regard to the class organization of economic elites. Schneider's (2002, 2004) wide-ranging comparative work on Latin American business organization underscores both the unity of elites in Mexico and Chile and the marked disunity of their Brazilian counterparts. Both Mexico and Chile boast encompassing national associations that emerged from the business community itself and effectively represent business as a class. In both cases, moreover, business has close ties to electorally competitive, programmatic right-wing parties (Luna and Rovira Kaltwasser 2014). Mexico's National Action Party (*Partido Acción Nacional* [PAN]) held the presidency from 2000 to 2012, and Chile's two major conservative parties – the Independent Democratic Union (*Unión Demócrata Independiente* [UDI]) and National Renovation (*Renovación Nacional*) – have generally held about 40% of the seats in Congress since 1990, as well as the presidency from 2010 to 2014.

In contrast, Brazil lacks encompassing national business associations (Schneider 2004). Although there are many entities representing business, even the broadest ones are limited to a particular sector and tend to be handicapped by internal divisions and lack of member engagement. Moreover, Brazil lacks a competitive party that is strongly pro-business. The party that seemed most likely to assume that role in the early years of democracy, the Party of the Liberal Front (*Partido da Frente Liberal* [PFL]; now called *Democratas*), has since been reduced to near irrelevance. The Party of Brazilian Social Democracy (*Partido da Social Democracia Brasileira* [PSDB]) does represent business to some extent, but it is more a centrist party than a true programmatic conservative party.

On the left, the differences are also significant. Brazil's union density is about 50% higher than in Chile or Mexico.[11] Brazilian labor also possesses encompassing organizations that more actively promote a progressive agenda. The Unified Workers' Central (*Central Única dos Trabalhadores* [CUT]), easily the largest union confederation, is clearly leftist and an important political actor, and there are two research institutions directly controlled by the labor movement whose work is commonly cited in news coverage and legislative debates.[12] In comparison, at least in recent years, labor organizations in the other two countries have had a more corporatist orientation and limited technical capabilities.

Comparing the electoral strength of the left among these countries is somewhat more complex. On the surface, Chile has had the strongest left, since a center–left coalition, known initially as the Concertation (*Concertación*) and later as New Majority (*Nueva Mayoría*), has been in office for most of the period since the return of democracy. However, these coalitions, especially the *Concertación*, were constrained by the combination of a cohesive right-wing bloc anchored by a business

[11] In 2006, the most recent year for which data are available for all three countries, union density was 17% of the employed labor force in Brazil, 11% of the employed labor force in Chile, and 10% of the economically active population (EAP) in Mexico (Fundação Perseu Abramo 2013, 3; Bensusán and Middlebrook 2013, 54; Dirección del Trabajo 2014, 11). The Mexican figure would be somewhat higher if it were calculated based on the employed work force, since the EAP includes unemployed workers who are seeking employment.

[12] These are the Inter-Union Department for Statistics and Socioeconomic Studies (*Departamento Inter-Sindical de Estatística e Estudos Socioeconômicos* [DIEESE]), which conducts socioeconomic research, and the Inter-Union Department for Parliamentary Advisory (*Departamento Intersindical de Assessoria Parlamentar* [DIAP]), which monitors Congress.

community committed to neoliberalism, electoral institutions favoring the right, and a popular sector lacking organizations capable of inducing or supporting a turn to the left (Posner 2008; Fairfield 2015). The result has been a brand of politics that, at least until recently, discouraged popular mobilization and demand-making.

Brazil's electoral left, led by the Workers' Party (*Partido dos Trabalhadores* [PT]), has held the presidency for less time (2003–2016) than Chile's center–left coalitions, but its ties to civil society have remained stronger and its rhetoric more leftist. Although the labor movement has a significant centrist wing, most unions continue to sympathize with the PT or other leftist parties, as do national movement organizations such as the Movement of Landless Rural Workers (*Movimento dos Trabalhadores Rurais Sem Terra* [MST]) and the National Union of Students (*União Nacional dos Estudantes* [UNE]). The PT has attempted to make peace with the private sector, but it has never accepted market-oriented policies to the extent that, for example, Chile's Socialists have. Today, the party is mired in a deep crisis. A massive corruption scandal and a protracted economic recession led to the congressional removal of President Dilma Rousseff in late 2016. Some of the PT's top leaders are facing criminal charges. Nevertheless, there can be little doubt that the PT has been the most influential political party in Brazil during the twenty-first century and will continue to be an important force in national politics.

Mexico clearly has the weakest electoral left. The country's main leftist party, the Party of the Democratic Revolution (*Partido de la Revolución Democrática* [PRD]), has never held more than about a quarter of the seats in either house of Congress and, more importantly, has never been able to capture the country's powerful presidency. A number of factors have thwarted the PRD's rise, including electoral fraud, internal factionalism, and lack of labor support. Even among the small group of workers who are unionized, there is more support for the centrist PRI than the PRD (Bensusán and Middlebrook 2013). In recent years the PRD has been weakened further by the defection of its most popular leader, Andrés Manuel López Obrador, and his National Regeneration Movement (*Movimiento de Regeneración Nacional* [MORENA]).

These differences in the balance of left–right power have shaped the tax burden. In Chile, as mentioned, the *Concertación* was able to pass a much-needed 1990 tax reform that raised revenues significantly. However, as Fairfield (2010, 2015) has argued, the combined power of business and conservative parties played a crucial role in keeping the tax burden stagnant thereafter. Some potential reforms were not even presented because policymakers understood that they would be forcefully rejected. A combination of defeat in the 2010 presidential election and the massive student protests of 2011–2012 prompted *Concertación* leaders to expand their coalition to the left and to push for a more significant tax reform to fund the expected increase in educational spending. That reform, approved in 2014, will eventually raise the tax burden, but to nowhere near the current level in Brazil.[13]

Conservative dominance has also contributed to persistently light taxation in Mexico, despite the more democratic character of politics since the 1990s (Ondetti 2017). The PRI governments of that decade were committed to currying business confidence (damaged during previous decades, as discussed later in the chapter) through liberalizing reforms, and business was equally committed to keeping taxation to a minimum. An implicit agreement resulted in which business accepted certain revenue-raising reforms in times of fiscal need, but on the condition that they not be used to fund major new spending commitments (Martínez-Vázquez 2001, 4–5). Given the PAN's pro-market ideology and ties to business, its victories in the 2000 and 2006 presidential elections virtually ensured that the tax burden would not substantially increase. PAN governments did seek to boost revenues to some extent, but their insistence on doing so primarily through indirect taxation both limited the scope of the proposed reforms and made them vulnerable to accusations of regressivity. Not surprisingly, their efforts largely failed. In 2013, President Enrique Peña Nieto of the PRI allied with the PRD to gain approval of a more balanced proposal. However, that reform was energetically opposed by all major business associations, as well as the PAN. Concessions made to both business and the PRD (with regard to indirect taxes) resulted in a reform that has had little impact on Mexico's tax burden (Unda Gutiérrez 2015).

In contrast, business resistance to taxation in Brazil has been tepid and fragmented. The sharp increase in the tax burden during the 1990s and early 2000s did not provoke a strong, coordinated repudiation from business. A private sector umbrella organization called Business Action (*Ação Empresarial*) was created in the 1990s and came to focus much of its attention on tax issues. However, it was never more than a loose network and was abandoned several years ago. Moreover, it did not demand that the tax burden be reduced, only that its growth be controlled and its structure simplified (Ferreira 2002, ch. 2). In the last decade, given

[13] Tax revenues are projected to increase by 3% of GDP by 2018.

the extraordinary level reached by the tax burden and rising concerns about its effects on competitiveness, business associations have frequently complained about both the tax load itself and the enormous costs of compliance.[14] While these complaints have contributed to some minor victories[15] they have not translated into unified political action.

Meanwhile, unions, movements, and left-leaning parties have played an important role in the growth of the Brazilian tax burden, not so much by championing higher taxation as through their strong defense of social spending, which has increased greatly since the democratic transition (Weyland 1996; Mendes 2014). Spending pressures, combined with the relative lack of counterpressure from business and the right, compelled the governments of the PSDB (1995–2002) and PT (since 2003) to seek more revenue. As Schneider discusses (see Chapter 5 in this volume), the 1988 Constitution, which created important new social policy commitments, especially in the area of pensions, is an important institutional source of these pressures (see also Melo et al. 2010). However, both the original design of the constitution and the way it has been implemented and amended reflect the strong support for generous social spending in civil society and the party system (Ondetti 2015).

A potential objection to this interpretation is that if labor and the partisan left were really more influential in Brazil than in Mexico or Chile, then Brazilian taxation would be more progressive. As noted earlier, direct taxes comprise a lower percentage of total tax revenues in Brazil than in the other two countries, especially Mexico. However, this objection is not supported by the wider literature. Scholars have frequently noted that the countries with the largest and most welfare-oriented public sectors tend to rely particularly heavily on regressive forms of taxation (Kato 2003; Timmons 2005; Beramendi and Rueda 2007). To the extent that redistribution occurs, it is mainly on the spending side (Mahon et al. 2015, 12). While an in-depth analysis of this tendency lies beyond the scope of this chapter, in broad strokes the literature suggests that it has to do with restrictions imposed by the private sector (Przeworksi and Wallerstein 1988; Timmons 2005). While capitalists may be willing to accept a heavy tax burden that is regressively financed or a light one that is progressively financed, it is difficult to

[14] This assertion is based on a series of field interviews conducted with leaders and top officials of major firms and business associations in June and July 2015.

[15] Perhaps the most significant was the nonrenewal of a federal financial transactions tax in 2007. However, much of the revenue lost was replaced by rate hikes on other taxes.

impose upon them a system that both collects large amounts of revenue and does so in redistributive manner. Governments that wish to construct extensive welfare states thus usually opt to rely heavily on regressive levies.

LINKING POWER RESOURCES TO PATH DEPENDENCE

Of course, this explanation begs the question of why the balance of political power in Mexico and Chile tilts more to the right than in Brazil. In addressing such differences, power-resource-oriented analyses tend to focus on socioeconomic structures, such as industrialization and urbanization (Stephens 1979; Huber and Stephens 2012). Such variables do play a role in these cases. Most significantly, the more sweeping character of economic liberalization in Chile and Mexico in recent decades helps to explain why labor is weaker in these countries than Brazil. Trade liberalization and privatization hit hard at workers in import-substitution industrialization (ISI) firms and public enterprises, who were typically among the most unionized, contributing to declining union density. Brazil's more moderate approach to liberalization, in contrast, helped to preserve overall density despite important shifts in the rate of unionization among different categories of workers (Fundação Perseu Abramo 2013).

Nevertheless, the most important factor in shaping the contemporary balance of left–right power is the enduring impact of certain historical events on elite attitudes and political organization. Specifically, I argue that the superiority of the right in Chile and Mexico can be traced to episodes in which left-leaning governments implemented major reforms that deeply menaced, but ultimately did not destroy, the private sector. These instances inculcated in economic elites a deep-seated apprehension of the state that led them to organize politically to prevent future threats. In Brazil, in contrast, no such episode ever arose and, as a consequence, business has remained complacent about state intervention in the economy. To a large extent, variation in labor strength is a derivative of this difference, since in Chile and Mexico the right has striven more consistently and effectively to weaken unions.

This argument is perhaps easier to make in the Chilean case, where the key historical episode, or "critical juncture," is more recent and dramatic. In the early 1970s Chilean elites were alarmed by the election of Salvador Allende, a Marxist, to the presidency and Allende's subsequent attempts to advance a transition to socialism amid intense popular mobilization

(Valenzuela 1978). While the previous president, Eduardo Frei of the Christian Democratic Party (*Partido Demócrata Cristiano* [PDC]), had initiated some notable redistributive programs, under Allende this reformist turn became a sharp veer to the left. His government expropriated numerous businesses and rural estates, boosted wages and social spending, imposed widespread price controls, and made friendly gestures toward socialist regimes elsewhere. The nearly three years under Allende's Unidad Popular government were a time of intense polarization and, eventually, high inflation and deep recession. Many Chilean elites undoubtedly became convinced that their country was heading toward Soviet- or Cuban-style communism. Not surprisingly, many also supported the brutal 1973 coup that established a military dictatorship.

The Allende experience had a lasting impact on elite political attitudes, intensifying their rejection of the statism and leftism that had been staples of Chile's politics prior to the coup (Silva 1993; Silva 1995; Pollack 1999). This effect was compounded by the eventual success of the radical market reforms implemented by the subsequent military regime (1973–1990) led by Gen. Augusto Pinochet. Although Chile's economy suffered through some difficult times under this regime, beginning in the mid-1980s it entered a period of rapid and sustained growth that would make it a darling of liberal economists.

Chilean business organizations reflected this transformation. Prior to the Allende period, many business people, especially in manufacturing, had been highly sympathetic to state intervention in the ISI mold. Others, especially in agriculture, preferred a more liberal tack. This disagreement, as well as more specific conflicts, divided business and detracted from the influence of its nominal peak organization, the Confederation of Production and Commerce (*Confederación de la Producción y del Comercio* [CPC]) (Schneider 2004). These divisions were also reflected to some degree in partisan loyalties. While some elites favored one of the two traditional conservative parties, others came in the 1960s to support the centrist PDC (Stallings 1978). These defections helped weaken the conservative parties, which merged in 1966 to form the National Party.

The experiences of the 1970s and 1980s ended up largely overcoming these divisions by unifying Chilean elites around an ideology that rejects state intervention in the economy (Silva 1995; Pollock 1999). This relative consensus was expressed in the greater political weight achieved by the CPC, which emerged during the democratic transition as the mouthpiece of the business community as a whole (Fairfield 2015). Business also lent its support to the creation in the 1980s of the UDI and *Renovación*

Nacional. While UDI differs from *Renovación Nacional* in being more socially conservative and *pinochetista*, both are viscerally committed to free markets and have strong business ties. Finally, elites backed the creation of think tanks, including the Center of Public Studies (*Centro de Estudios Públicos*) and Freedom and Developement (*Libertad y Desarrollo*), which became influential proponents of free-market policies.

In other words, the traumatic experience of the Allende government contributed to the subsequent rise of a cohesive, enduring right-wing bloc anchored by a business community strongly committed to economic liberalism. To be sure, Pinochet's radical reformism also contributed to that consensus by demonstrating the growth potential of a ruggedly liberal development path. However, the radical swing to the market would have been quite impossible had Allende not swung Chile sharply in the opposite direction first, fomenting a willingness among the country's economic elites to accept sweeping change (Silva 1993; Silva 1995).

This conservative bloc has proved effective not only in holding the line against statist economic policies, but also in preventing the revival of Chile's once strong and militant labor movement. Unions were dealt heavy blows under the military regime, including repression, trade-induced deindustrialization, and the adoption of an anti-union labor code (Winn 2004). Despite implementing some incremental reforms, Chile's democratic governments have fallen short of legislating changes that would substantially empower unions. While the politics of this failure are complex, there can be little doubt that the electoral strength of the right and the unity of business around a free-market ideology have played crucial roles (Posner 2008; Ensignia 2017).

In the Mexican case, path dependence is somewhat subtler but also more telling, given the persistence and gradual strengthening of business organization and antistate feeling over a longer period and under more diverse conditions.

The impressive organization of Mexican business today is the fruit of recurrent business–state conflicts (Martínez Nava 1984; Schneider 2002). During the second half of the twentieth century the private sector faced two governments – those of Adolfo López Mateos (1958–1964) and Luis Echeverría (1970–1976) – that sought to push economic policymaking in a more statist, social-democratic direction. The confrontation with López Mateos helped propel the 1962 creation of the Mexican Council of Businessmen (*Consejo Mexicano de Hombres de Negocio* [CMHN]), an organization that brings together the leaders of the country's largest firms.[16] Meanwhile, the more protracted struggle against Echeverría provoked the creation in 1975 of the Business Coordinating Council (*Consejo Coordinador Empresarial* [CCE]), an entity that unites all the major business associations and has become the most visible representative of Mexico's private sector. Business also confronted the state at the end of the presidency of José López Portillo (1976–1982), who nationalized the banking sector in an effort to contain the effects of the debt crisis. Alarm over this initiative encouraged business leaders to breathe new life into the PAN, which already existed but was of little electoral significance.

Nevertheless, the role of business in these episodes cannot be adequately understood without reference to an earlier conflict, which strengthened or created collective actors that would go on to play a major role in the growth of the political right. That was the conflict with the immediate postrevolutionary governments, most particularly that of Lázaro Cárdenas (1934–1940).

The Cárdenas years were a watershed in Mexican politics. The pioneering 1917 constitution, framed during the country's tumultuous revolution (1910–1920), had promised progressive, nationalistic change. However, the immediate postrevolution governments pursued these changes only halfheartedly. Rather unexpectedly, Cárdenas struck out in a new direction, implementing easily the largest agrarian reform in Latin American history until that time, the first major expropriations of foreign oil companies in the region, and measures to encourage union membership and activism. He also moved to diminish Catholic Church influence in education. Scholars have sometimes downplayed the significance of these changes, but by the standards of the time they were genuinely radical (Knight 1994; Gilly 2013). Cárdenas also used state intervention to encourage private investment. However, for business owners, especially those of the more established firms, this aspect was overshadowed by perceived threats to property rights and control over the labor force (Hamilton 1982; Martínez Nava 1984). For this reason, they joined Catholic activists and other conservatives in mobilizing to oppose the government, generating a rising tide of political conflict.

At the heart of this reaction were the industrialists of Monterrey, capital of the northern state of Nuevo León and Mexico's major manufacturing hub. Incensed by the government's assault on its privileges, the *regiomontano* elite reacted with sharp public rebukes, street protests, lockouts, and support for antilabor thugs and fascist groups (Saragoza

[16] Recently, CMHN changed its name to Mexican Council of Business, or CMN.

1988). In their attempts to articulate broader opposition to Cárdenas, they relied in part on the Confederation of Mexican Employers (*Confederación Patronal Mexicana* [COPARMEX]), an association that had originally been created in 1929, but which came into its own under Cárdenas. In 1939, with the 1940 election looming on the horizon, business people from Monterrey and other regions joined forces with Catholic activists to back the formation of the PAN, a party created with the singular purpose of combating *cardenismo* (Tirado 1985, 106–107).

In the face of rising conservative resistance, Cárdenas eventually backed off his reformism and facilitated the selection of Manuel Avila Camacho, a moderate with close ties to the military, as the candidate of his National Revolutionary Party (*Partido Nacional Revolucionario*), which would be renamed PRI in 1946. Cárdenas may well have feared that continued insistence on reforms might lead to a civil war and the rollback of his earlier achievements (Michaels 1970). During the 1940s and 1950s, Avila Camacho and his successors deepened this tentative turn to the right, discouraging strikes, holding down wage growth, sharply reducing land reform, and compensating the owners of expropriated oil companies.[17]

Beginning under Avila Camacho, the state also moved to weaken the more leftist currents within the labor movement (Collier and Collier 1991, 408–410). This effort intensified under Miguel Alemán (1946–1952), whose government strove to replace independent union leaders with *charros*, or ones subservient to the state and friendly to management (Middlebrook 1995, ch. 4). Through a combination of carrots and sticks, Mexico's labor movement, once among the strongest in Latin America, was gradually brought to heel.

The apparent cooperation between the state and private sector during these decades (and, to a somewhat lesser extent, the 1960s) has led some analysts to embrace the notion of a symbiotic "alliance for profits," in which business allowed the PRI to run the country relatively undisturbed and in return received ample opportunities for enrichment (Reynolds 1970; Thacker 2012). This perspective, however, risks obscuring the tensions that existed between the state and the private sector, as well as the partly coerced nature of the PRI's policy choices (Martínez Nava 1984; Tirado 1985; Gauss 2010). It was not easy for a party that framed

[17] Admittedly, Avila Camacho did pass Mexico's first significant social insurance law. However, the resources committed to it were quite modest and would largely remain so in future decades.

itself as the embodiment of a social revolution and possessed strong ties to popular organizations to maintain probably the stingiest welfare state of any middle-income Latin American country, while restraining real wage growth and responding only selectively to peasant demands for land. Such an orientation required a difficult balancing act.

We can understand the course the PRI navigated only if we appreciate that it was striving mightily to regain the confidence of a private sector that had not forgotten the injuries and insults suffered under Cárdenas (Shafer 1973; Martínez Nava 1984). Owners of large, well-established businesses, in particular, had been traumatized by what they viewed as a struggle for the survival of capitalism. Even if they acquiesced to the PRI's persistence in power, they were determined to prevent anything smacking of a return to *cardenismo*. Their "historical paranoia," as one scholar put it, made them "hypersensitive to the least expansion of the state presence in economic activities, and even more so to reformist projects" (Martínez Nava 1984, 81).

The hard core of resistance to state intervention was the Monterrey elite, or the "Monterrey Group," as it came to be known. It was largely during the struggle against Cárdenas that this crucial faction of Mexican business would acquire its impressive political cohesion and well-known determination to fight against state economic intervention, even if that meant open confrontation with the authorities (Saragoza 1988; Gauss 2010). The Monterrey Group's blend of economic liberalism and Catholic social conservatism was also imprinted upon COPARMEX, which gradually became an association of national scope. Although the members of these groups were not above accepting special favors from the state, they were philosophically opposed to state intervention in almost every form.

COPARMEX and the Monterrey Group tended to be especially combative, but they were by no means isolated. Both had strong ties to other associations, such as the corporatist entities representing commerce and industry (Shafer 1973; Gauss 2010). In the 1940s there emerged a faction of smaller industrial enterprises that, in sharp contrast to these groups, explicitly endorsed state intervention. Associated with a corporatist entity called the National Chamber of Manufacturing Industry (*Cámara Nacional de la Industria de Transformación* [CANACINTRA]), they backed the PRI more unconditionally than big business. However, CANACINTRA never became a truly major force. As an early student of Mexican business pointed out, CANACINTRA's perspective "has utterly 'failed' to win the hearts of Mexican business to it, and it has had no effect on private enterprise attitudes toward government intervention, except possibly to make them more suspicious of government" (Shafer 1973, 112). In contrast, the author argued, "the legendary business conservatism of Nuevo León has always had plenty of counterparts elsewhere" (Shafer 1973, 105).

During the 1940s and 1950s, big business, while accepting the basic thrust of PRI's pro-industrialization policy, worked to circumscribe the scope of state intervention (López Portillo 1995; Gauss 2010). Not only did it insist upon light taxation, snubbing attempts in both decades to increase the state's fiscal resources (Unda Gutiérrez 2010, ch. 5), it also sought to limit the state's role in other areas (Cypher 1990; Gauss 2010). Thus, although Mexico explicitly adopted the same basic ISI model that emerged elsewhere in Latin America during this period, its state enterprise sector remained smaller and its state development bank less active than in some other countries, including Brazil and Chile (Graham 1982; Etchemendy 2011, 293). Even Mexico's tariff protection tended to be lower than that of other large countries in the region (Graham 1982, 25; Ros 1993, 8–9).

The antistate mindset that grew out of the conflict with Cárdenas is crucial to comprehending subsequent developments in business–state relations and business organization. López Mateos and Echeverría proposed reforms that were not especially radical. If approved, they would simply have moved Mexico somewhat closer to countries such as Chile (even pre-Allende) and Uruguay, where the state was far larger and social policies more developed.[18] The reason that these episodes, especially the second, provoked large-scale business mobilization and lasting innovations in formal organization is because key business groups interpreted them through the enduring ideological prism arising from the conflict with Cárdenas. From this perspective, they became additional evidence confirming the *priista* state's dangerous expansive tendencies. This view, in turn, informed business's interpretation of the 1982 bank nationalization, which was seen as a further example of the PRI's hostility to private enterprise, rather than as a rational (if questionable) measure by an otherwise business-friendly president facing desperate circumstances.[19]

[18] For example, in both Chile and Uruguay, during the 1960s social security revenues and expenditures were about four times larger than Mexico's as a share of GDP (Mesa-Lago 1978, table 7–15).

[19] Prior to the bank nationalization, López Portillo had worked assiduously to restore business confidence, shaken by the conflict with Echeverría (Luna Ledesma 1992, ch. 3).

The enduring impact of the conflicts of the 1930s is clearly illustrated in the evolution of the CCE, Mexico's powerful peak business association. Even though it arose more than three decades after the Cárdenas presidency, the CCE shares much the same anti-intervention mentality embraced by big business during that era. This continuity is due to the fact that associations and networks deeply influenced by the struggle against cardenismo played a crucial role in creating it and steering its subsequent development. Due to their intense commitment to combating state economic interference, Monterrey-based firms directly provided about a third of the CCE's total funding in its early years. Even in the 1990s, half of the CCE's budget consisted of direct, voluntary contributions from individual firms, and three of the five biggest contributors were from Monterrey (Schneider 2002, 97). COPARMEX has also played a leading role in the CCE's development. For example, several CCE presidents (including the two most recent ones) have been former presidents of COPARMEX, despite the fact that, as a voluntary organization, it has fewer members than the corporatist entities. The CCE is thus an extension of an older network of antistate activism born during the anti-Cárdenas mobilizations and nourished by subsequent skirmishes between the state and capital.

The dynamic described earlier exhibits the self-reinforcing quality underscored by path dependence theorists, especially those, like Mahoney (2000) and Pierson (2000; 2004), who emphasize the crucial role that ideology and perceptions of legitimacy can play in such processes. The antistate beliefs and sentiments that emerged from the conflicts of the 1930s became embedded in enduring formal organizations and informal networks with great influence over the business community, especially big business. They shaped this sector's perceptions of subsequent state actions and, in turn, were reinforced by those perceptions. Opposition to state intervention became part of business's collective identity and was institutionalized in and propagated by an expanding network of organizations. In other words, the 1930s turned out to be a "critical juncture" that led the private sector along a self-reinforcing path of mistrust of the state and growing preparedness to resist it.

Brazil presents a sharp contrast to both Chile and Mexico. The private sector has never faced a government both willing and able to carry out major redistributive reforms. Getúlio Vargas, who led Brazil from 1930–1945 and 1950–1954 and is sometimes compared to Cárdenas and other "populists," was far more moderate than his Mexican counterpart (Collier and Collier 1991, ch. 5). He implemented no agrarian reform or high-profile expropriations of other businesses and his labor agenda was much more about controlling than mobilizing workers. The closest Brazilian analogue to Salvador Allende was João Goulart (1961–1964), who sought to implement rural land redistribution, progressive labor reforms, and the enfranchisement of illiterates. However, Goulart was both more moderate than Allende and politically weaker, having arrived in office as a result of the elected president's resignation and lacking either a legislative majority or a strongly organized support base. His reforms stalled in Congress, and he was overthrown in a bloodless coup after having achieved almost none of his major objectives.

This more benign political environment aided, in turn, in the development of a private sector relatively unconcerned with, and sometimes actively supportive of, state intervention. Many scholars have remarked on this aspect of Brazilian politics. For example, a study of industrialists between the 1930s and the 1970s concluded that "our research did not reveal an industrial elite opposed to state intervention in the economy. In some cases [the elite] even justified that intervention by the necessity of the state filling gaps the private sector could not" (Diniz and Boschi 1978, 191). Similarly, in her book on developmentalism in Brazil and Argentina during the 1950s, Sikkink (1991) argues that Brazil's more consistent adherence to this approach reflected a greater elite consensus on the benefits of state intervention. Finally, in a wide-ranging analysis of Brazilian interest group politics, Schmitter remarks on the comparative lack of elite resistance to the expansion of the state under Vargas and subsequent presidents (Schmitter 1971, 375–376).

In the 1970s some prominent business leaders did raise their voices against the growing presence of the state in the economy, but this "movement" was mainly a media initiative and reflected discontent with the military's tight grip on policy more than it did a rejection of interventionism per se (Diniz and Boschi 1978; Schneider 2004). Graham (1982) develops a telling comparison between this *desestatização* ("state retrenchment") campaign and business mobilization against Mexican president Echeverría during the same period. Despite the fact that Brazil's tax burden was more than double Mexico's and state firms played a larger role in the economy, the business reaction to Echeverría's reforms was far broader and its criticisms more sweeping. Graham argues that "in no way could either the criticism or the concessions be compared to the private sector offensive that had been launched in Mexico. The Brazilian private sector critics were weaker, more defensive in their posture and never went beyond the specifics of their complaints" (Graham 1982, 36).

Lacking an instinctive wariness about the state, Brazilian business also lacked a strong motivation to craft encompassing organizations capable of defending their general interests as a social class. Instead, they focused their energies on defending more specific interests (Schneider 2004). Even sector-wide entities tend to be divided and weak. The exception that proves the rule is agriculture, which faced a major scare in the mid-1980s when the incoming civilian government announced a sweeping, expropriation-based agrarian reform. Large landowners across the country quickly coalesced into a coalition called the Democratic Rural Union (*União Democratica Ruralista* [UDR]) and later created a large, cohesive caucus in the Brazilian Congress known as the *bancada ruralista* ("landowners' caucus"). Landowner resistance blocked much of the proposed reform, but later governments have kept the issue alive by conducting piecemeal expropriations in response to land invasions. Although the UDR is no longer active, the *bancada ruralista* remains a major force, one with no real analogue among other sectors of the economy. Property rights continue to be a key concern for the caucus but it is also active in other policy areas, such as farm credit and environmental protection (Costa 2012).

While many Brazilian business elites undoubtedly take a dim view of labor unions, their lack of determined opposition to state expansion has unwittingly provided labor with advantages not available to their counterparts in Chile and Mexico. For example, the state-driven industrialization policy of the military years, which enjoyed a great deal of private sector support, helped give rise to the "new union movement," which would in turn found the CUT and play a central role in creating the PT (Keck 1992). Furthermore, business's failure to decisively oppose some crucial aspects of the 1988 constitution, including generous pensions for public sector workers, arguably stimulated unionization by giving workers an additional incentive to organize to defend their interests.

The current context of heavy taxation and spending is perceived negatively by Brazilian elites, but the buildup has been gradual and largely (although not exclusively) based on indirect taxes, as discussed in detail by Schneider (Chapter 5, this volume). The "Brazil cost" resulting from taxes and rigid labor laws undermines industrial competitiveness. However, it is partially offset by tariff protection, subsidized credit, and other state-provided benefits, sometimes referred to as *bolsa empresário*, in ironic reference to the well-known social program *bolsa família*, which provides poor families with small cash transfers. Moreover, more than 13 years of PT rule did not produce anything that could be perceived as an existential threat to business or the rich. Although they engaged in considerable income redistribution, the PT-led coalitions respected private property and left labor relations essentially intact. Consequently, there has been no major break in the Brazilian tradition of nonconflictual relations between the state and economic elites.

CONCLUDING REMARKS

In this chapter I have explored the differences in the tax burden among Brazil, Chile, and Mexico. While natural resource wealth offers the most obvious solution to this puzzle, it is insufficient, since it cannot explain the huge gap between, on the one hand, Mexico and Chile, and on the other, Brazil. To complement it, I have developed an explanation emphasizing power resources and how they have been shaped by path dependence. Specifically, I have argued that the lower tax burdens in Mexico and Chile reflect the greater strength of right-wing forces in these countries compared to Brazil. The superiority of the right in the former two countries reflects, in turn, the impact of historical episodes in which leftist governments undertook major redistributive reforms that unwittingly pushed elites to embrace right-wing attitudes and to organize themselves to combat state intervention of all kinds.

To conclude the chapter, I touch briefly on two additional questions. First, to what extent can the arguments developed here shed light on the magnitude of the tax burden in other Latin American countries? Second, under what conditions might we expect established patterns of light or heavy taxation in the case study countries to change?

Of course, it is impossible to adequately assess the generalizability of the arguments in a few paragraphs. However, in the interest of demonstrating that the causal dynamics emphasized here are not limited to the case studies, I trace some rough parallels between these countries and two others: Guatemala and Uruguay. While Guatemala is among the most lightly taxed countries in Latin America, with revenues of around 12% of GDP in recent years, Uruguay is one of the three heaviest, with a tax burden approaching 30% of GDP. Nontax natural resource revenues cannot explain this difference, since neither country enjoys substantial flows of such revenues.

In consonance with the argument laid out above, there is considerable agreement among students of Guatemala that a key reason for the persistence of very light taxation is the political dominance of right-wing forces

(United Nations Development Program 2008, 467–499; Sánchez 2009). While Guatemala lacks a highly institutionalized right party such as those of Mexico or Chile, right-leaning groups clearly dominate elections. Just as importantly, Guatemala boasts arguably the most powerful peak business association in the entire region: the Coordinating Committee of Agricultural, Commercial, Industrial and Financial Associations (*Comité Coordinador de Asociaciones Agrícolas, Comerciales, Industriales y Financieras* [CACIF]). For decades, CACIF has fiercely and effectively combated efforts to strengthen tax capacity, ensuring that the state apparatus remains weak, except perhaps in its ability to repress groups that challenge the status quo (United Nations Development Program 2008).

While the force of the Guatemalan right cannot be explained with reference to only one factor, the scholarship suggests that, as in Chile and Mexico, countermobilization against an episode of strong redistribution played a key role in its development. Centered on an ambitious, expropriation-based land reform, President Jacobo Arbenz's (1951–1954) reform program sought to shift the balance of power and benefits in Guatemalan society in favor of the poor majority. However, the threat of change panicked elites, who overcame their traditional differences and joined forces with the military and the US government to secure the president's overthrow (Yashar 1997). This same basic coalition "would rule Guatemala for the next four decades" (Dosal 1995, 101). CACIF, which was formed shortly after Arbenz's fall, expressed the unified determination of Guatemalan business leaders to combat any possibility of a return to the state activism of the Arbenz years (Dosal 1995).

Guatemalan elites were obligated by international pressures during the 1980s to allow a transition to at least formal democracy, but they have continued to dominate politics through a blend of money, media control, and selective repression. While superficially riven by factionalism, elites enjoy an underlying unity based on their firm rejection of state economic intervention (Granovsky-Larsen 2017).

Uruguay, in contrast, resembles Brazil in terms of its relatively heavy taxation, the weakness of the right and the lack of any episode of radical redistribution in its history. The country's tax burden has increased significantly in recent years, at least partly due to reforms introduced by the center–left Broad Front (*Frente Amplio*), which has controlled the presidency since 2004. However, Uruguay has been among the most heavily taxed countries in Latin America since at least the 1950s (Ondetti 2015, 753). This tradition reflects the early, incremental growth of a welfare state that came to be very large. By the 1960s, Uruguay's social security system was rivaled within Latin America only by Chile's (Mesa-Lago 1978).

While Uruguay's precocious welfare state development sets it somewhat apart from Brazil, where the social security system emerged later, it shares with its neighbor the fact that the state has never threatened property on a large scale. The growth of social programs was advanced mainly by the social-democratic *batllista* current of the catch-all Colorado Party, which did not favor expropriatory land reform (Finch 1981, 10–11) and did not even have very strong ties to organized labor (Collier and Collier 1991, 438–456).

The relatively unthreatening character of the state probably explains why Uruguay, despite its diminutive size, does not have a peak business association (Schneider 2004, 40; Rius 2013). It may also explain why the closest thing Uruguay has had to a conservative party, the National Party, is more of a catch-all party than a programmatic right-wing party. The 1973 coup d'état did, to some extent, express elite discontent with the development model. However, that discontent was more a reflection of prolonged economic stagnation and growing social unrest than panic about radical policies (Notaro 2010). Moreover, even the 1973–1984 military regime did not have the determination or political support to reverse the tax burden growth of preceding decades (Ondetti 2015, 752).

In other words, Uruguay's relatively heavy tax burden, much like Brazil's, can be understood as a result of the fact that the state's reformism was never deep enough to provoke the rise of powerful actors committed to an antistate agenda. Uruguay's early development path was, as mentioned, more welfare-oriented than Brazil's, but in recent decades even that difference has eroded with the growth of Brazilian social spending.

To assert that differences in the tax burden reflect a path-dependent dynamic is not, of course, to suggest that they are impervious to change. The stability engendered by such processes is relative, not absolute. Based on the historical experiences of the case study countries, as well as Latin America more generally, one can envision at least two hypothetical paths to change, each corresponding to a particular status quo.

In the case of high-tax Brazil, an episode of state overreach in which a left-leaning government seeks to go beyond the limits of fiscal redistribution by restructuring property rights could potentially trigger a backlash strong enough to engender an enduring reactionary coalition, as in Mexico and Chile. With regard to the latter two countries, change could potentially be brought about by an external economic shock that delegitimizes the existing market-oriented development model and gives rise to a new period of statist policymaking protagonized by leaders with a nationalist discourse.

At the time of writing, however, neither of these scenarios seems very plausible. It is true that Brazil's center–left president was recently replaced by a center-right coalition that has advanced some significant reforms to moderate spending. However, this government lacks both internal cohesion and strong societal pressure to deepen these reforms. Moreover, given the fragmented and unprogrammatic character of the party system, it is hard to envision the next Brazilian government having both the power and the will to reorient the country's policies in a notably more liberal direction. More incremental change is not out of the question, but it would take many years of stagnant revenue growth for Brazil's tax burden to approximate the regional average, even for the higher-income countries.

While both have struggled with low growth rates in recent years, neither Chile nor Mexico currently faces a crisis sufficiently deep or prolonged as to threaten the basic development model. In fact, Chile recently elected a center-right president, who may well attenuate some of the statist reforms of recent years, including increased taxation. Mexican resentment against the current US government's hostility could potentially help López Obrador, with his nationalist discourse, win the presidency in 2018. Nevertheless, it is hard to envision how a government led by his small party would have the legislative influence to significantly alter Mexico's market-oriented development path. Moreover, López Obrador himself has repeatedly sought to assuage business fears by insisting that he intends only to make the state more efficient, not larger (Zavala 2017). Thus, the differences in the magnitude of the tax burden that this chapter has sought to explain seem likely to persist for years to come.

References

Aboites Aguilar, Luis. 2003. *Excepciones y privilegios: Modernización tributaria y centralización en México, 1922–1972*. Mexico: Colegio de Mexico.

Afonso, Jose Roberto. 2013. *A Economia Politica da Reforma Tributaria: o caso Brasileiro*. Washington, DC: Woodrow Wilson Center.

Arretche, Marta. 2012. *Democracia, federalismo e centralização no Brasil*. Rio de Janeiro: Editora FGV/Editora Fiocruz.

Astorga, Pablo, Ame R. Berges, and Valpy Fitzgerald. 2005. "The Standard of Living in Latin American During the Twentieth Century," *Economic History Review* LVIII (4): 765–796.

Bennett, Andrew, and Colin Elman. 2006. "Complex Causal Relations and Case Study Methods: The Example of Path Dependence," *Political Analysis* 14 (3): 250–267.

Bensusán, Graciela, and Kevin Middlebrook. 2012. "El Sindicalismo y la Democratizacion en Mexico," *Foro Internacional* 210 (4): 796–845.

2013. *Sindicatos y política en México: cambios, continuidades y contradicciones.* Mexico City: FLACSO/UAM-Xochimilco; CLACSO.

Beramendi, Pablo, and David Rueda. 2007. "Social Democracy Constrained: Indirect Taxation in Industrialized Democracies," *British Journal of Political Science* 37: 619–641.

Besley, Timothy, and Torsten Persson. 2013. "Taxation and Development." Center for Economic Policy Research, Working Paper.

Bird, Richard M. 1971. "Wagner's Law of Expanding State Activity," *Public Finance* 26: 1–26.

Brennan, Geoffrey, and James M. Buchanan. 1980. *The Power to Tax: Analytical Foundations of a Fiscal Constitution.* Cambridge: Cambridge University Press.

Cameron, David R. 1978 "The Expansion of the Public Economy: A Comparative Analysis," *American Political Science Review* 72 (4): 1243–1261.

Cárdenas, Mauricio. 2010. "State Capacity in Latin America." Global Political Economy and Development at Brookings, Discussion Paper.

Centrángolo, Oscar, and Juan Carlos Gómez Sabaíni. 2007. *Politica tributaria en Argentina: Entre la solvencia y la emergencia.* Santiago: ECLAC.

CEPALSTAT. n.d. Database of the United Nations Economic Commission for Latin America and the Caribbean: http://estadisticas.cepal.org/cepalstat/WEB_CEPALSTAT/estadisticasIndicadores.asp?idioma=e.

Chávez M., Marcos. "Las finanzas públicas en México, 1970–2000. Crónica del fracas de la política fiscal," in Luis Aboites Aguilar and Luis Jáuregui (eds.), *Penuria sin fin*, Mexico City: Instituto Mora, 211–302.

CIAT-IDB. n.d. Latin America and the Caribbean Fiscal Burden Database of the Inter-American Center of Tax Administrations and Inter-American Development Bank: https://publications.iadb.org/en/publication/13997/latin-america-and-caribbean-fiscal-burden-database.

Collier, Ruth Berins, and David Collier. 1991. *Shaping the Political Arena.* Princeton: Princeton University Press.

Corbacho, Ana, Vincente Fretes Cibils, and Eduardo Lora. 2013. *More than Revenue: Taxation as a Development Tool.* New York: Palgrave Macmillan.

Correa, Felipe. 2016. *Encadenamientos productivos desde la minería de Chile.* Santiago: ECLAC.

Costa, Sandra Helena Gonçalves. 2012. *A questão agrária no Brasil e a bancada ruralista no Congresso Nacional.* Masters thesis, University of São Paulo.

Cypher, James. 1990. *State and Capital in Mexico: Development Policy Since 1940.* Boulder: Westview Press.

Díaz, Jose, Rolf Lüders, and Gert Wagner. 2010. *La Republica en Cifras.* Santiago, Chile: Instituto de Economía, Pontificia Universidad Católica de Chile.

Díaz-Cayeros, Alberto. 2006. *Federalism, Fiscal Authority, and Centralization in Latin America.* Cambridge: Cambridge University Press.

Diniz, Eli, and Renato R Boschi. 1978. *Empresariado Nacional e Estado no Brazil*. Rio de Janeiro: Forense-Universitária.

Dirección del Trabajo. 2014. "Compendio de Series Estadísticas 1990-2013": www.dt.gob.cl/documentacion/1612/articles-62614_recurso_1.pdf.

Dosal, Paul J. 1995. *Power in Transition: The Rise of Guatemala's Industrial Oligarchy, 1871–1994*. Westport: Praeger.

Drake, Paul. 2009. *Between Tyranny and Anarchy: A History of Democracy in Latin America, 1800–2006*. Palo Alto: Stanford University Press.

Ensignia, Jaime. 2017. "Chile: a reforma trabalhista de Bachelet e o papel do sindicalismo," Teoria e Debate, no 161: https://teoriaedebate.org.br/2017/06/07/%EF%BB%BFchile-a-reforma-trabalhista-de-bachelet-e-o-papel-do-sindicalismo/.

Etchemendy, Sebastian. 2011. *Models of Economic Liberalization*. Cambridge: Cambridge University Press.

Fairfield, Tasha. 2010. "Business Power and Tax Reform: Taxing Income and Profits in Chile and Argentina," *Latin American Politics and Society* 52, no. 2: 51–71.

2015. *Private Wealth and Public Revenue in Latin America: Business Power and Tax Politics*. New York: Cambridge University Press.

Farfán Mares, Gabriel. 2011. "La economía política del estado rentista mexicano (1970–2010)," *Foro Internacional* 51, no. 3: 541–577.

Ferreira, Roberto. 2002. *A Reforma Essencial*. São Paulo: Geração Editorial.

Finch, M. H. J. 1981. *A Political Economy of Uruguay since 1870*. New York: St. Martin's Press.

Fitzgerald, Edmund V. K. 1978. "The Fiscal Crisis of the Latin American State," in John Toye (ed.), *Taxation and Economic Development*, London: Frank Cass, 125–158.

Flores-Macías, Gustavo. 2014. "Financing Security through Elite Taxation: The Case of Colombia's 'Democratic Security Taxes,'" *Studies in Comparative International Development* 49, no. 4: 477–500.

Fundação Perseu Abramo. 2013. "Densidade sindical e recomposição da classe trabalhadora no Brasil." Working Paper: http://sindsaudesp.org.br/download/fpa_comunica_3.pdf.

Gauss, Susan. 2010. *Made in Mexico: Regions, Nation, and the State in the Rise of Mexican Industrialism, 1920s-1940s*. University Park: Penn State University Press.

Gilly, Adolfo. 2013. *El Cardenismo: una utopía mexicana*. Mexico City: Ediciones Era.

Goggin, Malcolm L. 1986 "The 'Too Few Cases/Too Many Variables' Problem in Implementation Research," *The Western Political Quarterly* 39 (2): 328–347.

Graham, Douglass. 1982. "Mexican and Brazilian Economic Development: Legacies, Patterns, and Performance," in Sylvia Ann Hewlett and Richard S. Weinert (eds.), *Brazil and Mexico: Patterns in Late Development*, Philadelphia: Institute for the Study of Human Issues, 2–55.

Granovsky-Larsen, Simon. 2017. "Land and the Reconfiguration of Power in Post-Conflict Guatemala," in Liisa L. North and Timothy D. Clark (eds.),

Dominant Elites in Latin America: From Neoliberalism to the "Pink Tide," New York: Palgrave Macmillan, 181–204.

Hamilton, Nora. 1982. *The Limits of State Autonomy: Post-Revolutionary Mexico*. Princeton: Princeton University Press.

Huber, Evelyne, and John D Stephens. 2012. *Democracy and the Left: Social Policy and Inequality in Latin America*. Chicago: University of Chicago.

IBGE. 2006. "Estatisticas do seculo XX": https://seculoxx.ibge.gov.br/.

Karl, Terry L. 1997. *The Paradox of Plenty: Oil Booms and Petro-States*. Los Angeles: University of California Press.

Kato, Junko. 2003. *Regressive Taxation and the Welfare State*. Cambridge: Cambridge University Press.

Keck, Margaret E. 1992. *The Workers' Party and Democratization in Brazil*. New Haven: Yale University Press.

Knight, Alan. 1994. "Cardenismo: Juggernaut or Jalopy?" *Journal of Latin American Studies* 26 (1): 73–107.

Korpi, Walter. 1978. *The Working Class in Welfare Capitalism: Work, Unions, and Politics in Sweden*. London: Routledge & Kegan Paul.

Kurtz, Marcus J. 2013. *Latin American State Building in Comparative Perspective: Social Foundations of Institutional Order*. Cambridge: Cambridge University Press.

Lindert, Peter H. 2004. *Growing Public: Social Spending and Economic Growth Since the Eighteenth Century*. Cambridge: Cambridge University Press.

López Portillo, Felicitas. 1995. Estado e ideología empresarial en el gobierno alemanista. Mexico City: UNAM.

Luna Ledesma, Matilde. 1992. *Los empresarios y el cambio politico Mexico, 1970–1987*. Instituto de Investigaciones Sociales, UNAM.

Luna, Juan Pablo, and Cristobal Rovira Kaltwasser. 2014. *The Resilience of the Latin American Right*. Baltimore: Johns Hopkins University Press.

Mahoney, James. 2000. "Path Dependence in Historical Sociology," *Theory and Society*. 29: 507–548.

Mahon, James E. Jr., Marcelo Bergman and Cynthia Arnson. 2015. *Progressive Tax Reform and Equality in Latin America*. Washington, DC: Wilson Center.

Mahoney, James, and Daniel Schensul. 2006. "Historical Context and Path Dependence," in Robert E. Goodin and Charles Tilly, *The Oxford Handbook of Contextual Political Analysis*, Oxford: Oxford University Press, 454–471.

Martínez Nava, Juan M. 1984. *Conflicto Estado Empresarios*. Mexico City: Editorial Nueva Imagen.

Martínez-Vázquez, Jorge. 2001. "Mexico: An Evaluation of the Main Features of the Tax System." Georgia State University Working Paper.

Melo, Marcus Andre, Carlos Pereira, and Saulo Souza. 2010. "The Political Economy of Fiscal Reform in Brazil: The Rationale for the Suboptimal Equilibrium." IDB Working Paper 117.

Meltzer, Allan H. and Scott F. Richard. 1981. "A Rational Theory of the Size of Government," *Journal of Political Economy* 89, no. 5: 914–927.

Mendes, Marcos. 2014. *Por Que o Brasil Cresce Pouco*. Rio de Janeiro: Campus.

Mesa-Lago, Carmelo. 1978. *Social Security in Latin American: Pressure Groups, Stratification, and Inequality*. Pittsburgh: University of Pittsburgh Press.

Michaels, Albert. 1970. "The Crisis of Cardenismo," *Journal of Latin American Studies* 2, no. 1: 51–79.

Middlebrook, Kevin. 1995. *The Paradox of Revolution: Labor, the State, and Authoritarianism in Mexico*. Baltimore: Johns Hopkins University Press.

North, Douglass C. 1990. *Institutions, Institutional Change and Economic Performance*. Cambridge: Cambridge University Press.

Notaro, Jorge. 2010. "Estrategia de Desarrollo, Política Económica y Actores Sociales. Uruguay, 1968–1984," *Boletín de Historia Económica* 9: 31–40.

Ondetti, Gabriel. 2015. "The Roots of Brazil's Heavy Taxation," *Journal of Latin American Studies* 47 (4): 749–779.

2017. "The Power of Preferences: Economic Elites and Light Taxation in Mexico," *Revista Mexicana de Ciencias Políticas y Sociales* 62 (231): 47–76.

Patrucchi, Leticia, and Leonardo Grottola. 2011. "Estructura Tributaria, Ingresos Rentisticos y Regresividad en America Latina," *Leviathan* 2: 96–122.

Persson, Torsten, and Guido Tabellini. 2003. *The Economic Effects of Constitutions*. Munich Lectures in Economics. Cambridge, MA: MIT Press.

Pessino, Carola, and Ricardo Fenochietto. 2010. "Determining Countries Tax Effort," *Revista de Economia Politica* 195, no. 4: 65–87.

Pierson, Paul. 2000. "Increasing Returns, Path Dependence, and the Study of Politics," *American Political Science Review* 94 (2): 251–267.

2004. *Politics in Time: History, Institutions, and Social Analysis*. Princeton: Princeton University Press.

Pollack, Marcelo. 1999. *The New Right in Chile, 1973–97*. New York: St. Martin's Press, Inc.

Posner, Paul W. 2008. *State, Market, and Democracy in Chile*. New York: Palgrave Macmillan.

Przeworski, Adam and Michael Wallerstein. 1998. "Structural Dependence of the State on Capital," *American Political Science Review* 82 (1): 11–29.

Reynolds, Clark W. 1970. *Mexican Economy: Twentieth Century Structure and Growth*. New Haven: Yale University Press.

Rius, Andrés. 2013. "The Uruguayan Tax Reform of 2006: Why Didn't It Fail?" Washington, DC: Woodrow Wilson Center.

Rodden, Jonathan. 2003. "Reviving Leviathan: Fiscal Federalism and the Growth of Government," *International Organization* 57, no. 4: 695–721.

Rodrik, Dani. 1998. "Why Do More Open Countries Have Bigger Governments?" *Journal of Political Economy* 106 (5): 997–1032.

Ros, Jaime. 1993. "Mexico's Trade and Industrialization Experience Since 1960: A Reconsideration of Past Policies and Assessment of Current Reforms." Kellogg Institute. Working Paper.

Ross, Michael. 2001. "Does Oil Hinder Democracy?" *World Politics* 53 (3): 325–361.

Sánchez, Omar. 2009. "Tax Reform Paralysis in Post-Conflict Guatemala," *New Political Economy* 14, no. 1: 101–131.

Saragoza, Alex. 1988. *The Monterrey Elite and the Mexican State: 1880–1940*. Austin: University of Texas Press.

Schmitter, Phillippe. 1971. *Interest, Conflict and Political Change in Brazil*. Stanford: Stanford University Press.

Schneider, Aaron. 2012. *State-Building and Tax Regimes in Central America.* Cambridge: Cambridge University Press.

Schneider, Ben Ross. 2002. "Why is Mexican Business so Organized?" *Latin American Research Review* 37 (1): 77–118.

2004. *Business Politics and the State in Twentieth-Century Latin America.* Cambridge: Cambridge University Press.

Shafer, Robert J. 1973. *Mexican Business Organizations: History and Analysis.* Syracuse: Syracuse University Press.

Sikkink, Kathryn. 1991. *Ideas and Institutions: Developmentalism in Brazil and Argentina.* Ithaca: Cornell University Press.

Silva, Eduardo. 1993. "Capitalist Coalitions, the State, and Neoliberal Economic Restructuring: Chile, 1973–88," *World Politics* 45: 526–559.

Silva, Patricio. 1995. "Empresarios, neoliberalismo y transicion democratica en Chile," *Revista Mexicana de Sociologia* 57 (4): 3–25.

Stallings, Barbara. 1978. *Class Conflict and Economic Development in Chile, 1958–1973.* Stanford: Stanford University Press.

Stein, Ernesto. 1999. "Fiscal Decentralization and Government Size in Latin America." *Journal of Applied Economics* II (2): 357–391.

Stein, Ernesto, and Lorena Caro. 2013. "Ideology and Taxation in Latin America." IDB Working Paper.

Steinmo, Sven, and Caroline Tolbert. 1998. "Do Institutions Really Matter? Taxation in Industrialized Democracies," *Comparative Political Studies* 31 (2): 165–187.

Stephens, John. 1979. *The Transition from Capitalism to Socialism.* Basingstoke: Macmillan.

Stinchcombe, Arthur L. 1968. *Constructing Social Theories.* Chicago: University of Chicago Press.

Thacker, Strom C. 2012. "Big Business, Democracy, and the Politics of Competition," in Roderic Camp (ed.), *The Oxford Handbook of Mexican Politics*, Oxford: Oxford University Press, 313–334.

Thelen, Kathleen. 2003. "How Institutions Evolve: Insights From Comparative Historical Analysis," in James Mahoney and Dietrich Rueschemeyer (eds.), *Comparative Historical Analysis in the Social Sciences*, Cambridge: Cambridge University Press, 204–240.

Timmons, Jeffrey F. 2005. "The Fiscal Contract: States, Taxes and Public Services," *World Politics* 57: 530–567.

Tirado, Ricardo. 1985. "Los empresarios y la derecha en Mexico," *Revista Mexicana de Sociologia* 47 (1): 105–123.

Topik, Steven. 1987. *Political Economy of the Brazilian State, 1889–1930.* Austin: University of Texas Press.

Unda Gutiérrez, Mónica. 2010. "The Building of a Poor Tax State: The Political Economy of Income Tax in Mexico, 1925–1964." PhD dissertation, University of London, Department of Development Studies.

2015. "La reforma tributaria de 2013: los problemas de la Hacienda pública y la desigualdad en México." *Espiral: Estudios sobre Estado y Sociedad* 22 (64): 69–99.

United Nations Development Program. 2008. *Guatemala: Una Economía al Servicio del Desarrollo Humano?* New York: UNDP.

Valenzuela, Arturo. 1978. *The Breakdown of Democratic Regimes*. Baltimore: Johns Hopkins University Press.

Weyland, Kurt. 1996. *Democracy without Equity: Failures of Reform in Brazil*. Pittsburgh: University of Pittsburgh Press.

Winn, Peter. 2004. *Victims of the Chilean Miracle: Workers and Neoliberalism in the Pinochet Era, 1973–2002*. Durham: Duke University Press.

World Bank. 1984. "Chile: Economic Memorandum": http://documents.worldbank.org/curated/en/home

1961. "Current Economic Position and Prospects of Chile": http://documents.worldbank.org/curated/en/497811468027649657/Chile-Current-economic-position-and-prospects

1966. "Current Economic Position and Prospects of Chile": http://documents.worldbank.org/curated/en/120491468015836290/Main-report

1970. "Current Economic Position and Prospects of Chile": http://documents.worldbank.org/curated/en/629501468015835669/Main-report

Yashar, Deborah. 1997. *Demanding Democracy: Reform and Reaction in Costa Rica and Guatemala, 1870s – 1950s*. Redwood City: Stanford University Press.

Zavala, Misael. 2017. "AMLO lanza tres compromisos con empresarios," *El Universal*, July 12: www.eluniversal.com.mx/elecciones-2018/amlo-lanza-3-compromisos-con-empresarios.

5

Federalism and Taxation

Periods of Brazilian International Insertion

Aaron Schneider

Brazil collects around 34% of GDP in tax, among the highest levels in the developing world and above the level of a number of developed countries. This impressive level of tax occurs within the context of a complex federal system. Over time, tax collection and federalism have been marked by moments of coincident change, resetting federal arrangements and expanding the amount of revenue available. Such moments articulate new state–society relationships, exchanging revenues from dynamic sectors for outlays in priority areas, and new intra-elite relationships, settling disputes among regional elites and between regional and national interests. Such moments are rare, and they are separated by periods in which divergent reforms within federalism and tax gradually undercut federal fiscal bargains. These two orientations of change – coincident and divergent – reflect more fundamental dynamics of political elite and class dynamics. Coincident reform indicates the victory of rising elites over declining elites, defined in terms of their ability to lead a new period of capitalist development and insertion in the international economy. Divergent reform indicates stalemate or victory of declining political and economic elites, usually ensconced in the protections of federal jurisdictions and able to stymie state-building efforts required for new modes of accumulation.

The present chapter divides Brazilian development into four long periods defined by patterns of international insertion: agricultural export, import-substitution industrialization, industrial deepening, and liberalization. In each period, patterns of international insertion shift the structural relations among domestic sectors, strengthening elite and popular actors adapted to new periods of international insertion and weakening others.

Major tax reform and expanded fiscal capacity occur when federal bargains reaccommodate rival elites ensconced in regional jurisdictions in ways that are compatible with fiscal bargains. Fiscal bargains mobilize new revenues necessary for state capacity to shape international insertion.

The mix of social and fiscal variables considered here views public finance as a window into larger social processes. Combined attention to fiscal and federal arrangements prompts the label "fiscal federal sociology," drawing on the rich literatures of "fiscal sociology" (Martin et al. 2009; Schumpeter 1917) and "fiscal federalism" (Oates 1971). The sections that follow proceed by periods, concentrating on two characteristics: changing patterns of international insertion, and new fiscal federal relations as expressed in tax and federal institutions. To begin, it is useful to consider the social implications of international insertion and fiscal federal institutions of state–society mediation.

INTERNATIONAL INSERTION: RISING AND FALLING ELITE AND POPULAR SECTORS

When considering social relations, particular attention is given here to the way in which class structures of semiperipheral economies such as Brazil's are shaped by the international system. Approaches that highlight the link between external insertion and internal social dynamics include a variety of world systemic and structural approaches, highlighting the challenges to "late developers" in an integrated capitalist world (Gerschenkron 1962).

One challenge is the impact of international insertion on domestic social structures and politics. Elites leading sectors adapted to new patterns of international insertion rise in wealth and influence and seek to adapt state policies and institutions to further their dynamism. At the same time, they encounter declining elites atop sectors adapted to previous patterns of international insertion, many of whom are ensconced in preexisting institutions. In large, federal countries such as Brazil, these internal divisions among capitalist factions take a regional and political dimension, with rival factions finding room to survive moments of decline within subnational units. While popular sectors have tended to be constrained in the limited democracies of peripheral countries, certain patterns of international insertion require their labor and land, increasing their leverage. As a result, popular and middle sectors occasionally provide the political and social allies necessary for the victory of one or another elite aspirant to power (Reuschemeyer et al. 1992). As Ondetti demonstrates (Chapter 4 in this volume), the relative strength of the Left and the Right depends on the way rival elite and popular factions align. In Brazil, the existence of multiple jurisdictions fragmented both the organization and the policy impact of the Left, weakening the threat to the Right, who were therefore occasionally willing to accept greater state-building efforts in the form of tax.

MEDIATING STATE–SOCIETY RELATIONS: FISCAL FEDERAL BARGAINS

As international insertion prompts shifts in social relations, state institutions mediate rising and falling fortunes. In federal systems, two closely related state institutions filter social relations: tax and federalism. The literature on fiscal federalism has long argued for a close relationship between these two, and each has been treated by a rich tradition of theoretical literature on the nature of extraction and territorial organization of authority.

Considerations of tax capacity and tax structure, especially those drawing on fiscal sociological traditions, position tax as an indicator of state–society relations (Schneider 2012). As the chapters by Bergman and Mahon (3 and 8, respectively) in this volume suggest, how much revenue a state generates, through what bases, and from whom, depends critically on the ability of state actors to secure a political agreement around government priorities and apply administrative and coercive tools to secure compliance from contributors (see also Lieberman 2003). For late developers, mobilizing revenues requires political bargains among rising and falling elite and popular sectors in support of state activism for development (Brautigam et al. 2009).[1]

The language of bargains is also the way observers describe federal systems, which represent bargains among potentially rivalrous leaders of territorial jurisdictions (Hamilton et al. 1961). Federal agreements have been framed as efforts to come together around collective objectives, such as defense or a national market (Riker 1964); or to hold together a larger unit at risk of fragmentation, such as after decolonization or in the face of ethnic and internal diversity (Stepan 2000). In striking bargains among territorial leaders and delegating authority across jurisdictions and between levels of government, federal bargains allow the state to penetrate

[1] Alternatives to tax appear in the form of "fiscal illusions" to hide the amount extracted (Buchanan and Wagner 1977) or nontax revenues, such as natural resource rents (Ross 2014).

a territory (Ziblatt 2008). In this way, successful federal bargains are essential to the "infrastructural power" of the state to promote development (Mann 1984).

Fiscal bargains and federal bargains come together in what might be termed fiscal federal bargains. Such bargains grant subnational units the authority to collect revenues from certain tax bases while other revenue streams are mobilized at the national level. Transfers manage imbalances horizontally across subunits and vertically between the national and local levels. Successful fiscal federal bargains represent pacts that operate among both the potentially rivalrous leaders of different regions and levels of government as well as elites and popular sectors whose fortunes rise and fall according to different patterns of international insertion.

While successful promotion of new international insertions requires fiscal federal bargains to build state capacity, resulting changes to the interests and relative power of elite and popular actors can subsequently depart from the conditions that existed when the original fiscal federal bargain was set. For example, while the particularist electoral institutions described by Scartascini and Hallerberg (Chapter 6 in this volume) may have been convenient to the dominant regional oligarchies of the Old Republic, the demands of a growing urban sector would quickly outpace the capacity of retrograde institutions, calling for a new fiscal federal bargain adequate for industrialization.

Shifts in patterns of international insertion require new state capacities to sustain the dynamism of rising sectors while accommodating falling sectors and popular actors (Schneider 2012). The central argument here is that expansions in state capacity occur when fiscal federal bargains successfully accommodate new patterns of international insertion. A correlate is that disjunctures in fiscal federal bargains constrain state capacity and reflect the inability to accommodate rising and falling elites and popular sectors.

This suggests two kinds of changes to federalism and tax. Coincident reform occurs when both federal and tax institutions change together, including a major advance in revenue capacity and the reorganization of federalism to complement new state capacities. Such moments represent new accommodations between rising and falling elites and popular sectors as they are distributed across a country – a new fiscal federal bargain. Such moments are rare for two reasons. First, they are difficult, requiring broad bargains across highly varied elite and popular sectors. Second, coincident reform is only possible and necessary at critical moments of transition between patterns of international insertion, itself a rare occurrence.

Divergent reform occurs when the pace or direction of change in federalism operates independently of or contrary to the direction of change in tax. While taxation appears to require moments of coincident reform to achieve major advances, federalism has proven more malleable, shifting on its own and in gradual fashion, as regional authorities use their influence to force new bargains with the central government. Divergent federal reform is associated with two directions of change for tax. Lower tax capacity can result when declining elites adapted to prior patterns of international insertion ensconce themselves in regional units and shift power away from the national government to protect their privileges, undercutting national state capacity by weakening or blocking expansion in revenue capacity. Alternatively, rising elites may first achieve a degree of dominance at the local level, where they experiment with increased tax capacity to promote new international insertions, before scaling-up to undertake a coincident reform of both tax and federalism at the national level.

BRAZIL'S FOUR TAX PERIODS

In Brazil, the occasional disjuncture between fiscal and federal bargains produces unusual outcomes. For example, dynamics of federal competition among governmental units can end up "overfishing the common pool of national revenue," thereby undercutting fiscal solvency (Rodden 2006, xii). Also, fiscal dynamics can provide certain regions or levels of government with more buoyant and productive revenue streams, turning other actors into their dependents and upsetting federal bargains (Arretche 2012).

When one looks at the levels of tax as a percentage of GDP in Brazil since the beginning of the twentieth century, a few breakpoints stand out. After fluctuating around 10% of GDP during the Old Republic, revenues crept upwards during the 1920s, and settled at a new balance between 15% and 20% until 1960. Several more years of fluctuation followed until a moment of major reform under the military in the 1960s, stabilizing taxes at a new platform of around 25%, where they remained until about 1980. After once again entering a period of fluctuation, a new upward course was set after the 1988 Constitution and 1990s reforms, stabilizing between 33% and 37% since the late 1990s. Figure 5.1 shows the percentage of GDP collected in tax, with vertical lines indicating moments of significant change in the 1920s, 1960s, and 1990s.

While four main periods characterize the evolution of tax, there are slightly more moments of inflection within federalism. In addition to the three moments of change in tax, the federal system was subject to two

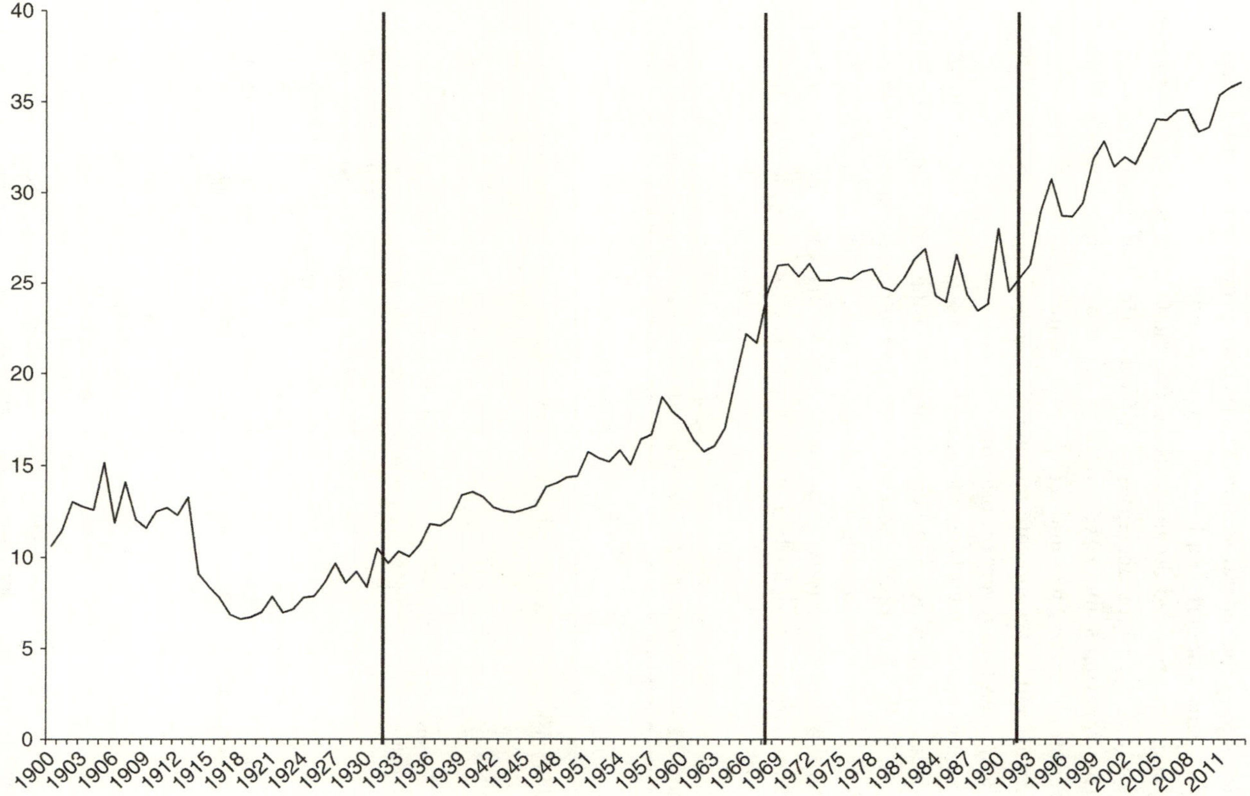

FIGURE 5.1 Brazil tax revenue as a % of GDP
Source: www.ibge.gov.br/ for 1900 to 2000 and www.ipeadata.gov.br/ for more recent years.

additional moments of adjustment, with the return to democracy in 1945 and the fiscal adjustment of the mid-1990s. Figure 5.2 offers one indicator of change in the federal system: the relative proportion of total receipts and expenses undertaken by the central government. The proportion of expenditures trended downwards during the Old Republic, only to rise steadily in the 1930s. Increases in federal share of expenditures stopped during the 1940s and 1950s, only to begin again in the 1960s, falling precipitously after 1988 and recuperating somewhat from the mid-1990s onward. Solid lines indicate moments of coincident reform; dotted lines indicate trends of divergent reform.

Simultaneous reworking of federal and fiscal bargains – coincident reform – requires accommodation among rising and falling elites, and occasionally also popular sectors. Divergent reform occurs between coincident reforms, indicating the ability of rival elites to undercut fiscal federal bargains. Periods of coincident reform mark four periods of fiscal federal bargains as described in Table 5.1. The following sections discuss

TABLE 5.1 *Four periods of international insertion, federalism, and tax*

Period	International Insertion	Federalism	Tax
Old Republic	Agricultural exports	Powerful state governments; weak central government	Subnational tax with federal expansion only to support states
Estado Novo and Populism	Domestic industrialization	Parallel federal bureaucracy to promote industrialization; oligarchic elites intact atop rural regions	Increase federal tax, especially through parallel bureaucracy; states control less buoyant revenues
Bureaucratic Authoritarianism	Industrial deepening	Centralized authoritarian government gradually accommodates regional allies	Mobilize new revenues and increase centralization, gradually increase transfers
Liberal Democracy	Stabilization, liberalization, commodity-dependence	Decentralization reversed by expanding federal programs and mandates	Rapid increase in federal revenues to pursue macroeconomic stability and expand social spending

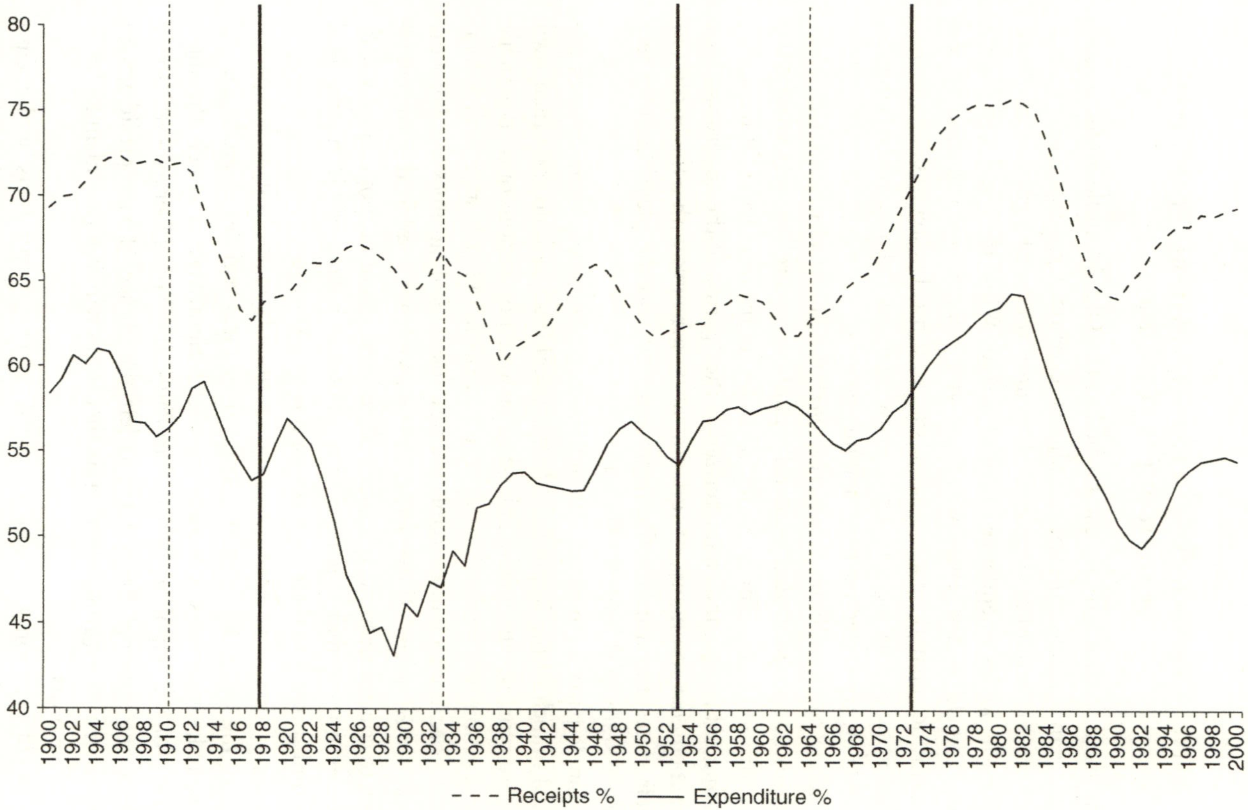

FIGURE 5.2 Central government share of total receipts and expenditures
Source: www.ibge.gov.br/ for 1900 to 2000 and www.ipeadata.gov.br/ for more recent years.

Brazil's four main periods, with distinct patterns of international insertion and corresponding federalism and tax arrangements.

FISCAL FEDERAL SUBNATIONAL STATE-BUILDING FOR AGRICULTURAL EXPORTS

The fiscal federal bargain established in the Old Republic aimed at sustaining an agricultural-export economy, essentially grafting a new federal pact among republican regional elites atop the fiscal structure inherited from the postindependence imperial period. While the fiscal and federal bargain held at first, there was a growing imbalance within the federal system (dominated by a few large states), a fiscal system maladapted to fluctuating export receipts, and a growing industrial and urban economy poorly incorporated into existing institutions.

In 1889, a military coup removed the monarchy, and the 1891 Constitution established a federal republic structured loosely around the constitution of the United States. Thus began the Brazilian Old Republic, lasting until 1930 and characterized as the "period of the governors," for the clientelist dominance of agricultural export elites within the borders of their states and a national government that was the plaything of a few strong state-level leaders (Abrucio 1998).

Single-party dominance characterized state regimes, in most cases the local branch of the Republican Party. Local leaders could raise their own security forces, which were unleashed on local populations once monarchic moderation was removed; "violence – at the municipal, state, and federal level – became an indispensable political instrument, at times involving the local armed forces" (Love 1982, 10–11). Violence combined with clientelism to control elections in which only around 3% of the population voted, and even those that voted did so in nonsecret ballots in which state-level incumbents wrote their own electoral rules (Abrucio 1998, 36).

Governors were drawn together nationally in an "oligarchic pact," managing the federation as a concert of local regimes (Love 1982, 8). The federation was a loosely managed hierarchy, in which the most powerful and populous states – São Paulo and Minas Gerais – effectively chose the national president and left the choice of vice presidents to secondary states, compensating smaller states with ministerial and administrative posts.

Brazil's economy remained focused on primary products, with incipient industrialization mostly an appendage to the export economy. Coffee accounted for approximately 75% of exports in 1924, and Rio was the world's most important coffee export center. Sugar and cotton also expanded, and Brazil was one of the world's leading exporters of cacao, providing also 90% of the world's rubber at the beginning of the twentieth century (Furtado 1972).

The Old Republic fiscal federal bargain depended on agricultural exports. State governors controlled the most important revenue source, the tax on exports, which also tapped interstate trade, as well as rural and urban property, industry, and professions. The central government controlled taxes on imports, rights of entry and departure of ships, stamp taxes, and federal services such as mail and telegraph.

For São Paulo and other major exporters, the arrangement guaranteed sufficient revenues to reproduce their agro-export economy and fortify the dominant local political elite. In moments of financial pressure, they could appeal to the federal level for support, which was always forthcoming, as they both controlled the national executive and could cajole the compliance of weaker states whose leaders were essentially dependent on the large states for the revenues to sustain their own clientelist regimes (Lopreato 2002, 9–11, 15–20). Large states could secure international loans, backed by the federal government, and made the most important public investments to support agricultural exports (Martinez Fritscher and Musacchio 2009). It was the São Paulo state coffee-marketing boards that managed prices by purchasing, and occasionally destroying, excess coffee stocks (Baer 2001, 20–21), and state public health and education systems emerged a decade before the national government (Love 2013). The poorer and weaker states were particularly vulnerable under this arrangement. Their international exports were minimal, and they were forced to rely on inefficient and distorting tax handles, such as taxes on exports to other states and taxes on sales and transport within their borders (Lopreato 2002, 18).

The central government played a limited role, except in rare moments when state elites divided and the agro-export model faced decline. This was the case after World War I, when trade slowdown temporarily weakened state oligarchies and convinced them of the need for a federal power with more significant political and administrative tools. In this window of opportunity, the national government imposed orthodox adjustment through expenditure cuts, tax increases, and revaluing the currency, restoring national credibility and subnational access to international markets (Lopreato 2002, 19).

The adjustment also set a precedent. It added items to which the consumption tax was applied, creating a tax on sales (1922), and taxing income (1924). Overall, Brazilian federalism in fiscal terms was characterized as follows. First, the size of government in terms of tax burden was small, at around 10% of GDP, even declining over time until a small rebound in the 1920s. Further, around one-third of the total was collected by states and municipalities, and their share increased over time.

The federal hierarchy was an unstable equilibrium built on a fiscal and political paradox. Elites from small and poor states were practically dependent on the federal government for resources, but federal authority was controlled by the large states, who were willing to expand federal power only in moments of downturn.[2] When international commodity prices collapsed in 1929, none of the entities within the federation had the tools to drive recovery, especially as incipient industrialization required state capacities that were nonexistent under the Old Republic. It would fall to the next government to establish a new fiscal federal bargain.

FISCAL FEDERAL PARALLELISM FOR INDUSTRIALIZATION

The new fiscal federal bargain that emerged in the 1930s erected a parallel architecture of central government state institutions and revenue streams to stimulate the urban and industrial economy. The new fiscal federal bargain tapped growing industrial sectors to fund state activism, but it was gradually undermined by shifting federal and fiscal dynamics which undercut central authority and by the 1960s had produced a fiscally unsustainable situation.

Industrialization during the 1930s resulted from public policies that included central government subsidies, trade protections, and tax incentives to build a domestic industrial sector (Furtado 1972). Industry overtook agriculture as the leading contributor to GDP (Baer 2001, 39), rising from 26% to 34.2% of GDP, while agriculture fell from 21.4% to 16.5%. By 1953, manufactured goods exports had surpassed primary goods (Baer 2001, 50). The pinnacle of this phase of industrialization came in the second half of the 1950s, when President Juscelino Kubitschek announced a Plan of Goals in which Brazil would grow "Fifty Years in Five" (Evans 1979: 30–54). The Plan identified priority sectors (energy, transportation, food, industries, education), in which the construction of a new capital, Brasília, was the symbol of centralized planning and finance, with a total cost of US$2.3 billion.

[2] "To an extent, the regime change of 1889 represented a 'capture' of the national government by São Paulo" (Love 2013, 115).

To direct the urban and industrial economies, the government constructed a parallel architecture of centralized institutions. State monopolies in key infrastructure and strategic sectors included the Institutes of Alcohol, Salt, and Forestry; and general cultural and research activities necessary for industrial and long-term planning were led by the Brazilian Geographic and Statistical Institute (IBGE) and the federal university system. In professional services, medicine, law, and engineering received stimulus and were integrated with industrial research and public works (e.g., the Merchant Marines and DNER). The jewels in the state enterprise sector were created between 1940 and 1945, including the National Steel Company (CSN); the largest mining enterprise in the world – the Valley of Rio Doce Company (CVRD); and the Electric Company of the Valley of São Francisco, somewhat modeled around the US Tennessee Valley Authority. Petrobras was created as a state-owned monopoly for the exploration and distribution of oil, and state enterprises controlled the extraction of other minerals. State enterprise budgets and personnel regulations were autonomous from the rest of the public sector, and they sought financing in international markets.

The 1934 constitution introduced by President Getúlio Vargas did not last long, but it laid out the architecture of a fiscal program to reorient revenues away from fluctuating export taxes and toward the urban and domestic economy. Vargas had risen to power in the midst of a split among Old Republic elites, and "he reaccommodated the regional elites in a new power scheme in which there were other actors involved, particularly, the *tenentes*," the military elites who had backed his rise (Abrucio 1998, 42).

His new fiscal federal bargain targeted revenues on consumption and income, and states gained taxes on sales and municipalities taxes on buildings, urban property, public parks, rural income, and municipal services (Varsano 1999, 3). The federal government retained the income tax, but it left the states in control of tax on property, transfer of property, services and professions, and the tax on exports. The most important tax innovation was a sales tax (IVC), which was meant to replace trade taxes, and was given to the governors (Skidmore 1999, 101).[3]

To consolidate and deepen these changes, Vargas staged a self-coup in 1937, codified in the constitution of the *Estado Novo*, or "New State." The *Estado Novo* constitution rested on the organic statist model of the

[3] Fiscal innovations made the system more rational, addressing distortionary taxes enacted by states under the Old Republic (Lopreato 2002, 23–24).

Polish Fascist regime with a greater role for the central government. It eliminated the elected position of governor and established an appointed interventor as the chief administrator of each state, chosen specifically from outside of the established political elite to ensure they acted on behalf of Vargas (Campello de Souza 1976, 14; Abrucio 1998, 45). Rather than eliminate clientelism, the Estado Novo forced clientelism into the service of the national government, in which interventors were the brokers of federal patronage and came to dominate state politics (Abrucio 1998, 46f).

There were concessions to regionalism, however. While the Estado Novo centralized resources, it did not significantly alter the tax powers outlined in the 1934 constitution, leaving significant fiscal power in the hands of states. In terms of expenses, the fiscal outlays that the central government absorbed were largely those associated with the agro-export model, taking over the task of smoothing the price of coffee and sugar and creating additional agencies with similar functions for salt, tea, cacao, and timber (Draibe 1985, 87–100).[4] Beyond these areas, however, most expenses of direct administration (education, health, transportation) remained in the hands of state and local authorities, and the sales tax gave them a stable, if unspectacular, new source of revenue. They collected approximately 3.02% of GDP in 1930, and approximately 6.28% of GDP in 1960. By the end of the 1930s, taxes rose to almost 14% of GDP, and the subnational level continued to be responsible for a little over a third of this total.[5]

Yet, Vargas and his allies were up to something more substantial, and the formal tax architecture summarized only a portion of their actions. More significant fiscal federal restructuring was the establishment of a parallel bureaucracy linked directly to Vargas and the office of the presidency, with its own political base of support, its own fiscal base, and its own expenditure powers. A corporatist system linked workers and business directly to the executive branch, registering and regulating which organizations were legally empowered to enter collective bargaining agreements, the terms of labor agreements, and a special legal system to adjudicate disputes (Collier and Collier 1979; Schmitter 1971).

[4] As Furtado notes, "Unconsciously, Brazil undertook an anticyclical policy of larger relative proportions than had been practiced in industrial countries until that time" (Furtado 1972, 192).

[5] Sources of revenue moved from the subnational to the national level included the Unified Tax on Combustibles and Lubricants (IUCL) and the tax on rural properties, though subnational unit revenues expanded in absolute terms as a result of economic growth.

The parallel administration also included a host of new agencies through which the central government promoted the industrial, urban economy. New ministries for Work, Education and Health, and Industry and Commerce were created, along with entities responsible for trade, credit, insurance, and monetary policy. Of critical importance was the Administrative Department of Public Service (DASP), a centralized bureaucracy with a degree of autonomy and capacity previously unseen in Brazilian public administration. The DASP had primary responsibility for guiding the national industrialization project, and it came to dominate public enterprises and central government institutions. It was established as an elite within the bureaucracy, recruited meritocratically, controlled hierarchically by the presidency, and operated as an "island of efficiency" within the public sector (Geddes 1994, 43–82).[6]

To sustain this effort, an alternative and parallel system of finance, not subject to regional pressures, drew revenues from dynamic urban sectors. The revenue instruments chosen were contributions on salary and transactions within productive processes, and the funds available were potentially abundant, as the urban sector was clearly booming. With corporatism, the number of employees covered by formal contracts, and therefore contributing to social insurance schemes, doubled overnight, from 844,000 in 1937 to 1.787 million in 1938, and their number increased steadily to 2.762 million by 1945, the end of the Estado Novo. By 1963, 5.711 million workers paid into the system, and only 1.271 million were retired and/or drawing benefits (around an 80/20 split). Even as the number of retirees crept upwards, surpluses were all but guaranteed so long as payouts did not keep pace with inflation (Lopreato 2002, 21).[7]

Surpluses decreased over time as the accumulated number of retirees increased, and the figures suffered severe fluctuations when a new currency was introduced to deal with inflation in the latter 1930s. Still, surpluses started as high as 70% of receipts from the first years of the Estado Novo, and remained at 23% even in 1963. As a result, the federal government could push revenues toward 18% of GDP without significant tax reform, simply by incorporating more workers into the network of

[6] In each state, an extension of the DASP operated to manage local complements of the import-substitution industrialization project (Abrucio 1998, 46), side-stepping regional elites while leaving their traditional practices intact (Faoro 1975).

[7] Additional revenue bases mobilized but outside the taxes shared with subnational units included income, imports, industry, services, industrial products, and fees on energy and transport earmarked for infrastructure investment.

contributory payments. Corporatism allowed Vargas to use the state to promote development and draw revenues from the most dynamic sectors.

The existence of parallel fiscal systems led some to label the Estado Novo a "patronage-oriented developmental state" (Lessa and Fiori 1984). Regional elites were coopted with material benefits that they distributed to their clients, and rising urban elites were coordinated through a centrally directed, parallel, administrative bureaucracy. Yet, divisions among the Vargas allies, pressure to democratize following World War II, and pressure from elites in the poorer states spelled the collapse of the Estado Novo fiscal federal bargain in 1945. In the return to democracy in 1945, the opposition took the first election, but Vargas himself won the 1950 election, and the partisan alliance he supported took the 1955 election as well.

The constitution of 1946 made few changes to the tax structure, though it set in motion a major change in federal bargains by shifting power and resources to subnational governments. Discretionary transfers to subnational governments and annual budget allocations were now fixed in a series of revenue-sharing formulas, varying according to geographic size, population, consumption, and production.[8] Among the federal taxes shared were federal income tax, consumption tax, and levies on electricity and mineral extraction. Municipalities gained control over stamp duties and taxes on professions, and state governments regained residual powers to tax.[9] In terms of proportions, the federal government share of total taxes fell to 60% in 1950, recuperating slightly during the 1950s only to fall again through 1964, when it dipped below 60% for the first time since before the Estado Novo.[10]

The most devastating handicap to the postwar industrialization effort was a chronic foreign exchange shortage. Declining prices for primary exports and a growing demand for imports led the central government to address the imbalance through a variety of stopgap mechanisms, including exchange-rate manipulation and tariffs, which both adjusted accounts and stimulated industry (Baer 2001, 55). Regional elites used their power

[8] 10% of income tax went to municipalities for spending on rural development (Lopreato 2002, 32).

[9] 3% of federal revenues went to the Amazon, 3% to the Northeast, and 1% to the São Francisco River Valley.

[10] Earmarks channeled revenues to regional elites but constrained them within federal development plans, "On one hand, the tax format assured freedom to member units to manipulate tax and fiscal policy to defend their interests, and on the other, to create federal mechanisms to support peripheral oligarchies, such that they could reproduce their form of domination at the local level" (Lopreato 2002, 34).

to erode both federal and municipal resources, increasing their share of revenues from 40% to 45% from 1952 to 1964 while the central government and municipal shares fell (Lopreato 2002, 39).[11] The resulting fiscal crisis was inherited by Janio Quadros, elected in 1960 on a platform of cleaning-up politics, but essentially handed a task made impossible by the stalemate among regional elite, partisan, and popular sectors. After Quadros resigned, the vice president took over in 1961 and attempted a wholescale redefinition of Brazil's relationship to the international economy, favoring small-scale capital and basic agricultural production for domestic consumption while confronting international capital with laws restricting profit repatriation, limiting capital outflows, and nationalizations (Baer 2001, 73).

His gamble was unsuccessful. Prices rose, political polarization increased, and the fiscal and monetary sustainability of the government decayed further (Cohen 1994, ch. 6; Stepan 1978, 110–138). "Congress had been transformed into an 'inflationary machine' which multiplied expenses and 'distortionary factors' of investments with the hypersensitivity to regional pressure capable of destroying the coherence and balance of plans and programs" (Campos 1975, 35–6, as cited in Abrucio 1998, 65).

FISCAL FEDERAL CENTRALIZATION FOR INDUSTRIAL DEEPENING

In response, the military seized power in 1964 and initiated a new fiscal federal bargain characterized by centralized, authoritarian coordination of industrial deepening. To increase rates of investment, the regime increased extraction, undertaking the most significant tax reform since the Old Republic while centralizing funds in the central government and state enterprises. Growth boomed, but increased political conflict forced the military to cede power and resources to regionally based elites, gradually undermining its fiscal federal bargain just as inflation and slowing growth worsened, leading up to democratization in 1985 (Stepan 1975, 97).

[11] Northern and Northeast states bristled: "The states that produce and export primary materials covered, in 1958, São Paulo's exports of 17 billion and imports of 57 billion, which is to say, 3.3 times more than the exports. We are forced to sacrifice yet again, foregoing taxes we are owed... and it is excessive!! It is an unbearable sacrifice!...The situation is strangling our economy while offering an abundance of financial benefits to others" (*A Gazeta*, São Paulo, 10/12/1959).

The military rejuvenated the system of parallel federal administration inherited from the Estado Novo. Centralized technical bureaucracy maintained support to national industrialists but now gave a leading role to multinational capital, brought in to scale-up the size and sophistication of national industry (Dreyfuss 1981, 73). The effect internationalized Brazilian industrialization with an infusion of external capital, technology, and ownership, as well as increased capacity to export (Evans 1979). Growth fell below 5% only twice in fifteen years, and was frequently above 10%, averaging 11.3% from 1968 until 1980.

Industry share of GDP increased from 34% to 44%, growing more than 12% per year, upgrading from traditional manufactures such as textile and clothing to more complex capital and intermediate goods, such as transport equipment, machinery, and electrical equipment (Baer 2001, 75–77, Appendix A1). State enterprises retained certain sectors, such as strategic intermediate inputs of steel, mining, and petrochemicals, as well as energy, public utilities, and banking (Rezende 1982).

When the first oil shock occurred in 1973, Brazil doubled-down its deepening strategy. The regime opted for large-scale projects in capital goods, steel, and infrastructure through the Second National Development Plan (PND II) (Barros de Castro and Pires de Souza, 1985), a strategy made possible by the availability of international finance in markets flush with petrodollars and offering low interest rates. Foreign borrowing increased, with net debt rising from US$6.2 billion in 1973 to US$31.6 billion in 1978, 63.3% of which was in the hands of the public sector.

These strategies of industrial deepening interacted in several ways with fiscal federal bargains. When the military had lost key states in the 1965 governor election, hardliners acted on their suspicion of the political class in general and of opposition governors in particular (Abrucio 1998, 61–62) to replace clientelist and populist regional elites with nontraditional technical administrators drawn from local states (Sallum Junior 1994, 2–3).[12] Abrucio and Samuels (1997) note that the men chosen to lead state governments were "governor-technicians," and the federal bargain was defined as "unionist-authoritarian," with limited civil society space and indirect elections for state governors and municipal mayors.[13]

[12] Collier refers to "a type of authoritarianism characterized by a self-avowedly technocratic, bureaucratic, nonpersonalistic approach to policy making and problem solving" (1979, 364–371, 399–400).

[13] Institutional Act Five of 1968 cut federal transfers in half, and made them conditional on federal approval of local investment plans. The 1967 tax reform diminished local revenues,

The military undertook a major fiscal reform in 1967, addressing a number of the problems that had accumulated since the 1930s and expanding revenues significantly (Varsano 1999). Major innovations on the revenue side were to eliminate cascading indirect taxes, improve income tax, simplify the tax system, eliminate double taxation of bases by different levels of government, and administrative reform. The reform of indirect taxes was highlighted by the ICM (Tax on Circulation of Goods), one of the first value-added taxes in the world, which replaced the sales tax (IVC). After hovering around 16% of GDP during the 1950s, revenues increased to approximately 25% of GDP.

The reform concentrated resources and authority in the federal government, but the bargain shifted after the mid-1970s. Regional elites had been alienated by governor-technicians and the campaigns run centrally from Brasília (Abrucio and Samuels 1997, 147), and they secured a majority of the vote in the 1974 election, doubling opposition Congressional representation to 165 of 364 seats, and raising their total to 20 in the Senate – almost a third of the 66 total. The regime responded by reorganizing both fiscal and federal arrangements. First, as Hagopian has observed, the military renewed their alliance with traditional clientelist elites in the states: "When the military was challenged to shore up its sagging support, it revitalized its alliance with the political elites" (1996, 14).

What emerged was a hybrid political form, combining elements of traditional clientelism with modern bureaucracy, distributing the material resources and privileges of a bureaucratic state to sustain both urban and rural clientelist networks.[14] The military also manipulated the party system, gradually opening competition for subnational and legislative offices, but doing so in ways that would fragment the opposition while encouraging regime unity and even expanding conservative representation, creating new states in rural regions and altering the formula for representation.

This coincided with the second national development plan, PND II, which sought to deconcentrate industries from the São Paulo–Rio corridor.

but to access federal discretionary grants states and municipalities had to provide their own matching funds and cover associated current expenses (Abrucio 1998, 62–68).

[14] "It creates a dualism within the state, in systems of interest representation, in the electorate, and in various realms of public policy... The bumping up of traditional against modern politics and each with economic constraints and opportunities 'contaminates' both. Their interaction produces hybrid political forms, and practices that are normally thought of as 'traditional' become 'modernized,' and the practices of the state and modern political parties are somewhat perverted by the presence and actions of traditional political elites" (Hagopian 1996, 17).

As Abrucio relates, "Geisel sought to make federalism more multipolar in economic terms, weakening the wealthiest states, especially São Paulo. In this way, the power of the strongest states – usually in opposition to the regime – were counterbalanced by the association between the Union and the emerging states" (1998, 85–86). While the military was able to slow its departure from power until 1985, it could not dictate the terms, and it was forced to increasingly shift resources to its clientelist allies in the rural and less-developed states.

In the context of inflationary shocks, rising oil prices, and depressed global trade, these federal changes undermined fiscal capacity: "The deceleration in economic growth, the increase in inflation and the increase in fiscal exemptions limited the receipts of state governments. Combined with rising debt service costs, they help to explain the situation of state finance and financial problems" (Lopreato 2002, 68). Attempts to recover investment with tax exemptions, preferences, and special regimes further eroded the fiscal base, which fell below 25% of GDP. Subnational governments were particularly afflicted, as centralized fiscal authority and absorption of concurrent subnational tax bases and rates made it impossible for states and municipalities to recover solvency.

Steps taken to patch fiscal shortfalls at the national level further prejudiced subnational accounts. The regime came to depend on earmarked levies on payroll and other transactions: compulsory federal savings funds, termed social contributions, including the Contribution toward the Social Integration Program (PIS), the Program for the Formation of the Public Sector Fund (PASEP), and the Social Investment Fund (FINSOCIAL) (Blanco 2002). Not quite taxes, and not shared with subnational units, they protected national revenues even as they worsened revenue quality with cumulative and distortionary charges. The result was a further centralization of resources; by 1980 the central government was collecting 80% of all revenues, and after transfers the federal share of available tax receipts rose from 40.6% to 51.6% while state shares fell from 46.3% to 35.2%.

As the military neared its exit in 1985, and in an effort to favor its allies in poorer and rural states, it reformed the transfer system: State Participation Fund (FPE) and Municipal Participation Fund (FPM).[15] Fund values were raised in 1980 to 11% of the total IR (income tax) and IPI (industrial products tax), in 1984 to 12.5%, and in 1985 to 14%,

[15] State incentives on the ICM tax were absorbed by the federal government, which also extended incentives on its industrial products tax (Lopreato 2002, 66).

with the FPM raised to 16%. Special portions of the transfers were reserved for the poorer and more conservative Northern, Northeastern, and Central-Western states (10% in 1976/1977 and 20% in 1978). Wealthier states secured increases in the ICM to 16% in 1982 and 17% in 1984, while the regime assumed the cost of ICM credits extended to enterprises in the North and Northeast.

The main benefits to wealthier states came through state enterprise investments, which tended to target already developed areas (Rezende 1982).[16] Further, they were more able to offer required matching funds (Lopreato 2002, 54) and had much stronger state banks to secure capital (Mora 2002). Total state external debt rose to US$22.8 billion, with US$18.3 billion owed by Southeastern states and US$8.1 billion by São Paulo alone (Abrucio 1998, 87).

The second oil shock of 1979 and the interest rate shock of the 1980s revealed the extent of the fiscal crisis. A rising import bill and cost of financing current and fiscal account imbalances severely constrained public accounts. Public investments had risen from 3% of GDP to 5% between 1964 and 1970, only to taper toward the end of the decade, dropping to 1.2% in 1988 (Bresser-Pereira 1996, 58). General economic stagnation signaled the end of debt-financed industrial deepening (Erber and Vermulm 1993), and fiscal incapacity and hyperinflation indicated the bankruptcy of the military fiscal federal bargain.

FISCAL FEDERAL ADJUSTMENT FOR LIBERALIZATION AND NEO-DEVELOPMENTALISM

The transition to democracy in 1985 opened space for pent-up demands, inscribed in the 1988 Constitution with mandates for increases in social spending. Still, ongoing fiscal crisis and hyperinflation meant that no new fiscal federal bargain appeared until the mid-1990s. When it materialized, it was underpinned by a steady increase in fiscal resources to finance social spending and macroeconomic stability, along with a federal bargain in which regional elites acted as the alliance partners of nationally dominant social forces. This fiscal federal bargain served to advance first a liberalizing and then a neo-developmentalist agenda, though the bargain would appear to have unraveled with the 2016 impeachment.

[16] Heads of the most important economic ministries tended to be drawn from wealthier states, giving them an additional advantage in the allocation of investments (Rezende 1982, 515).

Throughout the 1980s and into the 1990s, Brazil faced cycles of inflation and failed stabilization. Twelve stabilization plans were attempted, including five orthodox and six heterodox plans, and each failed plan only complicated stabilization further by embedding expectations of future inflation. A decided turn toward structural adjustment began under President Collor, elected in 1990, with trade liberalization and privatization, but his presidency was cut short by corruption scandals and impeachment. The next administration introduced a monetary shock, called the Real Plan, to break the cycle of inflationary expectations (Bresser-Pereira and Nakano 1987), and the 1994 election of Fernando Henrique Cardoso began a series of efforts at structural adjustment, including privatization, liberalization, and deregulation, as well as a stabilization strategy that raised revenues (Bresser-Pereira 1996).[17] The stabilization strategy eventually came to concentrate on an inflation-targeting regime known as the "tripé," in which the Central Bank and the Ministry of Finance use interest rates and primary fiscal surplus to keep exchange rates high, thereby controlling inflation.

These policies came on the heels of industrial slowdown during the debt crisis and evolved in response to a changed international environment of liberalized trade and capital markets. Instead of activist industrial policy, the Cardoso administration attempted to attract international capital with regulatory reform, high interest rates, and privatization – a development strategy dependent on international loans and investment (Bresser-Pereira 2010).

As Ondetti notes in Chapter 4, while the government decreased its direct investment, it shifted expenditure to fulfilling the commitments of the 1988 Constitution, significantly expanding social spending. These increases began in 1994 and took off after 2002, practically tripling social spending from 1995 to 2015 from 5% of GDP to close to 15%. For example, health expenditure almost tripled from 1995 to 2012, 260 billion reais to 680 billion reais, and health expenditure per capita almost quadrupled, from U$315 to U$1,118.[18]

To support this increase in social spending while sustaining the stabilization effort, the federal government expanded revenues. Increases in income taxes and the implementation of numerous contributions linked to social spending outlays more than compensated for decreases in tariffs as Brazil

[17] During the 1990s, total proceeds from privatization, including transferred debts, was $36.6 billion, led by $8.2 billion in steel, $6.9 billion in mining, $5.6 billion in electricity, and $4.0 billion in oil and gas (BNDES 2000).

[18] http://data.worldbank.org/data-catalog/world-development-indicators.

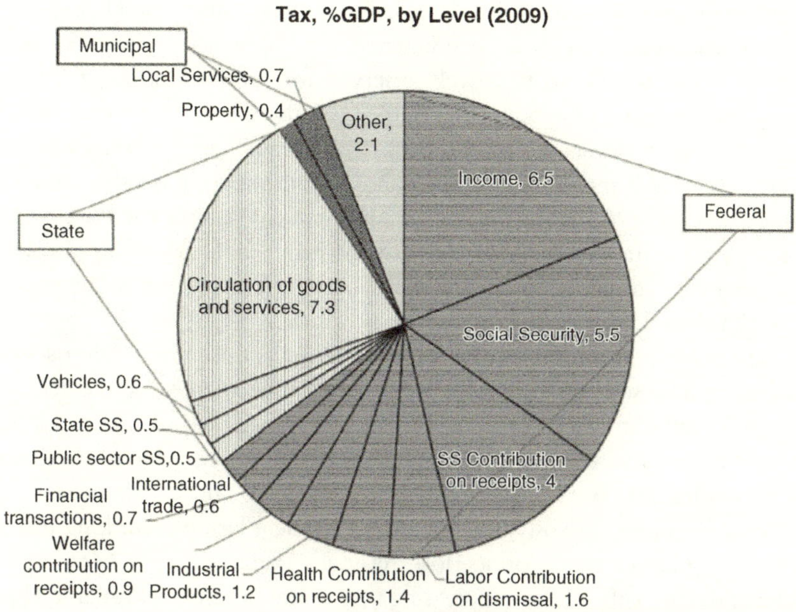

FIGURE 5.3 Tax revenue as a share of GDP by type and level of government, 2009
Source: Compiled with data from the Min. Fazenda, Receita Federal

liberalized international trade. As shown in Figure 5.1, from 1994 to 2010, taxes increased from 28.4 to 34.6% of GDP.

A glimpse at the distribution of taxes and their attribution to different levels of government highlights two patterns. First, the tax system has become increasingly complex, ranking Brazil among the countries in which tax compliance takes the greatest number of hours. The single largest tax is a tax on the circulation of goods and services attributed to the states, accounting for 7.3% of GDP.

With the states in control of the most important tax on consumption, the federal government focused much of its effort on income taxes and social contributions. As Figure 5.2 shows, by 2009 direct taxes were almost 60% of total revenues, up from barely 44% in 2000. As a percentage of GDP, this represented an increase from 13.6 to 17.8% (Afonso 2012). Social contributions increased from 8.95% of GDP in 1994 to 12.94% in 2010.[19] Social

[19] Contributions now include social security, a social security contribution on business receipts (COFINS), a contribution to unemployment benefits for dismissed workers (FGTS), a health contribution on receipts (CSS), a welfare contribution on receipts (PIS), a public sector social security contribution (CPSS), a contribution on profits toward social security (CSL),

contributions hold several attractions. First, while other federal taxes are shared with state and local governments, contributions are not.[20] Second, while contributions are putatively reserved for specific outlays, they are frequently available for other uses, either because the outlays would occur long in the future (as in social security) or because the outlays were not particularly well monitored. While contributions, as well as other indirect taxes, tend to be regressive, their most important characteristic in the context of democratization is that they carry the political legitimacy of a promise – government commits to increasing social spending in exchange for increased contributions.

The federal government increased fiscal effort to raise revenues for social spending and stabilize inflation, but it took time to rework the federal bargain. Subnational governments enjoyed greater fiscal resources as a result of constitutionally mandated decentralization, which raised the shares of federal taxes transferred to states to 21.5% and 22.5% to municipalities. Beginning in 1995, the federal government began reworking federalism to recover some of its lost revenues (Samuels 2003, 555–556). Municipalities suffered less, increasing their share of receipts available after transfers overall from 10.7% in 1988 to 18.3% in 2010. This increase came only partly at the expense of the federal government, which dropped from 62.5% of available receipts to 57%, and the rest came from the share of state governments, whose share fell from 26.8% to 24.7% of available receipts.

Prior to 1994, inflation had hidden subnational imbalances, and state governments especially used subnational state enterprises and banks to take on debt, which rose to US$95 billion by 1995 (Dillinger 1995).[21] These debts became unpayable as stabilization eliminated inflationary finance, federal retention of revenues lowered transfers, and high interest rates increased burdens (Alston and Mueller 2005). States were forced to accept bailouts that included ceilings on outlays, debt limits, and privatization (Webb 2004). Within a year, almost all state banks were eliminated or turned into development banks with circumscribed mandates. A 1999 Fiscal Responsibility

a contribution on fuel toward education and health (CIDE), and for a time there was a contribution toward education and health on financial transactions (CPMF).

20 20% of all federal revenues were separated from the pool of shared taxes and made available only to the federal government, first through the Social Emergency Fund and later through Disconnection of Receipts.

21 State banks obtained 38% of their capital through borrowing in 1988–1990, with 63–81% of their loans going to the state governments, who received only 2–5% of their total from private banks. State bonds were a poorly regulated area, allowing states to affect the monetary base through printing quasi-money.

Law placed limits on debt as a percentage of current receipts, a "golden rule" for credit that cannot exceed investments, a cap on personnel spending at 60% of current revenue, and limits on credit and new payment obligations in the final year of gubernatorial mandates (IMF 2001, 1).

The new fiscal federal arrangement greatly constrained state governments to fall within the national fiscal federal bargain of increased revenues for social spending and stabilization. Still, there was room in the bargain for regional elites, especially those drawn from poorer states. In the context of a fragmented party system, they were essential coalition partners to federal governments. Since 1989, the party of the president has had consistently low representation: never above the 99 out of 513 seats won in 1998, and as low as 41 seats under Collor's government. To deal with these issues, subsequent governments managed governance through "presidential coalitionism" (Abranches 1988), building legislative supermajorities that could withstand occasional defections. A host of interlocutors manage such coalitions, including single-issue caucuses, governors with leverage over state delegations, party leaders, and individual politicians with large vote-banks. To secure support, presidents deploy ministerial appointments, tens of thousands of federal jobs, and release of investments in the bailiwicks of legislators (Pereira et al. 2005). As the largest catch-all party, dominant in several poorer and rural states, the Party of the Brazilian Democracy Movement (PMDB) has proven itself to be the essential coalition partner to all governing parties, along with a scattering of additional clientelist and patronage-oriented additional parties (Nobre 2010).

Patronage for coalitional presidentialism remained within the fiscal limits of the inflation-targeting regime, which was further compatible with quite different development strategies. During Cardoso's presidency, international insertion depended on attracting foreign savings with high interest rates, liberalization, and privatization, and the main local counterparts able to intermediate international capital were local financial and service elites, sectors especially supportive of Cardoso's Party of Brazilian Social Democracy (PSDB) and its most important bases in São Paulo.

By contrast, when the Workers' Party won power in 2002, they gradually shifted to a more neo-developmentalist strategy of international insertion (Ban 2013). The first PT president, Lula, took advantage of rising prices of commodity exports to lower debt burdens, become less dependent on international capital, and use state spending and subsidized credit to boost the fortunes of large national companies, especially those commodity-processing firms able to compete internationally. The strategy remained within the limits of macroeconomic stability, even as it further expanded social spending, wage increases, and public employment, as Ondetti points out (Chapter 4 in this volume). Still, both the development with foreign savings and neo-developmentalist strategies maintained the fiscal federal bargain of raising revenues for social spending and macroeconomic stability and coalitional presidentialism dependent on alliances with clientelist elites drawn from poorer states.

The fiscal federal bargain of revenues for social spending and stabilization with patronage for coalitional presidentialism came undone during the second Workers' Party government of Dilma Rousseff, when commodity prices fell, growth slowed, and the president was unable to sustain either the fiscal or the federal side of the bargain. Attempts to restart growth with austerity policies only abrogated both the fiscal bargain of increased social spending and the federal bargain of patronage for allies. As Scartascini and Hallerberg's analysis of particularist electoral institutions might suggest (see Chapter 6 in this volume), it was precisely the elite from commodity producing states who were especially eager to jettison the Workers' Party coalition when the fiscal federal bargain no longer served their interests.

In 2016, Rousseff was impeached, and the incoming government has essentially thrown out the social commitment side of the fiscal bargain, introducing a constitutional amendment to lock-in spending freezes for twenty years. Revenues are unlikely to fall, as the government appears committed to the inflation-targeting stabilization regime, and it has continued with a coalitional strategy that includes favors to regionally dominant elites.

EXTENSIONS

Before concluding, it is worth considering how this model might travel to other developing-country federal systems. While the relatively small number and highly different circumstances make comparison difficult, the prominent position of federalism among developing countries suggests important insights. Among the five BRICS, at least four were federal systems (Brazil, Russia, India, and South Africa), and some have argued that China ought to be considered quasi-federal for its complex arrangement of local and regional governments (Weingast 1995). The case of India is particularly useful to consider, as neoliberal adjustment in India took a decidedly federal turn during the 1990s. With major reforms blocked by a fragmented parliament at the national level, state governments raced ahead in pursuit of liberalization. State-level elections, especially during the 1990s, increasingly turned toward local considerations, dominated by leading castes and communal configurations specific to particular regions (Yadav and Palshikar 2008). While liberalizing elites made limited progress on reforms at the national level, they successfully pressed to empower states within the federation, finding eager proponents of liberalization among dominant caste and communal groups in certain states who eventually scaled up their efforts to the national level, leading some to characterize Indian adjustment as "reform by stealth" (Jenkins 1999).

Closer to Brazil in Latin America, the Mexican case also affirms the role of federal dynamics in the elite compromises necessary for new international insertions. In Mexico, liberalization occurred in the context of the 1980s debt crisis and flagging oil prices that threatened the sustainability of the Mexican state, calling for a significant fiscal effort (Magaldi de Sousa and Maldonado 2015). Yet, that fiscal effort has largely failed to materialize, held in check at least in part by regional elites eager to liberalize but unwilling to mobilize additional revenues. Rather than participate in efforts to build state capacity to promote a new international insertion, subnational units essentially traded their revenue-raising power for guaranteed and expanded transfers (Díaz-Cayeros 2006). As a result, oligarchic subnational regimes have survived and even flourished under liberalization in Mexico, distorting the process of democratization while blocking efforts to build state capacity (Snyder 2000).

CONCLUSION

Brazil's state capacity in terms of fiscal extraction has progressed in qualitative leaps in response to new insertions in the international economy. These leaps have been marked by changing fiscal federal bargains to accommodate rising and falling elite and popular sectors. Moments of coincident reform of both tax and federalism mark the construction of a new fiscal federal bargain in which the state captures revenues made available by new patterns of international insertion and funds outlays undergirded by a political agreement among rival elites inscribed in federalism. Such moments have been rare, and more frequent have been moments of divergent reform in which bargains of tax and federalism work at cross purposes.

Moments of coincident reform were evident in the establishment of the first Republic, the Estado Novo of the 1930s, the military regime that began in 1964, and in the 1990s. While these moments of coincident reform help explain impressive gains in state capacity over the past century, they are interrupted by various moments of divergent reform. Some moments of divergence were forward-looking, as rising regional elites experimented with policies that would later be adopted at the national level. More often, divergent reform is backward-looking, as declining elites use regional jurisdictions to constrain national state capacity.

The combination of coincident and divergent reform helps explain two characteristics of Brazilian tax. First, the country mobilizes an impressive quantity of revenue, testament to repeated moments in which political institutions accommodated the shifting fortunes of rising and falling elite and popular sectors associated with new patterns of international insertion. Second, the country mobilizes revenue in a complex and regressive fashion, the legacy of repeated moments in which fiscal and federal bargains have worked at cross purposes.

The Brazilian case offers lessons as well as cautionary tales for other countries. New patterns of international insertion imply sources of dynamism and capital accumulation available for state revenues. Successfully tapping these resources requires a series of bargains between state and society and among political and economic elites. In Brazil, federalism inscribes bargains among elites, in horizontal accommodations among regionally diverse interests and vertical accommodations between higher and lower levels of government. At the same time, and closely related, fiscal arrangements strike bargains between state and society, exchanging revenues for outlays and other policies of importance to key social bases.

References

Abranches, Sergio. 1988. "Presidencialismo de Coalizao: O DilemaIs Institucional Brasileiro," *Revista de Ciencias Sociais* 31(1): 5–34.

Abrucio, Fernando. 1998. *Barões da Federação*. São Paulo: CEDEC.

Abrucio, Fernando and David Samuels. 1997. "A Nova Politica dos Governadores," *Kriterion:* Revista de Filosofia 40: 137–166.

Afonso, Jose Roberto. 2012. *Desafios do Federalismo Brasileiro*. Rio de Janeiro: Presentation.

Alston, Lee J. and Bernado Mueller. 2005. "Pork for Policy: Executive and Legislative Exchange in Brazil," *Journal of Law Economics and Organization* 22(1) (Spring): 87–114.

Arretche, Marta. 2012. *Democracia, Federalismo, e Centralizacao no Brasil.* São Paulo: Fiocruz/Ed. FGV.

Baer, Werner. 2001. *The Brazilian Economy.* Chicago: Greenwood Publishing Group. 5th edn.

Ban, Cornel. 2013. "Brazil's Liberal Neo-Developmentalism: New Paradigm or Edited Orthodoxy?" Review of International Political Economy 20(2): 298–331.

Barros de Castro, Antonio and Francisco Eduardo Pires de Souza. 1985. *A Economia Brasileira em Marcha Forçada.* Rio de Janeiro: Paz e Terra.

Blanco Cossio, Fernando Andrés. 2002. Ensaios sobre Federalismo Fiscal no Brasil. PhD Thesis. Rio de Janeiro: PUC-Rio.

BNDES. 2000. A Privatização no Brasil. Rio de Janeiro: BNDES.

Brautigam, Deborah, Odd-Helge Fjeldstad, and Mick Moore. 2009. *Taxation and State-Building in Developing Countries.* New York: Cambridge University Press.

Bresser-Pereira, Luiz Carlos. 1996. "Da administração pública burocrática à gerencial," in Luiz Carlos Bresser-Pereira and Peter Kevin Spink (eds.), *Reforma do Estado e Administração Pública Gerencial.* São Paulo: Editora, chapter 9.

2010. "Taxa de câmbio, doença holandesa, e industrialização," *Cadernos FGV Projetos* 5(14): 68–73.

Bresser-Pereira, Luiz and Yoshiako Nakano. 1987. *The Theory of Inertial Inflation: The Foundation of Economic Reform in Brazil and Argentina.* Boulder: Lynne Rienner.

Buchanan, James and Richard E. Wagner. 1977. *Democracy in Deficit.* New York: Academic Press.

Campello de Souza, Maria do Carmo. 1976. *Estado e Partidos Políticos no. Brasil (1930 a 1964).* São Paulo: Alfa Omega.

Cohen, Youssef. 1994. *Autoritarismo e Corporativismo no Brasil.* New York: Academic Press.

Collier, David. 1979. *The New Authoritarianism in Latin America.* Princeton: Princeton University Press.

Collier, David and Ruth Berins Collier. 1979. "Inducements versus Constraints: Disaggregating Corporatism," *American Political Science Review* 73(4): 967–986.

Díaz-Cayeros, Alberto. 2006. *Federalism, Fiscal Authority, and Centralization in Latin America.* New York: Cambridge University Press.

Dillinger, Bill. 1995. "*Brazil – State Debt: Crisis and Reform,*" World Bank Report 14842-BR. Washington, DC: World Bank.

Draibe, Sonia. 1985. *Rumos e Metamorfoses: Estado e industrialização no Brasil: 1930–1960.* Rio de Janeiro: Paz e Terra.

Dreyfuss, René A. 1981. 1964: A Conquista do Estado. Petrópolis: Vozes.

Erber, Fábio Stéfano and Roberto Vermulm. 1993. *Ajuste estrutural e estratégias empresariais.* Brasília: IPEA.

Evans, Peter. 1979. *Dependent Development: The Alliance of Multinational, State and Local Capital in Brazil.* Princeton: Princeton University Press.

Faoro, Raymond. 1975. *Os Donos do Poder.* São Paulo: Editora Globo.

Furtado, Celso. 1972. *Formação Economica do Brasil.* Rio de Janeiro: Saraiva.

Geddes, Barbara. 1994. *Politician's Dilemma*. Berkeley: University of California Press.
Gerschenkron, Alexander. 1962. *Economic Backwardness in Historical Perspective*. New York: Cambridge University Press.
Hagopian, Frances. 1996. Traditional Politics and Regime Change in Brazil. New York: Cambridge University Press.
Hamilton, Alexander, James Madison, and John Jay. 1961. *Federalist Papers*. New York: New American Library.
IMF. 2001. "Brazil: ROSC – Fiscal Transparency," *IMF Country Report 01/217*. Washington, DC: IMF.
Jenkins, Rob. 1999. *Reforms by Stealth: Democratic Politics and Economic Reform in India*. New York: Cambridge University Press.
Lessa, Carlos and J. L. Fiori. 1984. "Houve uma política nacional-populista?" Anais, XII Encontro, ANPEC.
Lieberman, Evan. 2003. *Race and Regionalism in the Politics of Taxation in Brazil and South Africa*. New York: Cambridge University Press.
Lopreato, Francisco Luiz. 2002. *O Colapso das Finanças Estaduais e a Crise da Federação*. São Paulo: Editora UNESP-IE.
Love, Joseph. 1982. *São Paulo in the Brazilian Federation*. Stanford: Stanford University Press.
2013. *The Brazilian Federal State in the Old Republic: Did Regime Change Matter*. Working Paper. Lemann Institute for Brazilian Studies.
Magaldi de Sousa, Mariana and Claudia Maldonado Trujillo. 2015. *La Integración de Políticas Públicas para el Desarrollo: Brasil y Mexico en Perspectiva Comparada*. Ciudad de Mexico: CIDE.
Mann, Michael. 1984. "The Autonomous Power of the State: Origins, Mechanisms, Results," *European Journal of Sociology* 25(2): 185–213.
Martin, Isaac, Ajay K. Mehrota, and Monica Prasad, 2009. *The New Fiscal Sociology*. New York: Cambridge University Press.
Martinez Fritscher, Andé C. and Aldo Musacchio. 2009. "Endowments, Cost of Capital, and Fiscal Federalism" *NBER Working Paper 15411*. Cambridge, MA: NBER.
Mora, Mônica. 2002. "Federalismo e Dívida Estadual no Brasil," *Ipea Texto para Discussão 866*. Rio de Janeiro: IPEA.
Nobre, Marcus. 2010. "O Fim da Polarização," Revista Piaui: http://piaui.folha.uol.com.br/materia/o-fim-da-polarizacao/.
Oates, Wallace. 1971. *Fiscal Federalism*. New York: Harcourt Brace Jovanovich.
Pereira, Carlos, Timothy Power, and L. Rennó. 2005. "Under What Conditions do Presidents Resort to Decree Power? Theory and Evidence from the Brazilian Case," *Journal of Politics* 67(1): 178–201.
Reuschemeyer, Dietrich, Evelyn Huber Stephens, and John Stephens. 1992. *Capitalist Development and Democracy*. Chicago: Chicago University Press.
Rezende, Andre Lara. 1982. *Recessão e Ajuste Estrutural o Brasil Diante Da Crise da Divida Externa*. Rio de Janeiro: Paz e Terra.
Riker, William H. 1964. *Federalism: Origin, Operation, Significance*. Boston: Little Brown.

Rodden, Jonathan. 2006. *Hamilton's Paradox: The Promise and Perils of Fiscal Federalism.* New York: Cambridge University Press.

Ross, Michael. 2014. "What Have We Learned about the Resource Curse," *Annual Review of Political Science* 18: 239–59.

Sallum Júnior, Brasilio. 1994. "Transição política e crise de Estado," *Lua Nova* 32: 133–167.

Samuels, David J. 2003. Ambition, Federalism, and Legislative Politics in Brazil. New York: Cambridge University Press.

Schmitter, Phillippe. 1971. "Still the Century of Corporativism?" *Review of Politics* 36(1): 85–31.

Schneider, Aaron. 2012. *State-building and Tax Regimes in Central America.* New York: Cambridge University Press.

Schumpeter, Josef. 1917. "The Crisis of the Tax State." Reproduced in Swedberg, Richard. 1991. *Joseph A. Schumpeter, The Economics and Sociology of Capitalism.* Princeton: Princeton University Press.

Skidmore, Thomas. 1999. *Brazil: Five Centuries of Change.* New York: Oxford University Press.

Snyder, Richard. 2000. *Politics after Neoliberalism: Reregulation in Mexico.* New York: Cambridge University Press.

Stepan, Alfred. 1975. *The Military in Politics: Changing Patterns in Brazil.* Princeton: Princeton University Press.

1978. *The State and Society: Peru in Comparative Perspective.* Princeton: Princeton University Press.

2000. "Federalism and Democracy: Beyond the US Model," *Journal of Democracy* 10(4): 19–34.

Varsano, Ricardo. 1999. *A evolução do sistema tributário Brasileiro ao longo do século: Anotações e reflexões para futuras reformas.* Rio de Janeiro: IPEA.

Webb, Steven. 2004. "Fiscal Responsibility Laws for Subnational Discipline: the Latin American Experience," *Policy Research Working Paper Series 3309.* Washington, DC: World Bank.

Weingast, Barry. 1995. "The Economic Role of Political Institutions: Market-Preserving Federalism and Economic Development," *Journal of Law, Economics and Organization* 11(1) (April): 1–31.

Yadav, Yogendra and Suhas Palshikar. 2008. "Ten Theses on State Politics in India," *Seminar* 591 (November): 1–15.

Ziblatt, Daniel. 2008. *Structuring the State: Formation of Italy and Germany and the Puzzle of Federalism.* Princeton: Princeton University Press.

6

Particularistic Political Institutions and Tax Neutrality in Latin America*

Mark Hallerberg and Carlos Scartascini

President Michelle Bachelet entered office in 2014 with a broad agenda meant to reduce inequality. Her platform included a tax reform, which she introduced to Congress within months of gaining office. It advocated an increase in corporate income tax rates as well as the end of many exemptions for businesses. The proposed tax system, therefore, was expected to be more neutral in the way that it treated income from labor and capital than the system that it would replace. The reform then entered Congress. She enjoyed a clear majority in both legislative chambers. Yet it was more difficult to pass the reform than observers expected. The compromise that emerged included the possibility of corporate income tax payers keeping tax breaks but facing slightly higher marginal rates.[1]

In this chapter, we focus on the reasons for, and the dynamics of, the process of reform that leads to a more or less "neutral" tax system. By their very nature, more "neutral" systems are more economically efficient and treat more of the population equally, while less neutral systems are less economically efficient and favor specific constituencies in society. Such reforms have been on the agenda of economists and international organizations such as the International Monetary Fund for decades, and indeed they constitute one understudied part of the so-called Washington Consensus that remains relevant well after the "consensus" ended. Empirically, Lora (2007) is the best documentation of reforms, but without any explanation of their timing or depth. Mahon (2004) is one of

* We would like to thank José Cheibub, Philip Keefer, Shane Martin, Guillermo Rosas, Gisela Sin, and Ernesto Stein for helpful comments.

[1] *The Economist*, July 2014. Arenas (2016) describes the reform process in detail.

the rare studies that tries to explain neutral tax reforms across the region in a multivariate framework. He finds that past inflation, explicit IMF conditions, new administrations, and more authoritarian governments (among others) make such reforms more likely. But, as the inclusion of authoritarian regimes suggests, he considers the predemocratic period for many countries in his study that runs 1977–1995. Arenas (2016) brings a few recent reforms to life by interviewing the Ministers leading those reforms and describing the difficulties that arise when going from the drawing board to Congress.

In this chapter, we seek to explain actual *changes* in the neutrality of the tax system in Latin American democracies. Tax systems are the result of decades of tax legislation, and there are clear issues of identification when one regresses variables such as partisanship and preelectoral years on attributes of a given tax system. Our focus is therefore on reforms that affect the overall level. This chapter uses a new dataset the authors created for all Latin American democracies over a fifteen-year period (1990–2004) that codes tax reforms according to whether they increase or decrease the neutrality of the tax system. Among the characteristics of the tax system that increase neutrality are the broadening of tax bases, the equalization of tax rates across goods and sources of income, and the elimination of tax incentives that treat different people, goods, economic sectors, or activities differently.[2]

We follow an increasingly nuanced literature that examines the relationship between political institutions and policy outputs and argues that more encompassing institutions lead to better policy. The logic is that policymakers who need to focus on the needs of most of the population will create and implement policies for the broader good, while policymakers who care only for a narrow constituency will design policies to reward the narrow group. We examine fragmentation of the party system and of government. Given the relevance that tax reforms have within the legislative agenda, we focus especially on the incentives that the electoral system creates for legislators to push for specific tax breaks for their constituencies. More personalistic systems will be more likely to lead to reforms that erode neutrality, and this tendency will be exacerbated prior to legislative elections. We contrast the incentives of legislators with those

[2] We do not consider explicitly the reduction in marginal tax rates in our definition of tax neutrality. It is much harder to identify whether the reduction in the marginal rate increased neutrality than the more clear-cut cases we are incorporating in the definition and posterior measures.

of the president for increasing tax neutrality. The president is elected in a nationwide district and is more likely to propose and to support tax reforms that benefit more of the population, and to do so immediately following an election. These dynamics fit the expectations of theorists from American politics who note how the separation of powers may affect policy outcomes (Hansen 1998).

We begin with a discussion of the theoretical expectations. We present a story about how two crucial actors in the policy process – the president and the legislature – interact. The simple premise is that these actors want to reward their constituencies, and that the electoral calendar is important. We then present an ordered logit analysis for the region for 1990–2004 that predicts when tax reforms that either increase or decrease neutrality are more likely to occur. Despite our theoretical expectations, the partisanship of the president and whether there was an election in the previous year does not affect tax neutrality. However, tax incentives for particular groups in society were more common when the electoral system encouraged a personal vote. It is no coincidence that the four Finance Ministers from Latin America who have pushed for "broadening" tax reforms indicate that the hardest parts of the reform were going through Congress and dealing with the pressures coming from the private sector. As Fairfield (Chapter 7) points out, those discussions usually led to exceptions and special treatments that were not designed in the original bills (see also Arenas 2016). This evidence is similar to the descriptions in Bonvecchi et al. (2014) about tax reforms in Argentina.

Not related to the political game, we find that reforms that broadened the tax base were more likely during financial crises. This finding suggests that all types of presidents and legislatures agree on such a reform when they are especially short of needed revenue.

NEUTRAL TAX SYSTEMS AND TAX REFORM

There are two common ways to judge any tax system. Horizontal equity refers to whether the system treats a given tax unit the same. If a value-added tax levies a rate of 19% on coffee but 7% on milk, then the same tax treats two goods differently. Taxing all goods sold at the same rate would increase horizontal equity. Vertical equity refers to the distributional impact of the tax system. The reduced rate on dairy means that a good that children consume proportionally more would be cheaper (everything else equal) than a good that adults consume less.[3] This example illustrates tradeoffs between "horizontal" and "vertical" equity. Yet one can imagine that the tradeoff can come at different points. In some countries, a tax system could be generally flat, with exemptions only for the worst off in society. In another system, exemptions could be the rule, with each industry (or even each firm) facing a different tax rate. These systems tend to be less efficient. Tax neutrality tends to be more associated with horizontal equity than vertical equity.[4]

Given that every tax system has horizontal inequities, and given that more "neutral" tax systems are also more economically efficient and are presumed to lead to higher economic growth, proposals to simplify tax systems have been common for several decades in a wide variety of preexisting tax systems. While such proposals were originally associated with the political right (e.g., Feldstein 1976), and the most radical versions of "flat taxes" remain most popular with right parties (Appel and Orenstein 2013), over the past two decades reforms to make the tax system more neutral became part of the political platforms of the political left as well (Agell et al. 1999). It is also reported that for those who favor more redistribution, the argument is that it is better to do it on the expenditure side. There are fewer economic distortions, which in turn lowers economic growth and means there is a smaller overall pot, than when redistribution occurs on the tax side.

In terms of economic growth, an OECD study entitled *Tax Policy Reform and Economic Growth* reinforced the argument that base broadening is associated with higher growth. In contrast, the study found that the effect of tax incentives for research and development "on productivity appear to be relatively modest" (Organization for Economic Cooperation and Development 2010, 24). In sum, among economic experts and on bipartisan committees, there is a surprising consensus that governments should pass reforms to make tax systems more neutral.[5]

[3] If there is little competition, producers may instead charge a price that maximizes income, which could mean that the price of milk would be the same to the end consumer regardless of the tax rate. This complication is relevant for a systematic analysis of the relative tax burden, but is not relevant for the illustration of vertical tax equity.

[4] Moreover, in the extreme cases in which neutrality favors proportional instead of progressive tax systems, it could lead to increases in vertical inequity (at least as presented by Burman 2013).

[5] The best-known measure is the Tax Reform Act of 1986 in the United States. For recent proposals and additional discussion of the benefits that would arise from more neutral tax systems, see National Commission on Financial Responsibility and Reform 2010 for the

If there is a rough consensus across the political spectrum and among experts about the benefits of more neutral tax systems, what explains the frequency of such reforms? To examine this question, we need to define such a reform. Concretely, such a reform includes one or more of the following. First, it broadens the tax base, which means that a given tax covers more of a potential source of revenue. As such, the state can generate more revenue with the same tax rate. An increase in the base of the corporate income tax, for example, means that more corporations face the same regulations under the same tax so it reduces the incentives for firms to incorporate one way rather than another purely for tax reasons. We measure changes in the base of the corporate and personal income as well as the value-added tax. To this category of base broadening we add other reforms that increase efficiency. Value-added taxes (VAT) represent a more efficient way of generating revenues from sales than cascading sales taxes (which may create, for example, an artificial incentive for vertical integration.) The introduction of the tax in countries where they were not in place as of 1990 increases tax-system efficiency. Similarly, a broad administrative tax reform tends to work in the same direction. It not only makes it easier for the government to collect revenues, it also makes it more likely that the tax administration will treat taxpayers more equally than systems captured by a few. These last types of reforms are rare, however.

Second, we examine explicit tax incentives. By their very nature these incentives are targeted to some, and their introduction reduces tax neutrality. Conversely, their removal increases neutrality. All the variables are trichotomous, with (−1) indicating that the reform made the tax system less neutral, 0 that there was no reform, and 1 that the tax system became more neutral.[6]

Table 6.1 presents the data for our formulations of the dependent variable. The information comes from our coding of Price Waterhouse Cooper's annual reports from 1990 to 2004 on tax changes in Latin American countries.[7] We measure whether there was a reform that

United States; Mirrlees et al. 2011 for the United Kingdom; and Tanzi 2013 for Latin America and the Caribbean.

[6] There are rare cases where there were reforms that went both ways. We then determined the overall direction of the reform. For example, for the tax-broadening variable, there were three such observations.

[7] Unfortunately, Price Waterhouse Coopers did not publish this data between 2005 and 2009, which is why our dataset ends in 2004. See Focanti et al. (2016) for more detail about the dataset.

TABLE 6.1 *Tax reforms that change the neutrality of the tax system, 1990–2004*

	Decrease	No Change	Increase
Total Country-Years, Changes	65 (25%)	148 (56%)	49 (19%)
Of which			
Base Broadening (CIT, PIT, VAT)	7 (3%)	245 (93%)	10 (4%)
Change in Personal Income Tax	13 (5%)	226 (86%)	23 (9%)
Changes in Incentives (positive number fewer incentives)	29 (11%)	225 (86%)	8 (3%)

This table indicates the country-years with reforms that decreased or increased the efficiency of the tax system. There is the possibility of more than one type of reform in a given year, so the types of reforms do not sum up to the total efficiency changes. The aggregate total includes other changes to other taxes, such as to the excise tax, where there is not enough variance to include separately in the analysis that follows. The percentages displayed are across the row and rounded to the nearest number.

decreased or increased the neutrality of the tax system in a given country year.[8] In aggregate, there were more decreases than increases of tax neutrality, or 25% of country-years versus 19% of country-years. There are differences in the type of reform. Conscious efforts to broaden tax bases were relatively rare, occurring in only 3% of country-years. In contrast, the introduction of incentives was almost four times more common than their elimination, or 11% of the time instead of 3%.

There are also country differences. For base broadening, while most countries have at most one change, Venezuela has a reform that either increases or decreases the base in six different years. Moving to personal income taxes, Chile had four years where it increased the neutrality of its personal income tax and no years where it decreased the neutrality. Argentina, in contrast, had three years where it decreased the same tax's neutrality and one year where it increased the neutrality. Three countries – Bolivia, Paraguay, and Uruguay – had no reforms that affected the neutrality

[8] It is important to note that the total number of reforms we measure is larger than what is reported here, but some of them, such as the changes in tax rates, are not included in the definition of changes to tax neutrality in the way defined in this chapter.

of the personal income tax. Concerning incentives, more than half of the countries in the sample introduced incentives that reduced neutrality in multiple years.[9]

INCENTIVES, POLITICAL INSTITUTIONS, AND PARTICULARISTIC POLICIES

Tax neutrality favors efficiency in the economy as it reduces the distortions in economic decisions that taxation may cause and the waste of resources that comes from trying to reduce tax payments. As such, more neutral taxes help to raise revenues for providing necessary public goods in the least costly fashion. Additionally, neutral taxes tend to be more horizontally equitable as they treat different people, firms, activities, and economic sectors more equally. On the contrary, less neutral systems tend to be correlated with particularistic benefits that help some at the expense of others. Many consider support for targeted policies as "pork barrel" behavior. Why politicians would want to benefit specific constituencies is the subject of some debate; in his study of Brazil, for example, Samuels (2002) argues that legislators provide "pork" not to win votes directly but to win money that can then be used to influence elections. The question we ask is whether institutional differences explain why policies targeted to specific interests vary across our dataset of Latin American countries.[10] We presume that decision-making processes that are broad are more likely to result in broader policy outcomes than decision-making processes that are narrow.

To understand what we mean, consider the traditional counterargument. Pluralist theories of interest groups (e.g., Truman 1951) contend that groups who represent particular interests should compete with one another, and that what will emerge will be a good policy outcome. This is because the interests of each group are aggregated into a whole. This implies that several particularistic policies are fine so long as most groups are heard and the benefits are spread out across the population in the form of many groups receiving something.

[9] The comparisons here are for the entire period, and because we have data for El Salvador only for seven years it is not included in these summary statistics but is included in the empirical analysis.

[10] See also Pop-Eleches and Pop-Eleches (2012).

There are two classic responses to these pluralist theories, however, which help to explain our argument.[11] The first is the collective action problem that Olson (1965) identifies and discusses. When an individual decides whether to join a group, she assesses the costs and benefits. As the size of a group increases, the marginal benefit the additional person contributes to the group declines. Some groups are more likely to form and to overcome collective action problems than other groups. In particular, small groups that receive concentrated benefits can organize more easily than large groups that receive diffuse benefits. In tax policy, tax breaks (or "tax expenditures"), tax incentives, or differential tax rates for specific groups in society increase their marginal benefit a great deal, while cutting those tax breaks improves the typical tax payer only a little because the per person benefit of eliminating a tax break is small. Given a collective action problem, tax reforms that reduce tax breaks for specific groups, which amount to broadening the tax base, are especially hard for governments to implement because the winners – the general population – are not as likely to organize as the losers –the special interest groups that lobbied for it in the first place.[12]

The second response to the Truman argument is another type of "problem" in the literature, namely the common pool resource (CPR) problem. A given group or representative of a group considers the benefits and costs for that group. Consider a situation where the benefits accrue fully to the group but the costs come out of a common pool of money, such as a national treasury. The costs to the group are small for each additional unit of benefit. If the group gets what it requests, it will request more spending than if it had to pay for all of the spending itself. Moreover, if the various group requests are simply aggregated, the aggregate level of spending is larger – and larger than anyone in any group would want.[13] The key factor is, in Perotti and Kontopoulos' (2002, 191) words, "the degree to which the costs of a dollar of aggregate expenditure are internalized by individual decision-makers."

[11] The arguments here can also be presented in terms of the debate between Donald Wittman (political markets are as efficient as economic markets) and the Public Choice School (political markets have imperfections so political outcomes are not the result of perfect competition). For a summary, see Caplan (2005).

[12] The best anecdotal book on the battle between lobbyists and advocates for taxpayers in general remains Birnbaum and Murray's 1988 *Showdown at Gucci Gulch*. Crespi et al. (2014) provide a discussion of the issue for Latin America in the general context of productive development policies, with tax policy – particularly tax incentives – as one of the main policies.

[13] For a formal model, see Hallerberg et al. (2009).

Note, however, that the discussion of CPR problems usually focuses on the expenditure side, not the revenue side. These models assume that the "common pool" of funds is exogenously given. To the extent that a CPR problem pushes up expenditures, and taxation policies are only a reaction to increased spending, a CPR problem on the expenditure side could lead to pressure to increase the overall tax burden. Yet this logic still does not get at the composition of the tax changes. Moreover, as Mankiw (2010), among others, argues, "tax expenditures are best viewed as a hidden form of spending." The introduction of tax incentives are these type of tax expenditures, and if there is a greater CPR problem there should be more tax incentives introduced, all else being equal.

So, one can conceptualize the relationship between political institutions and tax outcomes. Political institutions can increase or decrease the degree of collective action problems. Smaller collective action problems lead to more involvement of different groups in decisions. This should lead to more broad-based tax systems. Similarly, political institutions can increase or decrease the extent of the CPR problem, with smaller CPR problems again leading to more broad-based tax systems. In practice, we consider types of political institutions that are particularly relevant, with three of them testable using our dataset.

Why would politicians think it in their interests to make a tax system more neutral?[14] To answer this question, one needs to consider the policy-making process that characterizes Latin American democracies (e.g., Stein et al. 2008). In our dataset, all countries are presidential systems. The president, as a rule, introduces major legislation, which is then discussed in Congress.[15] Most countries in the region have two chambers. The president usually approves what emerges from Congress. Writing about the American system, Hansen (1998) suggests that the aggregation of voter preferences on taxation across the president, the House, and the Senate depends upon the aggregation process for votes. The president is the only actor in the process who has a nationwide constituency; hence, she is most likely to care about "general" policy prescriptions. The House,

[14] The most general relevant institutional difference is between presidential and parliamentary democracies (Persson et al. 2000; Persson and Tabellini 2000) but while these arguments are of interest, our dataset is composed of presidential democracies in Latin America, so we cannot test directly whether parliamentary systems have higher taxes and more particularistic tax systems.

[15] Even if constitutionally one of the chambers is in charge of drafting and introducing legislation, it is usually the executive who tends to draft the legislation with the highest chances of going through. See, for example, Bonvecchi et al. (2014).

in contrast, has smaller, more concentrated electoral districts, and it will be the most partisan of the three chambers. The Senate, finally, "effectively weights citizens' preferences by the inverse of the population of the state in which they reside" (Hansen 1998, 520). Following this logic, the question then is the relevant "n" that appears in the denominator for the "three chambers." While there are differences in how presidents are elected in Latin America, we have the same expectation as in the United States concerning reform – the president has the broadest potential base of votes, and she is most likely to propose base broadening reforms.[16]

One can still question, however, when those reforms would take place. We anticipate that presidents propose broad reforms in the first year of their terms when they have the most political capital. In her discussion of neoliberal reforms more generally, Stokes (1999) notes that such reforms generally came in the initial period after a president was elected. In the case of base-broadening reforms, the logic is the same – the expectation is that that they increase the potential growth of the economy, and they take some time to have a beneficial effect. Presidents therefore make such reforms early in their terms. We would expect that a change in president increases the likelihood of a base-broadening reform.

This "cyclical" argument assumes, however, that there are no partisan differences in the way presidents respond – or, put another way, that all new presidents have the same preference to increase tax neutrality. This would be consistent with some recent scholarship for the region that suggests that party labels do not have the same meaning as in other regions; Stokes (1999) suggests that presidents tend to adopt the same economic policies, while Lupu (2014) argues that having few policy differences among parties in Latin America in the 1980s and 1990s affected voter (or brand) allegiance to them. At the same time, taxation is an inherently redistributive tool. Even if parties do not differ substantively on other dimensions, they may still choose to tax their opponents more than their supporters. They may also have goals they can only reach with revenue.

[16] One executive-level variable that does vary significantly across the presidential systems in Latin America is the number of cabinet ministers. More ministers could increase the CPR problem – examining an OECD dataset from 1970 to 1995, Perotti and Kontopoulos (2002) argue that more cabinet members leads to more government transfers as well as higher budget deficits, while Wehner (2010), using a larger set of countries, finds that larger cabinets generally lead to higher spending. In unreported results, we examine whether cabinet size affects tax neutrality, but we find no significant results. Data comes from the Cross National Time Series Archive dataset, which is available at www.databanksinternational.com/ (see Banks and Wilson 2018).

The predictions, therefore, should be conditional on partisanship. Stein and Caro (2013) argue that the Left systematically raises total revenues as a percentage of GDP when it comes to power in Latin America. The example of President Bachelet at the start of this chapter fits this story – Left parties interested in expanding the size of the state may see the closure of loopholes as a relatively quick way to raise money. This would mean that Left Presidents support base broadening in any period. Right governments, in contrast, may be content with the size of the state. Moreover, as Fairfield points (Chapter 7 in this volume), businesses are, as a rule, more likely to back Right parties. Yet we anticipate that presidents of both the Right and the Left will support tax cuts for their constituencies, with the Left supporting exemptions under the VAT and the right the use of tax incentives.[17] We therefore test the hypothesis that the Left closes more loopholes, but because both sides like exemptions we would not be surprised if partisanship does not matter in the analysis.

H1: Left Presidents are more likely to promote an increase in tax efficiency than Right governments.

We rely on the Murillo et al. (2010) dataset for the coding of presidential partisanship, which has a five-point scale from Left (1) to Center (3) to Right (5). There are presidents for the five possible types of partisanship, although the modal president (43% of the sample) is "Center Right."

Whether a president gets her way on policy depends upon the preferences of the legislature. Those preferences, in turn, depend upon how Latin American legislatures are elected, which means that electoral systems are of interest, as well as their composition and the number of veto players. Concerning electoral systems, there are two basic types. Under plurality, the population votes for an individual who comes from a given political party. The number of candidates, or district magnitude, under pure plurality is one. While there is no pure plurality system in Latin America, one can also think of other systems that are similar; in Chile, for example, the top two vote-getters receive seats in Congress. The other common type of electoral system is proportional representation. Voters support a given political party. Candidates, in turn, appear on a given

[17] In unreported results, we explore a conditional relationship. Right governments will have been in office in most countries in previous periods, which suggests that the tax system, on average, will be closer to the preferences of the political right. There would then be less reason to change the system. This leads to a conditional relationship depending on partisanship on the effects of a new president. We find no such relationship when looking at results with interaction terms.

party list. The share of candidates on a list who are elected depends upon the share of the vote.

To understand why electoral systems are relevant, consider whether a candidate is more likely to be elected if she proposes a basket of goods that include broad-based policies, or whether it is better for electoral success to promise targeted policies to specific constituencies. There are two competing, and contrasting, responses. The first is consistent with the "collective action" problem. Persson and Tabellini (2000) focus on accountability of the given legislator under different systems. They contend that rents are higher under closed list PR, where voters can only vote against a given party, than under open list PR or plurality systems, where voters can punish directly a given legislator. Rents are therefore higher under closed list PR electoral systems. Bawn and Thies (2003), in an article that develops the collective action logic, suggest that the extent to which the "unorganized" receive representation depends on the electoral system, but they go beyond the simple "PR-plurality" to consider whether voters cast ballots directly for a given representative. They find that closed list PR is more disposed to organized interests than plurality.[18] This difference evaporates under electoral systems where voters cast ballots for both the party and candidate. In Latin America, the key distinction would be between closed-list and open-list PR, where voters select the order of the candidates on a party list.

The second perspective on electoral systems is consistent with the "CPR problem," and it has different predictions than the collective action perspective. Following Hansen (1998), the key question from this perspective is what proportion of the overall tax take does a given policymaker have to consider? Parties may focus mostly the tax burden on their constituencies. As a very rough approximation, consider how the electoral system affects incentives in an election of a 150-member legislature, with three parties that each win one-third of the vote. Under closed-list PR, one would expect the party to be worried about the tax burden on about 33% of the (voting) population. Under open-list PR, however, the proportion is much smaller: a candidate may win with only 1/150 of the vote, or 0.6% of the population. Under plurality, the proportion of the tax burden is even smaller – one only needs to win the most votes in 1 of 150 districts. This type of logic explains why specific benefits in the form of corruption are more common under open-list than closed-list PR in a country such as

[18] Kunicova and Rose-Ackermann (2005) suggest that corruption is higher under PR systems than under plurality.

Italy (Golden and Picci 2008). Similarly, Rickard (2009) finds that plurality electoral systems have more narrowly targeted transfers than proportional representation systems, where parties representing a larger swath of the population are the main actors who gather votes, although parties do seem more prone to changes in demand for more narrow transfers in PR systems.

Chang and Golden (2007) argue that the principal determinant of whether open or closed list PR leads to more particularistic policies, which they measure as corruption, is district magnitude – the incentive to target particularistic interests goes up under open PR but decrease under closed PR. This argument, in turn, is based on Carey and Shugart's (1995) discussion of the "personal vote" versus the "party vote." For our purposes, the more a candidate cares about a personal vote versus a party vote, the greater the extent of the CPR problem, so the details of how to measure the personal vote are important. The first structural factor that affects the personal vote, Carey and Shugart argue, is the interaction between whether there is an open- or closed-list system and district magnitude. When open, district magnitude increases the personal vote – there is a smaller and smaller share of the total party vote a candidate would have to win in order to gain a seat. The opposite is true under a closed list system. It becomes harder to identify the role of one candidate if she comes from an electoral district that will have 150 winners in it. They also examine three further variables. The first, *pool*, is whether party leaders determine which candidates appear on a party list. If leaders determine the list, they score the personal vote as a "0." Argentina is an example of a country where the party determines which candidate appears where on the list. If leaders propose the list but voters can reorder it, the score is "1." Finally, if voters determine the order of the list the score is "2." The second relevant variable is *ballot*. If pooling of the vote is at the party level, the score is "0." If the pooling is at the subnational level, the score is "1," while if pooling is at the candidate level the score is "2." The final variable is "vote." If someone has only one vote, this is scored as "0," if a person has multiple votes this is scored as "1," and if one can only vote at the subparty level, such as only for an individual, this is scored as "2." Carey and Shugart then aggregate these numbers, with the personal vote the weakest when they aggregate to "0" and the strongest when they aggregate to "6."

Others have examined the relationship between how personalistic an electoral system is and policy outputs. Hicken and Simmons (2008) found that an increasing personal vote reduces the efficiency of education spending, but does not affect its level. Concerning fiscal policy outputs, Hallerberg and Marier (2004) argue that budget deficits are worse in Latin American countries with personalistic electoral systems that do not have centralizing fiscal institutions to counterbalance, while Edwards and Thames (2007) contend that spending on public goods declines under such electoral systems. Mukherjee, Yadav, and Béjar (2014) note that more personalistic systems give greater voice to concentrated special interests – in developing countries, concentrated banks are successful in pushing for capital account liberalization that benefits them where there are particularistic electoral institutions but not where there are more party-centered electoral systems.

There are two ways to calculate the personal vote for empirical analyses that are both based on Carey and Schugart (1995). Johnson and Wallack (2010) compute a thirteen-point ordinal scale.[19] They code ballot, pool, and votes; they use those values to set the original scale; and they weight the outcome by the importance of a given electoral tier if there is more than one. They compute separately the magnitude of the average district as well as the magnitude for the average legislator. Hallerberg and Marier (2004) have a similar overall ranking of Latin American electoral systems, but they differ from Johnson and Wallack by including district magnitude directly in the index. First, they log the district magnitude measure – a change from 1 to 3 has a bigger effect than a change from 150 to 152. Second, they aggregate Carey and Shugart's three measures and, to avoid division by 0 in the next step, they add "1" to the number. They then add the logged district magnitude for countries with open-list systems to the initial aggregated number and divide district magnitude from the aggregated number where there are closed lists. This follows the intuition that increasing district magnitude strengthens parties under closed lists but leads to further fragmentation under open lists. Finally, to rescale the number to run from 0 (lowest personal vote) to 1 (highest personal vote), they divide through by 10. There are minor differences in coding in the original datasets that we correct for, and we rely on the more direct measure of district magnitude in our regressions (or on the coding scheme from Hallerberg and Marier [2004]).[20] The pairwise correlation between

[19] This, in turn, is based on Wallack et al. (2003) and updates the original dataset.

[20] In particular, the original Hallerberg and Marier coding for Mexico was more party-centered, while they missed a reform of the Bolivian electoral system. The Johnson and Wallack (2010) dataset does not capture all changes in electoral systems for Colombia and Peru. The version used in this chapter includes changes both for Bolivia and Mexico.

the original Johnson and Wallack (2010) measure and the one we use here is 0.64. Given that the correlation between the personal vote index in the upper and lower house is about 0.9 in the Johnson and Wallack dataset, we include in the analysis the personal vote index just for the lower house. The online appendix[21] presents the data for Latin American democracies from 1990 through 2005. More countries have party-based systems, although there is substantial variation. The country with the lowest index score is Bolivia (through 1996) at 0.04, while the highest scores are for Colombia (1990–2001) at 0.78 and Brazil (entire time period) at 0.73.[22] These scores indicate the potential size of the CPR problem in Congress.

This discussion leads to the following hypothesis:

H2: More particularistic electoral systems lead to less neutral tax reforms.

So far, the discussion has been about presidential action after entering office, which occurs after the election. There is reason to expect that there will be political business cycles concerning tax reforms that affect tax neutrality *before* elections. Presidents may want to remind populations that they are acting in the best interests of the general population. At the same time, they may be appealing to a marginal group whose support is necessary to win a plurality. We will include whether there is a presidential election in the analysis, but the prediction is not clear. Major tax reforms, however, are notoriously hard to organize in electoral years when cooperation among veto players tends to break down (Stein et al. 2008). Nevertheless, consistent with Hansen (1998), we expect that:

H3: Neutral tax reforms are more likely prior to presidential elections.

The opposite relationship is expected for legislative elections – incumbents are elected to support targeted tax changes that will benefit supporters, and they all come from smaller districts than the one the president has. We anticipate that legislatures decrease tax neutrality prior to elections:[23]

[21] Online appendix available at http://flores-macias.government.cornell.edu/Data.html.

[22] Data for this variable are comes from Hallerberg and Marier (2004), which in turn is updated (and sometimes corrected) with data from Payne, Zovatto, and Mateo Díaz (2007) and from a dataset made available to the authors by John Carey.

[23] We also considered a conditional relationship, where the effect of legislative elections would increase the greater the size of the personal vote. In unreported results that include interaction effects, we do not find this relationship.

H4: Tax reforms that erode neutrality are more likely prior to legislative elections.

While our prediction is that weakened parties found under such electoral systems lead to a more particularistic tax system, one should note that there is a literature looking at other types of reform that would argue that greater fragmentation will make *any* change in policy more difficult. Haggard and Kaufman (1994) anticipate that strong parties are needed to push through reforms after a transition to democracy. Similarly, Ames (2001) contends that the personalistic nature of the political system made reforms in Brazil especially difficult.

The mention of parties brings one to a third explanation – namely, the number of partisan veto players. In a highly influential work, Tsebelis (2002) argues that an increase in the number of such players should decrease the amount of any reform. Hallerberg and Basinger (1998; see also Basinger and Hallerberg 2004) present empirical evidence on changes in taxation in OECD countries that is consistent with Tsebelis (2002). The first article focuses in particular on responses to the 1986 tax reform in the United States, which increased the efficiency of the American tax system and would seem to be especially relevant for this chapter. Yet there is not a consensus on veto players, reforms, and public finance. Bawn and Rosenbluth (2006), in their study of the effects of the number of parties in government, argue that larger parties internalize more costs so that one-party governments have more beneficial effects than multiparty systems. They therefore have lower spending than multiparty governments. Gehlbach and Malesky (2010) similarly find that increasing the number of players leads to *more* reform when the status quo is no reform, and the logic has implications for the discussion of which interests gain a say in policy discussions – when there are many relevant veto players, it may be too costly for special interests to block general reforms.[24] This work, in turn, follows Hellman (1998), who also argued that increasing the number of veto players makes reforms more likely, not less, because it is harder for small organized interests to block changes.[25]

While these arguments seem contradictory, they do yield different testable effects of veto players. The Hellman/Gehlbach and Malesky approach is about organized interests blocking reforms that erode existing

[24] The Gehlbach and Malesky definition of "veto players" focuses on "separation of powers" rather than "separation of purpose" (2010, 959).

[25] See also Lindvall (2010) and Tommasi et al. (2014).

benefits (or rents) that they accrue if the status quo is maintained. There is not a prediction about the ability of organized interests to get more benefits than they are already collecting. This implies an asymmetric effect of veto players – change that leads to a generalized improvement in the system is more likely under many veto players, not just one, but there is no reason to believe that one or many players will make the introduction of more tax breaks more or less likely. Basinger and Hallerberg (2004), however, are most interested in tax competition and in how quickly a given government reacts to tax adjustments in other countries. They would expect simply less change from the status quo the greater the veto-player distance.

We measure veto players based on the "checks" variable from the World Bank database for the first case.[26] Our expectation is:

H5: An increase in checks makes any reform less likely.

A final variable is a banking crisis. As Reinhart and Rogoff (2009) indicate, countries that face a banking crisis need additional revenue quickly both to bail out troubled banks and to stabilize the economy through more activist fiscal policy. Crises also represent "windows of opportunity" to introduce reforms. Alesina and Drazen (1991) suggest that crisis periods also may allow governments to resolve "wars of attrition" where different constituencies in government refuse to bear the burden of adjustment. A tax reform that eliminates incentives and broadens the base, all else being equal, increases the tax burden on the various constituencies. We include the online version of their dataset, which includes the latest additions to their dataset, and not the version that appears in their 2009 book.[27]

H6: Financial crises make reforms that increase tax neutrality more likely.

ADDITIONAL VARIABLES AND MODEL SPECIFICATION

There are economic variables that may also affect the neutrality of reforms that should be included. The level of economic development makes some types of taxes more feasible than others, such as the income tax. Growing GDP per capita implies a wider tax base, making reforms meant to capture

[26] Note that Calvo (2014) finds that one-party control of the legislature or the lack of such control is most relevant in this context, so in robust tests we also examined whether one party controls the relevant chambers. The results did not change.

[27] See www.reinhartandrogoff.com/data/.

a bigger tax base more probable (Chelliah 1971, as cited in Profeta and Scabrosetti 2010, 21). We include the lagged GDP per capita of a country. Inflation pushes incomes above statutory rates without the individual or company necessarily increasing their real incomes, and this in turn may lead individuals to pressure the government to reform rates. This variable was the most important in Mahon's (2004) study of efficient tax reforms in the region over the period 1977–1995. Another control is the top maximum personal income tax rate; countries with high rates may have more inefficient taxes than countries with lower personal tax rates and face more pressure to introduce efficient reforms. The country's reliance on international trade may affect the tax base.

The IMF may play an important role in the introduction of neutrality-enhancing reforms. Such reforms may be part of conditions the Fund imposes on countries in exchange for loans. We are somewhat skeptical of this variable; it is hard to know when conditionality "caused" a given reform and when a government requests that the Fund includes a given reform as a conditional factor so that it can shift blame from the government to the Fund. Nevertheless, Mahon (2004) finds that explicit mention of tax reform by the Fund increases the likelihood that a country enacts the reforms. Rather than code the mentions of tax reform in conditionality for the reasons given above, we include a variable for whether a country is under an IMF program. There should be a substantive difference because countries under a program are more likely to be subject to IMF pressure, which did in this period advocate the types of base broadening we are trying to measure.

The IMF variable also addresses another possible explanation. In the early 1990s, the "Washington consensus" was in vogue. The broad goal in terms of economic policy was to introduce more market-oriented economic policies (Williamson 1990), which in turn were meant to spur economic growth. Reforms to make the tax system more neutral were one of the parts of the consensus (e.g., Stokes 1999; 2001; Biglaiser 2002). One would expect that countries under an IMF program would be more likely to follow these reforms.

In terms of model specification, we want to explain both increases and decreases in overall tax system neutrality. We code reforms three ways – a decrease in neutrality (–1), no change (0), and an increase (1). This suggests an ordered logit model. We include a count variable that refers to the time since the last fiscal reform. Our initial intention was to include it for specification reasons.[28] But there may be reasons why a given

[28] Beck et al. (1998) argue that this variable addresses serially correlated errors.

government has a predilection for making the tax system more, or less, neutral. We also do not have a reliable way to measure total "neutrality," and this variable creates a history of previous behavior. Note that the empirical setup makes the model equivalent to a Cox proportional hazard model. We also include the absolute number of such reforms as a count over time. We also employ standard errors clustered by country as well as year dummies to capture possible time effects.

The empirical model is:

$$P(taxneutrality = -1,0,1)|(PresIdeology_{t,i}, PersonalVote_{t,i}, ElectYearPres_{t,i}, ElectYearLeg_{t,i}, checks_{t,i}, FinCrisis_{t,i}, CONTROLS_{t,i})$$

Table 6.2 presents the marginal effects of the ordered logit equation according to the type of reform. We are interested in whether certain variables make a reform that decreases or increases tax neutrality more likely. To do this, we display the results both for predictions of a reform that decreases neutrality and that increases neutrality. Given the nature of the process we are trying to estimate, where the dependent variables present relatively little variance and most of the independent variables, particularly our main variable of interest, are slow moving, finding high significance is difficult.

Some variables have effects that are consistent with the hypotheses introduced earlier. The extent of the personal vote has a clear effect on the introduction (−1) or repeal (1) of tax incentives in the tax code. A move from the electoral system with the lowest personal vote, which is found in Bolivia in the early 1990s at 0.037, to the highest personal vote, which was in Colombia prior to the 1993 constitutional reform, would increase the probability of an introduction of a tax incentive by about six percentage points per year and decrease the probability of abolishing an existing incentive by about two percentage points per year. While the signs on the marginal effects are in the expected direction in the other equations (i.e., positive for a decrease in neutrality and negative for an increase), this variable is not statistically significant. Given that incentives are the tax tool that we examine that is easiest to target, the result that the electoral system variable is significant in only this equation makes intuitive sense.

Similarly, financial crises mean it is more likely that a government broadens the tax base. Countries experiencing such a crisis are five percentage points more likely to broaden the tax base and about four percentage points less likely to narrow the tax base. At the same time, we do not find significant results for the effects for more common political variables, such as the partisanship of the president or either presidential or legislative

TABLE 6.2 *Increase neutrality?*

VARIABLES	(1) Broaden Base	(2) Broaden Base	(3) PIT	(4) PIT	(5) Incentives	(6) Incentives
	−1	1	−1	1	−1	1
Ideology of the President	0.006	−0.008	0.012	−0.018	0.008	−0.003
	(0.006)	(0.008)	(0.015)	(0.021)	(0.018)	(0.006)
Personal Vote	0.039	−0.057	0.021	−0.031	0.085**	−0.027**
	(0.038)	(0.059)	(0.033)	(0.051)	(0.034)	(0.012)
Presidential Election (Lag)	−0.017	0.026	0.009	−0.014	0.065	−0.021
	(0.025)	(0.037)	(0.039)	(0.059)	(0.062)	(0.021)
Legislative Election (Lag)	0.003	−0.004	−0.019	0.029	−0.062	0.020
	(0.012)	(0.017)	(0.033)	(0.050)	(0.051)	(0.017)
Checks and Balances	0.002	−0.003	−0.005	0.007	−0.003	0.001
	(0.003)	(0.005)	(0.006)	(0.009)	(0.008)	(0.002)
Banking Crisis	−0.038**	0.057***	0.013	−0.020	−0.077	0.025
	(0.018)	(0.018)	(0.019)	(0.031)	(0.055)	(0.020)
GDP Per Capita PPP 2005 (Lag)	−0.000	0.000	−0.000	0.000	0.000***	−0.000**
	(0.000)	(0.000)	(0.000)	(0.000)	(0.000)	(0.000)
Inflation (Lag)	0.000	−0.000	−0.000**	0.000***	−0.000**	0.000**
	(0.000)	(0.000)	(0.000)	(0.000)	(0.000)	(0.000)

(continued)

TABLE 6.2 *(continued)*

VARIABLES	(1) Broaden Base	(2) Broaden Base	(3) PIT	(4) PIT	(5) Incentives	(6) Incentives
Trade % of GDP (Lag)	-0.000	0.000	-0.001**	0.001***	0.000	-0.000
	(0.000)	(0.000)	(0.000)	(0.000)	(0.000)	(0.000)
Any IMF Program	0.016	-0.023	-0.001	0.002	0.022	-0.007
	(0.022)	(0.034)	(0.025)	(0.038)	(0.035)	(0.011)
# of previous reforms	-0.036***	0.054***	-0.032***	0.048***	-0.102***	0.033***
	(0.013)	(0.014)	(0.009)	(0.014)	(0.015)	(0.011)
Time Since Last Reform	-0.007*	0.010*	-0.005	0.007	0.015***	-0.005**
	(0.004)	(0.005)	(0.005)	(0.008)	(0.005)	(0.002)
Observations	248	248	248	248	248	248

*** p<0.01, ** p<0.05, * p<0.1

elections. The story about President Bachelet that opened the chapter does seem to be mostly anecdotal – we do not find evidence that partisanship explains this particular case.

Other effects on tax neutrality are not evident. Despite the urging of the IMF to make systems more neutral, whether a country is under an IMF program does not make it more likely that such reforms are adopted. Different levels of checks and balances do not seem to have an effect. Elections, whether presidential or legislative, do not mean that such a reform is more or less likely. The partisanship of the president is not relevant in these specifications. One plausible explanation for this finding is that the difference between the left and the right did not matter for economic policy in practice (e.g., Stokes 1999). Indeed, as Saiegh (2010) argues, most Latin American political parties are hardly programmatic. Another, however, concerns differences specifically on the neutrality of taxes. As already noted, by the 1990s there was a general consensus on the left and on the right about the desirability of more neutral tax systems, all else being equal. Indeed, in other work using the same time period, set of countries, and dataset (Hallerberg and Scartascini 2017), we also find no partisan effects on who bears the burden of tax reforms.

There is also an intriguing effect of including previous reforms across all specifications. Increasing the number of reforms that reduce the efficiency of the tax system reduces the likelihood of a future such reform. At the same time, there is a dynamic that as the number of previous reforms that increase neutrality goes up, it is more likely in future periods to have an additional such reform. We do not have the microlevel data to explain these results, but one conjecture is that there is a limit to how many holes one can create in a given system before it is not worth undermining further. There may also be only so many politically important interest groups, and once they get their breaks there is less pressure on the government to provide more. At the same time, places that have more neutrality-enhancing reforms may be more aware of their benefits, and may have bureaucracies that make such reforms a priority. Taken together, the main political finding concerns the design of the electoral system rather than the timing of elections or the political persuasion of the president.

CONCLUSION

Why do some countries have policies mostly targeted to specific constituencies while others have policies targeted mostly to the general population? This question gets at the heart of any debate about the quality of democracy, and it is especially relevant for the democracies of Latin America. After the wave of democratization and redemocratization in the late 1980s and early 1990s, the discussion moved from whether democracies are inherently better than autocracies at reducing inequality and in generating better economic growth to a discussion about the variance in the quality of democracy in the region (e.g., O'Donnell et al. 2004). This, in turn, has led to a proliferation of indices and measures of the quality of democracy. The focus of some of these works is on inputs and on the institutions of a given political system in particular. Beetham et al. (2008, 26), for example, ask whether a given democratic political system matches agreed values. Others include specific outputs, such as on the economy, protection of the environment, gender equality, and health (Campbell et al. 2011). There have been concerns that Latin American politics are somehow "different," that parties do not deliver to their constituencies what they promise in elections (e.g., Stokes 1999; Lupu 2014).

In this chapter, we find evidence that the most frequently used method to increase or decrease the neutrality of the tax base – namely, the abolition or introduction of incentives that can be targeted to specific constituencies – depends in part on the design of an institution all democracies have – namely, the electoral system. Those systems that encourage a party vote over an individual vote will pass fewer tax incentives over time. Those with a more personalistic electoral system will have more incentives. This means that the fragmentation of preferences that the electoral system creates affects the fragmentation of the tax system. For champions of more neutral tax systems, it appears that a financial crisis represents a better opportunity to widen the tax base.

One should also consider the findings, and nonfindings, of this chapter in comparison to work other types of tax reforms. In Hallerberg and Scartascini (2017), we examine determinants of reforms that increase or decrease tax burdens rather than tax neutrality. Consistent with the findings in this chapter, that study finds that financial crises make tax increases more likely, with this chapter indicating that one mechanism to raise revenue is through a broadening of tax bases. At the same time, they find that preelectoral periods make increases in tax burdens much less likely. This carries over to financial crises – governments, even in crisis, do not want to introduce such reforms.[29]

[29] Based on this insight, in unreported results we reran the equation for the broadening of the tax base listed in columns 3 and 4 above with an added interaction term to examine the effects of financial crises conditional on whether there was an upcoming legislative

The finding on the lack of effects of other political variables, such as on partisanship, are also consistent with work in Hallerberg and Scartascini (2017) on whether tax burdens increase or decrease. Instead of partisanship, we find that an exogenous shock such as a financial crisis and political institutions such as the extent to which the electoral system encourages a personal vote were more relevant to an understanding of whether governments are more likely to introduce reforms to change the neutrality of the tax system. Reformers of tax systems should think about the benefits and costs of reforms of electoral systems as well.

References

Agell, Jonas, Peter Englund, and Jan Södersten. 1999. "Tax Reform of the Century – the Swedish Experiment," in Joel Slemrod (ed.), *Tax Policy in the Real World*. Cambridge: Cambridge University Press, 331–352.

Alesina, Alberto and Allan Drazen. 1991. "Why Are Stabilizations Delayed?" *American Economic Review* 81: 1170–1188.

Ames, Barry. 2001. *The Deadlock of Democracy in Brazil*. Detroit: University of Michigan Press.

Appel, Hilary and Mitchell Orenstein. 2013. "Ideas Versus Resources: Explaining the Flat Tax and Pension Privatization Revolutions in Eastern Europe and the Former Soviet Union," *Comparative Political Studies* 46(2): 123–152.

Ardanaz, Martín and Carlos Scartascini. 2013. "Inequality and Personal Income Taxation: The Origins and Effects of Legislative Malapportionment," *Comparative Political Studies* 46(12): 1636–1663.

Arenas, Alberto. 2016. *Sostenibilidad fiscal y reformas tributarias en América Latina*. Santiago: CEPAL and IDB.

Banks, Arthur S. and Kenneth A. Wilson. 2018. Cross-National Time-Series Data Archive. Databanks International. Jerusalem, Israel.

Basinger, Scott and Mark Hallerberg. 2004. "Remodeling the Competition for Capital: How Domestic Politics Erases the Race-to-the-Bottom," *American Political Science Review* 98(2): 261–276.

Bawn, Kathleen and Frances Rosenbluth. 2006. "Short versus Long Coalitions: Electoral Accountability and the Size of the Public Sector," *American Journal of Poliical Science* 50(2): 251–265.

Bawn, Kathleen and Michael F. Thies. 2003. "A Comparative Theory of Electoral Incentives : Representing the Unorganized Under PR, Plurality and Mixed-Member Electoral Systems," *Journal of Theoretical Politics* 15(1): 5–32.

election. We find a grouping of countries toward the center of the legislative distribution near where the effects of financial crises are positive and significant, but the effect declines to zero as the legislative election variable moves toward one. So while legislative elections alone do not increase or decrease the likelihood of more neutral tax reforms, they do block such reforms during a financial crisis if they are imminent enough.

Beck, Nathaniel, Jonathan N. Katz, and Richard Tucker. 1998. "Taking Time Seriously: Time-Series-Cross-Section Analysis with a Binary Dependent Variable," *American Journal of Political Science* 42(4): 1260–1288.

Beetham, David, Edzia Carvalho, Tod Landman, and Stuart Weir. 2008. *Assessing the Quality of Democracy: A Practical Guide*. Stockholm: International Institute for Democracy and Electoral Assistance.

Biglaiser, Glen. 2002. *Guardians of the Nation? Economists, Generals, and Economic Reform in Latin America*. South Bend: University of Notre Dame Press.

Birnbaum, Jeffrey and Alan Murray. 1988. *Showdown at Gucci Gulch: Lawmakers, Lobbyists, and the Unlikely Triumph of Tax Reform*. New York: Vintage.

Bonvecchi, Alejandro, Javier Alvaredo, Ernesto Calvo, Maximiliano Castillo, and Juan Carlos Gómez Sabaíni. 2014. "Measuring the Political Economy of Tax Lawmaking: A Methodology and Evidence from Argentina," Working Paper 433. Washington, DC: Inter-American Development Bank.

Burman, Leonardo. 2013. "Pathways to Tax Reform Revisited," *Public Finance Review* 41(6): 755–790.

Calvo, Ernesto. 2014. *Legislator Success in Fragmented Congresses in Argentina: Plurality Cartels, Minority Presidents, and Lawmaking*. Cambridge: Cambridge University Press.

Campbell, David, Paul Pölzlbauer, Thorsten Barth, and Georg Pölzlbauer. 2011. *Democracy Ranking 2011 (Scores)*. Vienna: Democracy Ranking. [Data originally accessed at www.democracyranking.org/en/index.htm; data no longer available at time of writing].

Caplan, Bryan. 2005. "From Friedman to Wittman: The Transformation of Chicago Political Economy," *Econ Journal Watch* 2(1): 1–21.

Carey, John M. and Matthew S. Shugart. 1995. "Incentives to Cultivate a Personal Vote: A Rank Ordering of Electoral Formulas," *Electoral Studies* 14(4): 417–439.

Chang, Eric and Miriuam Golden. 2007. "Electoral Systems, District Magnitude, and Corruption," *American Journal of Political Science* 37(1): 115–137.

Chelliah, Raja. 1971. "Trends in Taxation in Developing Countries," *IMF Staff Papers* 18: 254–331.

Crespi, Gustavo, Eduardo Fernandez Arias, and Ernesto Stein. 2014. *Rethinking Productive Development*. Washington, DC: Inter-American Development Bank and Springer International.

Edwards, Martin and Frank Thames. 2007. "District Magnitude, Personal Votes, and Government Expenditures," *Electoral Studies* 26(2): 338–345.

Feldstein, Martin. 1976. "On the Theory of Tax Reform," *Journal of Public Economics* 6(1–2): 77–104.

Focanti, Diego, Mark Hallerberg, and Carlos Scartascini. 2016. "Tax Reforms in Latin America in an Era of Democracy," *Latin America Research Review* 51 (1): 132–158.

Gehlbach, Scott and Edmund J. Malesky. 2010. "The Contribution of Veto Players to Economic Reform," *Journal of Politics* 72(4): 957–975.

Golden, Miriam and Lucio Picci 2008. "Pork Barrel Politics in Italy, 1953–94," *American Journal of Political Science* 53(3): 268–289.

Haggard, Stephan and Robert R. Kaufman. 1994. *The Political Economy of Democratic Transitions*. Princeton: Princeton University Press.

Hallerberg, Mark and Scott Basinger. 1998. "Internationalization and Changes in Tax Policy in OECD Countries: The Importance of Domestic Veto Players," *Comparative Political Studies* 31(3): 321–353.

Hallerberg, Mark and Patrick Marier. 2004. "Executive Authority, the Personal Vote, and Budget Discipline in Latin American and Caribbean Countries," *American Journal of Political Science* 48(3): 571–587.

Hallerberg, Mark and Carlos Scartascini. 2017. "Explaining Changes in Tax Burdens in Latin America: Do Politics Trump Economics?" *European Journal of Political Economy* 48: 162–179.

Hallerberg, Mark, Rolf Strauch, and Jürgen von Hagen. 2009. *Fiscal Governance: Evidence from Europe*. Cambridge: Cambridge University Press.

Hansen, John Mark. 1998. "Individuals, Institutions, and Public Preferences Over Public Finance," *American Political Science Review* 92(3): 513–531.

Hellman, Joel S. 1998. "Winners Take All: The Politics of Partial Reform in Postcommunist Transitions," *World Politics* 50(2): 203–234.

Hicken, Allen and Joel Simmons. 2008. "The Personal Vote and the Efficacy of Education Spending," *American Journal of Political Science* 52: 109–124.

Johnson, Joel and Jessica Wallack. 2010. "Electoral Systems and the Personal Vote," https://hdl.handle.net/1902.1/17901, Harvard Dataverse, V1.

Kunicova, Jana and Susan Rose-Ackerman. 2005. "Electoral Rules as Constraints on Corruption," *British Journal of Political Science* 35(4): 573–606.

Lindvall, Johannes. 2010. "Power Sharing and Reform Capacity," *Journal of Theoretical Politics* 22(3): 1–18.

Lora, Eduardo. 2007. "Trends and Outcomes of Tax Reform," in Eduardo Lora (ed.), *The State of State Reform in Latin America*. Palo Alto and Washington, DC: Stanford University Press, the World Bank, and the Inter-American Development Bank, 185–212.

Lupu, Noam. 2014. "Brand Dilution and the Breakdown of Political Parties in Latin America," *World Politics* 66(4): 561–602.

Mahon Jr., James. 2004. "Causes of Tax Reform in Latin America, 1977–95," *Latin American Research Review* 39(1): 3–30.

Mankiw, Gregory. 2010. "The Blur Between Spending and Taxation," *New York Times*, November 20.

Mukherjee, Bumba, Vineeta Yadav, and Sergio Béjar. 2014. "Electoral Particularism, Bank Concentration, and Capital Account Liberalization in Developing Democracies," *Comparative Political Studies* 47(6): 851–877.

Mirrlees, James, Stuart Adam, Tim Besley et al. 2011. *Tax by Design*. Oxford: Oxford University Press.

Murillo, María Victoria, Virginia Oliveros, and Milan Vaishnav. 2010. Dataset on Political Ideology of Presidents and Parties in Latin America. Columbia University: www.columbia.edu/~mm2140 and www.columbia.edu/~vo2110.

National Commission on Fiscal Responsibility and Reform. 2010. "The Moment of Truth": www.taxpolicycenter.org/briefing-book/moment-truth-report-national-commission-fiscal-responsibility-and-reform-december-2010.

O'Donnell, Guillermo, Jorge Vargas, and Osvaldo Iazzetta (eds.). 2004. *The Quality of Democracy: Theory and Applications*. South Bend: University of Notre Dame Press.

Olson, Mancur. 1965. *The Logic of Collective Action*. Cambridge: Harvard University Press.

Organization for Economic Cooperation and Development. 2010. *Tax Policy Reform and Economic Growth*. Paris: OECD.

Payne, Zovatto, and Matteo Díaz. 2007. *Democracies in Development: Politics and Reform in Latin America*. Washington, DC: Inter-American Development Bank.

Perotti, Roberto and Yianos Kontopoulos. 2002. "Fragmented Fiscal Policy," *Journal of Public Economics* 86(2): 191–222.

Persson, Torsten and Guido Tabellini. 2000. *Political Economics: Explaining Economic Policy*. Cambridge: MIT Press.

Persson, Torsten, Gerald Roland, and Guido Tabellini. 2000. "Comparative Politics and Public Finance," *Journal of Political Economy* 108: 1121–1161.

Pop-Eleches, Cristian and Grigore Pop-Eleches. 2012. "Targeted Government Spending and Political Preferences," *Quarterly Journal of Political Science* 7(3): 285–320.

Profeta, Paola and Simona Scabrosetti. 2010. *The Political Economy of Taxation: Lessons from Developing Countries*. Cheltenham: Edward Elgar.

Reinhart, Carmen and Kenneth Rogoff. 2009. *This Time is Different*. Princeton: Princeton University Press.

Rickard, Stephanie. 2009. "Strategic Targeting: The Effect of Institutions and Interests on Distributive Transfers," *Comparative Political Studies* 42(5): 670–695.

Saiegh, Sebastian. 2010. "Active Players or Rubber Stamps? An Evaluation of the Policymaking Role of Latin American Legislatures," in Carlos Scartascini, Ernesto Stein, and Mariano Tommasi (eds.), *How Democracy Works: Political Institutions, Actors, and Arenas in Latin American Policymaking*. Washington, DC: Inter-American Development Bank, 47–76.

Samuels, David. 2002. "Pork Barreling is not Credit Claiming or Advertising: Campaign Finance and the Sources of the Personal Vote in Brazil," *The Journal of Politics* 64(3): 845–863.

Stein, Ernesto and Lorena Caro. 2013. "Ideology and Taxation in Latin America," Inter-American Development Bank Working Paper IDB-WP-407 (May).

Stein, Ernesto, Mariano Tommasi, Carlos Scartascini, and Pablo T. Spiller. 2008. *How Politics Shapes Policies*. Washington, DC: Inter-American Development Bank.

Stokes, Susan. 1999. "What Do Policy Switches Tell Us about Democracy?" in Adam Przeworski, Susan Stokes, and Bernard Manin (eds.), *Democracy, Accountability, and Representation*. Cambridge: Cambridge University Press, 98–130.

Stokes, Susan. 2001. *Mandates and Democracy: Neoliberalism by Surprise in Latin America*. Cambridge: Cambridge University Press.

Tommasi, Mariano, Carlos Scartascini, and Ernesto Stein. 2014. "Veto Players and Policy Adaptability: An Intertemporal Perspective," *Journal of Theoretical Politics* 26(2): 222–248.

Truman, David. 1951. *The Governmental Process: Political Interest and Public Opinion*. New York: Knopf.

Tanzi, Vito. 2013. "Tax Reform in Latin America: A Long Term Assessment." Paper prepared for the XXV Regional Seminar on Fiscal Policy, ECLAC, Santiago (Chile).

Tsebelis, George. 2002. *Veto Players: How Political Institutions Work*. Princeton: Princeton University Press.

Wallack, Jessica, Alejandro Gaviria, Ugo Panizza, and Ernesto Stein. 2003. "Political Particularism Around the World," *World Bank Economic Review* 17(1): 133–143.

Wehner, Joachim 2010. "Cabinet Structure and Fiscal Policy Outcomes," *European Journal of Political Research* 49(5): 631–653.

Williamson, John. 1990. *The Progress of Policy Reform in Latin America*, Volume 2. Washington, DC: Institute for International Economics.

7

Taxing Latin America's Economic Elites

Tasha Fairfield

The idea that progressive taxation plays a central role in redistribution might strike many as intuitive. In fact, median-voter models, which continue to generate extensive research and debate in political science, generally start from this premise. Yet until recently, there has been a surprising dearth of research on tax policy and redistributive politics in Latin America. Scholarship on inequality in the region has tended to focus on the politics of social policy and the spending side of the redistributive equation (e.g., Garay 2016; Pribble 2014). Meanwhile, literature on advanced welfare states (Steinmo 1993; Wilensky 2002; Kato 2003) and economic analyses downplayed the relevance of progressive taxation for reducing inequality. Scholars of advanced democracies identified regressive consumption taxation as forming the backbone of the welfare state, which fit well with the view from mainstream economics that revenue should be raised with the economically efficient value-added tax (VAT) rather than direct taxes on income and profits, which would distort decisions about work effort and investment and thereby undermine growth. The standard prescription was to effect redistribution through spending alone.

Groundbreaking work by Thomas Piketty, Emanuel Saez, and their collaborators has shifted the terms of the debate on taxation and inequality. Their research makes a compelling case that progressive taxation can raise significant revenue in highly unequal societies – revenue that can in turn finance social spending and improve the welfare of lower-income groups (Piketty and Saez 2006). They also illustrate that progressive taxation can be an important redistributive tool in its own right (Piketty et al. 2013). Both of these contributions are of great potential importance in Latin America, where weak tax capacity – documented in Flores-Macías' Introduction to this volume – has often constrained spending and economic elites bear a notoriously low tax burden.

Methods pioneered by these same innovative economists have shed light on how little economic elites actually contribute to state coffers in Latin America. Estimates from tax return data, which provide far better information than household surveys on income at the top end of the distribution, suggest that the top 1% of Chileans earn more than 23% of income and profits but pay an effective tax rate of only 15% (Fairfield and Jorratt 2016). For Colombia, Alvaredo and Londoño (2013) estimate similarly high top income shares but an even lower effective tax rate of just 7%, although methodological differences preclude direct comparison with the Chilean figures. Even in Uruguay, one of Latin America's historically most equitable countries, the top 1% receives 13% of the pie but pays an effective tax rate of only 14% (Burdín et al. 2014, 40). By comparison, the top 1% paid 21% in the US in 2004 (Piketty and Saez 2006) and 31% in Germany in 2005 (Bach et al. 2013).

In light of these remarkable figures, the question of how and when Latin America's unequal democracies can tax economic elites becomes all the more salient. I have aimed to address this question (e.g., Fairfield 2015a) by focusing on three countries that adopted broad-base VATs with comparatively high rates in the aftermath of structural adjustment: Chile, Argentina, and Bolivia. When confronting revenue needs, policymakers in these countries by necessity often considered tapping into the under-taxed income and profits concentrated at the pinnacles of society.

My research strategy entails close examination of policymaking processes, including the critical but often overlooked stages of agenda formulation and proposal design, which helps pinpoint how economic elites – especially business actors – influence tax policy decisions. This approach complements historical accounts of tax capacity that operate at a more macro-level of analysis (e.g., chapters by Ondetti (4) and Schneider (5) in this volume). While we know a good deal about the historical origins of key sources of business power including partisan linkages and organization (Gibson 1996, Schneider 2004), few studies have examined exactly how business influences policy processes and how much scope governments have to enact progressive reforms when facing different configurations of business power. Detailed process tracing and comparative analysis of multiple tax policymaking episodes in essence form the microfoundations for my aggregate-level characterizations of how business power varied across the countries studied, as well as broader insights about structural and political factors that strengthen or weaken business power over time – both short-term and long-term.

The remainder of this chapter gives an overview of my theoretical framework, arguments, and findings. The final sections contribute thoughts on future directions for research on progressive taxation in the region in relation to literature on public opinion and on money in politics.

DEMOCRACY, INEQUALITY, AND REDISTRIBUTION

Debate on democracy and redistribution in political science ranges between two polar positions. On the one hand, a large body of research builds from a median-voter oriented view of politics that expects democratic policymaking to foster redistribution in unequal societies (Meltzer and Richard 1981; Boix 2003; Acemoglu and Robinson 2006). On the other hand, some scholars argue that economic elites get what they want almost all of the time. Winters (2011) focuses on super-rich individuals and identifies exorbitant wealth as an almost invincible source of power, when it comes to the core issue of wealth protection – which in democracies primarily involves curtailing progressive taxation. Culpepper (2011) advances an intermediate argument; he finds that the interests of big business prevail almost uniformly when the issue area has low salience, but maintains that policymakers respond to voters on high-salience issues, which he expects to include taxation.

Contrary to traditional median-voter approaches, I find that voters rarely play a leading role in the politics of progressive direct taxation. Progressive direct taxation by and large involved debate between political elites and economic elites, with electoral incentives mattering at the margins. However, economic elites did not always secure their preferred policy choices, even on manifestly low-salience tax issues. In fact, I observe substantial variation in the extent to which policymakers were able to legislate tax reforms targeting the resources of economic elites – across countries, over time, and depending on the subset of economic elites affected (e.g., different sectors of corporate taxpayers).

I explain this variation in the scope and fate of revenue-raising tax reform initiatives by analyzing business power. Business, broadly defined, plays a key role in tax politics. Taxation is a core issue for business. Firms and capital owners make decisions about employment and investment in response to tax policy that may have significant consequences for society at large. And business associations are organized actors that may represent not only the interests of businesses, but also those of wealthy individuals – which is not surprising given the extreme concentration of ownership and the extensive, family-controlled *grupos* which characterize Latin America's "hierarchical" capitalism (Schneider 2013).

BUSINESS POWER

Building on recent efforts to revive the study of business power,[1] I have aimed to refine the classic concepts of instrumental power and structural power. Instrumental power (Mills 1956; Miliband 1969) is the capacity to engage in deliberate political actions. I take a power resources approach by identifying specific sources of instrumental power that help predict when business interests will shape policy decisions. One set of instrumental power resources can be described as relationships with policymakers that enhance access and create bias in favor of business and economic elites more broadly. Examples include partisan linkages, where business forms a core constituency for conservative and/or right-wing parties (Gibson 1996), and recruitment into government, where business representatives hold important positions in the executive branch. Another set of instrumental-power resources comprises four key resources: organization, media access, expertise, and, of course, money. Each of these sources of power enhances business's ability to make the deliberate political actions it undertakes more effective. It is important to stress here that political activities such as lobbying should not be conflated with power. Instead, the relationships and resources described above serve as indicators of instrumental power – these "sources" of power help predict how effective business's political engagement will be. If business lacks sources of power, lobbying – however intensive – may achieve little influence. That is, we should not expect lobbying from a position of weakness to bear results. Clearly specifying and assessing sources of power is therefore critical for analyzing influence.

Instrumental power provides a useful overarching concept that accounts for many different potential constellations of political resources. It also distinguishes political modes of business influence from a very different channel of influence associated with what has been labeled as business's structural power.

Structural power arises from the profit-maximizing behavior of firms and investors (Block 1977; Lindblom 1977; Przeworski and Wallerstein 1988; Winters 1996). If policymakers anticipate that a reform will hurt

[1] See especially Hacker and Pierson (2002).

investment, they may rule it out for fear of harming growth and employment. Structural power requires no organization or political action; instead, market signals coordinate how individual firms and investors react in the economic arena. Whereas many treatments of structural power focus on capital mobility vs. sunken costs, or a sector's economic importance, or other easily measured and clearly "structural" factors,[2] I have argued that faithfully operationalizing the concept of structural power requires reconciling its "structural" underpinnings with the importance of policymakers' perceptions and expectations (Fairfield 2015a,b).

The nuance lies in the fact that structural power operates through policymakers' *anticipations* about how firms and investors will respond to a particular reform. Policymakers must believe that the reform under consideration will actually create negative investment incentives or other economic problems that will have significant deleterious consequences for growth or other development goals. If that is not the case, then structural power is either weak, in that the contemplated reform will not create problematic market signals, or it is simply irrelevant – if policymakers do not anticipate negative investment consequences, they will not act to forestall them by discarding or amending the reform under consideration. Of course, policymakers might subsequently ascertain that the reform actually did provoke negative investment responses – in other words, business's structural power in retrospect was actually strong, but policymakers mistakenly perceived it to be weak ex-ante. In such cases, the reform might be amended in business's favor during subsequent iterations of policymaking. But even in these cases, perceptions and anticipations are central to how and when structural power operates. Investment might fall after a particular reform, but causally linking that outcome to the reform may be a nontrivial matter; even professional economists may draw different conclusions.

This approach to operationalizing structural power places heavy empirical demands on scholars, including substantial fieldwork and, where possible, interviews with key policymakers. If the goal is to *predict* policy decisions and policy outcomes across a large number of cases, scholars might understandably prefer to replace structural power with more easily measured "structural" variables such as capital mobility.

[2] See, for example, Monaldi on oil taxation (Chapter 2 in this volume), which focuses on structural characteristics of the sector such as sunken costs of investment. For a power-centered treatment of the Bolivian case that takes into account policymakers' perceptions, see Fairfield (2015a, ch. 8).

However, if the goal is to *explain* actual policy decisions and policy outcomes that have occurred in salient cases, we cannot sidestep the question of perceptions and anticipated reactions – the classic concept of structural power cannot be operationalized as a purely objective variable. Moreover, given that anticipated reactions and perceptions clearly affect policy outcomes, it would be unscientific to exclude this subjective dimension from the analysis. Unfortunately for advocates of parsimony and generalizability, structural power is highly variable; capital mobility in itself does not ensure strong structural power, and policymakers in any given instance may disagree on the likely economic consequences of a particular reform. The world of social science is complex, and explanation of empirical reality is as important as (and probably a more attainable goal than) accurate prediction of outcomes across time and space.

It is important to emphasize that both instrumental power and structural power can influence agenda formulation via anticipated reactions; likewise, both types of power can act during subsequent stages of policymaking. These points are often overlooked in the literature on business politics. For example, instrumental power is usually understood to operate through direct, readily observable actions; however, when business has strong and multiple sources of instrumental power, policymakers may anticipate that attempting a reform will entail major political conflict, and they may rule it out as infeasible or not worth the costs (Fairfield 2010). In such cases, business need not undertake any overt political action in order to influence policy outcomes. Structural power, in contrast, is usually viewed as restricting the agenda, but it can also matter later on. For example, even if the executive-branch authors of a tax increase do not believe that it will negatively impact investment, legislators may well harbor concerns and hence make concessions to business during deliberations in Congress (Fairfield 2015b). In addition, simply announcing a tax reform proposal could precipitate market-coordinated disinvestment, which may in turn motivate policymakers to update their evaluations of structural power and heed greater attention to business demands.

Instrumental power and structural power are distinct concepts – they correspond to different means of influence: instrumental power is political, structural power has to do with market reactions. However, they can be mutually reinforcing. Consider what I call "structural enhancement of instrumental power." When business's structural power is strong, policymakers may institutionalize business's existing sources of instrumental power or even grant business new sources of instrumental power. For example, concerns over investor confidence or attempts to curtail capital flight may compel governments to appoint finance ministers from business circles (recruitment into government). Conversely, instrumental power may enhance structural power; in other words, business may actively deploy its sources of instrumental power to augment policymakers' perceptions of structural power. When business' instrumental power is strong, deliberate political actions such as lobbying and media campaigns can increase concern over investment, or even create concern among policymakers who initially did not anticipate any negative economic consequences in response to a proposed tax reform. Of course, business actors regularly argue that tax increases will hurt investment, but policymakers do not always believe these claims. The key point is that concrete sources of instrumental power – such as media access, close relationships with policymakers, and technical expertise – make it more likely that policymakers will take those arguments seriously, rather than writing them off as self-serving or lacking credibility.

A NOTE ON ALTERNATIVE TREATMENTS OF BUSINESS POWER

Culpepper and Reinke (2014, 431) have advocated an alternative treatment that separates instrumental and structural power into "strategic capacities" that "have to be deliberately exercised in order to be effective," and "automatic capacities" which "work through the anticipation … of policymakers." However, I argue that this approach introduces conceptual problems that undermine the analytical leverage of the business power framework.

Regarding instrumental power, the authors' distinction between "strategic capacities," exemplified by "lobbying," versus "automatic capacities," exemplified by "pro-business policymakers" (Culpepper and Reinke 2014, 432), overlooks the fact that any given instrumental-power resource may act indirectly, through anticipated reactions, or directly, through deliberate business actions. While we might usually think of lobbying as having a direct effect on the policy process, as noted earlier, the mere anticipation of a concerted lobbying campaign, predicated on strong sources of instrumental power such as money and organization, could be enough to dissuade a government from even proposing a tax increase that business opposes (Fairfield 2010) – in which case lobbying would count not just as a "strategic capacity," but also as an "automatic capacity." Conversely, there are certainly instances where business must deliberately and actively engage with "pro-business policymakers" in order to make sure their preferences are understood and translated into policy – in which case "pro-business policymakers" should be treated not just as an "automatic capacity," but also as a "strategic capacity." The proposed conceptual distinction thus dissolves.

Turning to structural power, the distinctions between "automatic" and "strategic" are equally unclear. On the one hand, Culpepper and Reinke (2014, 488–489) identify "disinvestment" as an "automatic resource" that works through policymakers' anticipations. On the other hand, they define "strategic structural power" as "deliberate use of economic power," which they also describe as a "bargaining resource." On the first point, it is hard to see why disinvestment would fall under one category but not the other. Anticipation of disinvestment can certainly influence policy decisions through an "automatic" pathway, yet an overt threat of disinvestment would have to count as a strategic "bargaining resource." Business may even intentionally curtail investment as a political strategy for influencing policy decisions, as occurs in capital strikes – a clear instance of "deliberate use of economic power."[3] On the second point, the authors seem to have in mind any overt statements by business that explicitly invoke their (purported) structural power. There is a valid point here: structural power need not be *strictly* "automatic," in that business may need to undertake some communication efforts to activate this source of power. However, this observation does not provide any added analytical leverage for understanding when structural power does or does not affect policy outcomes. Furthermore, Culpepper and Reinke's approach risks conflating strategies and bargaining positions with underlying sources of power that make those strategies or bargaining positions effective, as opposed to empty threats or detectable bluffs. Business can always threaten to disinvest or take other actions in the economic sphere that run counter to policymakers' wishes, but those threats are only effective if policymakers believe it would actually be in business's economic interest to follow through on those actions post facto. Business threats are credible when policymakers anticipate that disinvestment is a market-rational response to policy change – and/or when business can use strong sources of instrumental power (e.g., technical expertise) to augment policymakers' perceptions of their structural power, as discussed in the previous section.

[3] I argue that capital strikes require *politically* coordinated economic protest, as opposed to market-rational economic behavior. As such, capital strikes are best understood as an exercise of instrumental power, rather than structural power (Fairfield 2015a, b).

The analytical advantage that Culpepper and Reinke (2014, 448–449) attribute to their notion of "strategic structural power" is that it "can [be] observed through its effect in negotiations, of which there is an empirical record," whereas studying "automatic structural power" requires the more difficult challenge of "assessing what is going on inside the heads of policymakers." Unfortunately this advantage is illusory. First, negotiations between policymakers and business often take place behind closed doors without public records – especially in developing countries – such that there are not necessarily any differences regarding the ease of obtaining empirical evidence to assess business influence. Second, and more importantly, focusing primarily on "strategic power" (whether structural or instrumental) shifts attention away from agenda formulation and anticipated reactions, which leads to multiple analytical perils in assessing business influence (Hacker and Pierson 2002; Fairfield 2015a,b). If structural and/or instrumental power is strong enough to shift the set of policies under consideration toward business preferences, focusing only on concessions made during negotiations after a policy has been proposed can lead us to significantly underestimate the extent of business influence (Fairfield 2010). Finally, ascertaining policymakers' (and business's) motives, perceptions, and strategic calculations – i.e., "getting inside their heads" – is critical for assessing business influence at any and all stages of the policymaking process.

Ultimately, distinguishing between "strategic capacities" and "automatic capacities" is unnecessary, once we recognize that (1) both types of power can act at different stages of policymaking – agenda setting or subsequently – through either anticipated reactions or observable actions and responses (whether in the political arena or in the economic arena), and (2) that instrumental power and structural power can be mutually reinforcing.

EXPLAINING VARIATION IN BUSINESS INFLUENCE

I argue that business interests shape policy decisions when either instrumental power or structural power is strong. The more types of power and the more sources of power business enjoys, the more significant and consistent business influence will be. Regarding instrumental power, I further argue that the more institutionalized relationships with policymakers, such as partisan linkages, will afford more consistent influence than less-institutionalized relationships, such as recruitment into government or informal ties to policymakers. In the latter cases, whether business interests prevail will depend much more on the characteristics and motivations of the specific policymakers in question. Of the other instrumental-power resources, I find that organization plays a particularly important role in explaining variation across my cases.

The argument plays out across the countries I analyze as follows. In Chile, during the primary time period I examine (1991–2009), business's strong instrumental power kept key tax reforms off of the agenda, even in the absence of structural power. Instrumental power arose primarily from strong business organization and partisan linkages to right parties, which enjoyed strong representation in Congress. Particularly during the Lagos administration (2000–2006), government policymakers anticipated that tax reforms targeting the resources of economic elites would provoke costly political battles involving coordinated opposition from business associations and their right-party allies that might well end in legislative defeat. The difficulty of legislating even modest progressive tax reforms dissuaded government policymakers from proposing more significant initiatives that they otherwise viewed as desirable and appropriate.

In Argentina, in contrast, business's weak instrumental power facilitated more significant direct tax increases. Governments in the 1990s and early 2000s were able to include various progressive tax initiatives among their revenue-raising tools, along with reforms that provided greater powers for the tax administration to control evasion, including broad access to bank information for the purpose of cross-checking taxpayers' declarations. Successive reforms contributed to a steady increase in direct tax revenue in Argentina, whereas tax revenue held essentially constant in Chile until the copper boom produced an exogenous increase (i.e., without any substantial tax policy changes). However, an examination of sectoral tax policy in Argentina reveals interesting variation, which can also be explained by examining business power at this level of analysis. Despite the weakness of business at the broader cross-sectoral level, finance and agriculture enjoyed substantial instrumental and/or structural power during specific periods that allowed them to block or defeat tax reforms that specifically affected their sectors.

In Bolivia during the early 2000s, when raising revenue became salient on the national agenda, business power shared the stage with an additional explanatory factor: popular mobilization. Business power interacted with popular mobilization (in occasionally surprising ways) to produce variation across different tax policy initiatives. Strong business associations with ties to Bolivia's traditional – albeit besieged – political parties were able to preclude higher taxation of income and wealth, yet large royalty increases were imposed on multinational hydrocarbons companies despite opposition from domestic business associations. While the details are complex, the Bolivian cases illustrate first, that business power plays an important explanatory role even in this very different and highly volatile political context; and second, that in unusual circumstances, popular mobilization in favor of redistribution can counterbalance or even overwhelm business power, leading to substantial tax increases on economic elites that otherwise would have been highly unlikely.

The business power framework also explains significant tax policy change over time at the within-country level. Sectoral tax politics in Argentina provides a salient example. Economic crisis, changes in development models, and alterations in government that led to greater proximity or isolation between policymakers and particular business sectors play a central role in driving variation in sectoral business power over time, which in turn explains the extent and timing of, for example, tax agency access to bank information for auditing purposes in Argentina. We also observe major change over time in Chile, when we consider developments under the second Bachelet administration (2014–2017). Whereas under previous center–left governments at most marginal tax increases were legislated, the Bachelet administration initiated a radical income-tax overhaul in 2014. Business's weaker instrumental power contributed to this change; the right's electoral losses in Congress made business's partisan linkages less effective for influencing policy decisions. At the same time, the student movement, which staged major protests and raised redistributive issues in 2011 and 2012, acted to counterbalance business power (discussed further in the next section).

BUSINESS'S STRATEGIC CALCULATIONS

As the Bolivia overview and recent developments in Chile suggest, analyzing business's strategic calculations along with business power is critical for understanding prospects for progressive direct tax increases. Business's strategic behavior has played a key role in the literature on democratization (Wood 2000; Makgetla and Shapiro 2016; Boylan 1996, and of course the formal modeling literature), but literature on business politics and the welfare state has sometimes paid insufficient attention to the ways that business's immediate or "induced" policy preferences may be shaped by the strategic landscape and the power of other social actors (Hacker and Pierson 2002; Korpi 2006).

Generally speaking, business and economic elites have a first-order preference for low taxation. Where revenue needs are imperative, they prefer using the VAT over taxes on income, profits, and wealth. However, the political context may compel business actors to accept measures they might otherwise oppose (Schneider [Chapter 5 in this volume] makes related points with regard to fiscal federalism). Popular mobilization plays an important role in altering business calculations about whether to resist or accept policy change. When popular mobilization emerges around redistributive issues, business elites may decide to accept reform rather than mobilizing their sources of power to resist, as occurred in the early stages of Chile's 2014 tax reform in the context of recent student protests for free higher education financed by taxing the rich (Fairfield 2015b). In such situations, business may anticipate that policy change will diffuse social pressure and restore order. Even if they view that scenario with skepticism, business elites may recognize that policymakers will prioritize responding to popular demands rather than business preferences for those same reasons, as well as for the sake of preserving their continuity in power. The scope of policy change business will tolerate depends on how sustained, organized, and disruptive social mobilization is. It is worth emphasizing, however, how rarely I observed the dynamic where social movements mobilize to demand progressive taxation – in only two out of the more than thirty cases examined in my book.[4]

Similar dynamics can occur in the absence of popular mobilization when policymakers perceive electoral incentives to promote progressive taxation, or when electoral considerations take regressive revenue-raising options off the agenda. For example, in Chile following the massive 2010 earthquake, President Piñera calculated that raising revenue for reconstruction by increasing the corporate tax would provide him with a highly desirable boost in public support, in a context where his government had been characterized as run by and for big business. Multiple factors contributed to the instrumentally powerful business associations' decision to accept the tax increase, but strategic calculations that refusing to open their pocketbooks after the natural disaster would elicit public opprobrium and could provide an opportunity for the left to push for a much more significant corporate tax increase was an important contributing

[4] In several cases, however, nonbusiness sectors mobilized against tax increases that they perceived (sometimes mistakenly) would affect them.

factor (Fairfield 2015a, ch. 9). Similarly, in Mexico, in a context of extremely tight electoral competition and the manifest unpopularity of increasing the VAT, President Calderón opted to satisfy revenue needs by taxing business instead. As in Chile, Mexican business elites accepted the corporate tax increase instead of using their ample sources of instrumental power to resist, in part because they recognized that their preferred VAT alternative was politically infeasible for policymakers (Fairfield and Garay 2017).

However, in cases where electoral incentives and public opinion drive progressive tax reform, the scope of policy change will be narrow; organized interests (whether business associations or social movements) tend to have a much greater impact on policymaking than unorganized voters (Hacker and Pierson 2010).[5] Both the Piñera and Calderón corporate tax increases were modest compared to the much more significant tax increases legislated on hydrocarbons in Bolivia (2005) and on economic elites in Chile (2014) in contexts of widespread ongoing or recent social mobilization.

REFLECTIONS ON PUBLIC OPINION ABOUT TAXING ELITES

Literature on advanced democracies debates the influence of voters and public opinion on economic policy decisions. In contrast to arguments that voters carry little import (Hacker and Pierson 2010), recent work has advocated an "electoral turn" in political economy to investigate how electoral coalitions and voter preferences shape social protection and economic policy regimes (Beramendi et al. 2015; Hall 2014). With regard to taxation, one might expect broad-based taxes such as the VAT to be high-salience issues where public opinion would matter for policymakers. And while income taxes in Latin America are definitely not broad-based – the vast majority of voters earn less than the minimum taxable income – polls show high levels of support for the principle of progressive taxation – 76% of the population, as Bogliaccini and Luna (Chapter 9 in this volume) show.[6]

[5] For development of this perspective with respect to taxation and social policy in Latin America, see Fairfield (2015a), Garay (2016), and Fairfield and Garay (2017).

[6] Similarly, the 2012 LAPOP (SOC1) survey question found that 59% of respondents preferred the most progressive of three tax burdens comparing how much a rich person and a poor person should pay for every 100 currency units earned. CEP (2009) found that 64% believed upper-income individuals should pay a larger or much larger proportion of income in taxes than lower-income individuals.

Yet my research suggests that progressive direct tax reforms in Latin America are often low-salience issues for nonelite voters, and that public opinion on these matters tends to be ill-formed, in accordance with findings in US politics (Bartels 2008; Graetz and Shapiro 2005). Even in Chile, where tax reforms were covered extensively in the media, many politicians I interviewed perceived that nonelite voters in their districts simply were not interested (Fairfield 2015a, 286). One member of Congress went so far as to assert: "The immense majority of people never ask you about your position on tax issues. I have been a member of the Budget Committee for eight years. If you ask me if I think any of my actions in the Budget Committee has caused me to win or lose votes, I would have to say zero" (quoted in Fairfield 2015a, 110). In many of the tax reform cases I analyzed, public opinion polls were not even conducted. Extractive resource taxation (e.g., copper in Chile and hydrocarbons in Bolivia) is a notable exception where surveys could be more easily located and public opinion tended to strongly favor tax increases. The difference is that mineral resource taxation tends to stoke nationalist sentiments when multinational companies dominate the sector. To a certain extent, "soaking the rich" in these contexts may be popularly understood as taxing extractive industries.

Much thought has been devoted to analyzing why nonelite voters might not support policies that are in their own economic best interest, including progressive taxation (e.g., Bartels 2008; Kaufman 2009). An important factor I wish to highlight is that taxation tends to be a highly complex, technical policy area, which means that voters rarely understand the consequences of policy change. Reform-minded policymakers can mobilize public support by emphasizing the importance of progressive taxation for fairness and equity and by designing reforms to clearly target economic elites while leaving the majority of citizens untouched. Other strategies, such as linking to visible social-spending benefits, can clarify that progressive tax reform will make a positive contribution to the welfare of nonelite taxpayers, who might not otherwise view tax increases on economic elites as relevant to their lives (Fairfield 2013). But business actors can also manipulate public opinion, by framing the same reforms as bad for growth and employment, or by fostering misperceptions regarding who will actually bear the tax burden. Instrumental-power resources, including media access and technical expertise, are extremely useful to these ends.

As an example, consider the Bachelet administration's 2014 income-tax overhaul initiative. Several survey organizations tracked public opinion on this far-reaching tax reform during the most intensive months of debate in Congress. The tax reform was explicitly intended to raise revenue from business and wealthy economic elites; tax agency studies indicated that the reform would primarily affect the top 1% and would make small and medium businesses better off than under the prevailing system. However, the Chilean tax system, with its integrated corporate and personal income tax and complicated system of deferred taxation for retained profits, as well as the proposed reform itself, were so complicated that there was ample scope for opponents to foster misperceptions regarding tax incidence, as well as concern over unwanted economic consequences.[7] Remarkably, the survey firm CADEM (2014) found that 68% of Chileans believed the tax reform would hurt the "middle class," and 57% thought they would personally have to pay more taxes as a result. Pervasive denunciations by business and the right in the media are likely responsible for these misperceptions; the government's inadequate communication campaign contributed as well. Meanwhile, despite the reform's high media salience, polls suggested that ordinary Chileans did not view it as a priority issue. Only 5% of respondents selected the tax reform as deserving greatest effort among eight other policy areas; health care, an issue with much more direct impact on citizens' daily lives, came out on top (CADEM 2014).

Future research on public opinion and progressive direct taxation in Latin America might fruitfully examine not just the factors that influence how voters at large respond to reform proposals (e.g., survey experiments on priming and earmarking, ascertaining which design features make taxes more visible), but also the ways that business interests and reform proponents seek to strategically deploy opinion polls during the policy-making process, along the lines described by Birney et al. (2008). Equally important would be more research on when public opinion becomes relevant at all in tax debates, and how decisive a role it plays. In my own research, I have found that strategies for mobilizing public opinion can make a difference for legislating progressive tax reforms, but where business power is strong, they matter only at the margins.

BUSINESS POWER AND THE DIRECT ROLE OF MONEY

Money is a source of instrumental power that distinguishes economic elites from all other actors. However, its direct role in politics and policy-making can be difficult to study, especially in Latin America where data on

[7] On the latter, see Fairfield (2015b).

lobbying and campaign finance contributions are not publicly available. Partly for that reason, I focus on other sources of instrumental power in my research (especially organization, which helps to explain a significant amount of variation across tax reform cases). Nevertheless, the direct role that money plays as a power resource merits more attention. Scholars including Luna (2010), Yadav (2011), and Boas et al. (2014) have made headway despite the limitations. In Chile, the recent business campaign contribution/tax evasion scandal uncovered in the Penta case – in which employees of Chilean holding Grupo Penta colluded with employees of the tax revenue service to carry out tax fraud and channeled funds toward political campaigns – may produce more tangible evidence on the inner workings and scope of money politics, as well as providing a fascinating case study of the right's effort to regroup and reign in the scope of the tax agency's operations. Moreover, Winter's (2011) innovative research on oligarchy demonstrates that ample insights can be gained even in the absence of hard quantitative data.

Winters (2011) identifies various types of oligarchy, which he defines as the politics-of-wealth defense. While his case studies do not include Latin American countries, they fall under the category of civil oligarchy, like the US, where the state protects property rights, and the primary threat to oligarchic wealth is progressive taxation. In his analysis of money politics and taxation in the US, Winters emphasizes the role of the "income-defense industry" – the lawyers, lobbyists, tax accounts, and other professionals who earn their living by helping to ensure that oligarchs pay a low tax burden. These professionals serve as agents for their oligarchic principals; when it comes to tax legislation, the interests of the lobbyists and tax advisors are automatically aligned with those of their wealthy clients. Oligarchs simply spend a tiny fraction of their fantastic wealth, and the income-defense industry does the work of inserting tax benefits into legislation, exploiting existing loopholes on the oligarchs' behalf, and so forth.

Does Winters' (2011) perspective on the income-defense industry elucidate tax politics in Latin America? Oligarchs everywhere are certainly able to exploit tax loopholes with the help of accountants and consultants, but the existence of those loopholes is a policy question. The key issue is therefore what role the income-defense industry plays in policymaking processes. In the countries I have studied, I do find evidence of tax accountants and professional associations participating in policy debates. They often serve on business association advisory boards or business associations' research departments, they present their views on legislation in congressional committees, and they opinionate in the press, generally expressing views very similar to those of business and upper-income individuals. Professional associations representing the income-defense industry were especially visible in Chile's 2014 reform. Congressional hearings featured a myriad of such groups all opposing the reform and especially the proposed elimination of the "taxable profits fund" (FUT). As the then director of the tax agency commented, becoming a tax accountant required taking three courses dedicated explicitly to the FUT, with "a FUT manual thicker than the Bible."[8] It is hardly surprising that professionals with so much training invested in the prevailing tax system would oppose the reform. The interests of business owners and tax professionals in preserving the FUT system were clearly aligned.

However, the activities of "income-defense" professionals can be subsumed under the broader instrumental-power resource of technical expertise. In Chile's 2014 reform, I argue that technical expertise helped sew concern not only about how investment would respond, but also about the legality and administrative feasibility of the new income tax system (Fairfield 2015b). The barrage of criticism from business's tax consultants and technical advisors overwhelmed governing-coalition senators; the Finance Ministry was surprisingly slow to respond, partly because the top expert had been allocated to directing the tax administration rather than negotiating the reform through Congress. A congressional informant explained: "There is an argumentational imbalance. Every time there is a hearing, they hit us and hit us and hit us ... and what am I to do? I don't have answers. But also, I have genuine concerns."[9] Even in this case, however, the role of business organization and the unified lobbying and media campaigns strike me as more important than the income-defense professionals in their own right. Structural power mattered in this case as well (Fairfield 2015b). Even in the absence of the very numerous technical-association presentations in Congress, the most likely counterfactual is that business would have won similar concessions.

It is important to note that Winters (2011) defines oligarchs as individuals, not corporations. To the extent that wealthy individuals and corporations are distinct actors, Winters' emphasis on money as the ultimate

[8] Michel Jorratt, Comisión de Presupuesto y Hacienda, June 30, 2014 (congressional hearing).

[9] Interview: Finance committee member, June 13, 2014.

source of power and the role of the income-defense industry in policymaking would be significantly different from my approach of subsuming the latter under technical expertise. In Latin America, however, where business elites and oligarchs as per Winters' definition are closely interrelated, family-controlled groups are common, and few companies are publicly traded, the distinction may matter less. Business associations in Chile and in Bolivia defended not only the tax interests of firms and corporations, but also the tax interests of upper-income individuals and business owners. In some sense, business associations themselves could be viewed as agents of the oligarchs – the owners of the large *grupos* who prefer to stay above the political fray.[10] The structural and political factors that lead wealthy individuals and business to coalesce, diverge, or complement one another as political actors are also worthy of further investigation.

CONCLUSION

In sum, Latin American elites remain substantially under-taxed, despite progress in recent decades in countries such as Argentina. Understanding prospects for raising revenue from the top of the income distribution requires examining economic elites' sources of power, both instrumental and structural. Economic elites have different configurations of power resources in different countries, and when either their instrumental power or their structural power is strong, they will be able to influence policy decisions. Instrumental and structural power are not constants, however, and opportunities for progress do arise that astute policymakers can take advantage of. Future research could complement our existing body of knowledge by finding creative ways to examine the direct role of money as a source of power and the role of the income-defense industry in tax politics, as well as the role of public opinion and social movements in efforts to tax economic elites. Particularly in a time of falling commodity prices and austerity – as noted in the Introduction – these are pressing intellectual and practical questions.

[10] When I asked former president Lagos if the heads of these *grupos* were active in tax policy discussion, he replied: "No, no. … they are not in the front lines of the battle, never" – that role instead falls to the business peak associations and to legislators with close ties to big business. Interview: September 2006.

References

Acemoglu, Daron and James Robinson. 2006. *Economic Origins of Dictatorship and Democracy*. New York: Cambridge University Press.

Alvaredo, Facundo and Julieta Londoño. 2013. "High Incomes and Personal Taxation in a Developing Economy: Colombia 1993–2010," Commitment to Equity Working Paper 12.

Bach, Stephan, Giacomo Corneo, and Viktor Steiner, 2013. "Effective Taxation of Top Incomes in Germany," *German Economic Review*, 14(2): 115–137.

Bartels, Larry. 2008. *Unequal Democracy: The Political Economy of the New Gilded Age*. Princeton: Princeton University Press.

Beramendi, Pablo, Silja Hausermann, Herbert Kitschelt, and Hanspeter Kriesi (eds.). 2015. *The Politics of Advanced Capitalism*. New York: Cambridge University Press.

Birney, Mayling, Ian Shapiro, and Michael Graetz. 2008. "The Political Uses of Public Opinion," in Ian Shapiro, Peter A. Swenson, and Daniela Donno (eds.), *Divide and Deal*. New York: New York University Press.

Block, Fred. 1977. "The Ruling Class Does Not Rule," *Socialist Revolution* 33: 6–27.

Boas, Taylor, Daniel Hidalgo, and Neal Richardson. 2014. "The Spoils of Victory: Campaign Donations and Government Contracts in Brazil," *Journal of Politics* 76(2): 415–419.

Boix, Carles. 2003. *Democracy and Redistribution*. New York: Cambridge University Press.

Boylan, Delia. 1996. "Taxation and Transition: The Politics of the 1990 Chilean Tax Reform," *Latin American Research Review* 31(1): 7–31.

Burdín, Gabriel, Fernando Esponda, and Andrea Vigorito. 2014. "Inequality and Top Incomes in Uruguay." World Top Incomes Database Working Paper 2014/1.

CADEM. 2014. *Encuesta No. 21 de Plaza Pública*, Santiago, Chile, June 9. Centro de Estudios Públicos (CEP). Various years. Santiago, Chile.

Centro de Estudios Públicos (CEP). Various years. Santiago, Chile. Working Papers.

Culpepper, Pepper. 2011. *Quiet Politics and Business Power*. New York: Cambridge University Press.

Culpepper, Pepper and Raphael Reinke. 2014. "Structural Power and Bank Bailouts in the United Kingdom and the United States," *Politics & Society* 42(4): 427–454.

Fairfield, Tasha. 2010. "Business Power and Tax Reform: Taxing Income and Profits in Chile and Argentina," *Latin American Politics and Society* 52(2): 51–71.

2013. "Going Where the Money Is: Strategies for Taxing Economic Elites in Unequal Democracies," *World Development* 47: 42–57.

2015a. *Private Wealth and Public Revenue in Latin America: Business Power and Tax Politics*. New York: Cambridge University Press.

2015b. "Structural Power in Comparative Political Economy: Perspectives from Policy Formulation in Latin America," *Business and Politics* 17(3): 411–442.

Fairfield, Tasha and Candelaria Garay. 2017. "Redistribution under the Right in Latin America: Electoral Competition and Organized Actors in Policymaking," *Comparative Political Studies* 50(14): 1871–1906

Fairfield, Tasha and Michel Jorratt. 2016. "Top Income Shares, Business Profits, and Effective Tax Rates in Contemporary Chile," *Review of Income and Wealth* 62: S120–S144.

Garay, Candelaria. 2016. *Social Policy Expansion in Latin America*. New York: Cambridge University Press.

Gehlbach, Scott. 2008. *Representation through Taxation: Revenue, Politics, and Development in Postcommunist States*. New York: Cambridge University Press.

Gibson, Edward. 1996. *Class and Conservative Parties, Argentina in Comparative Perspective*. Baltimore: Johns Hopkins University Press

Graetz, Michael, and Ian Shapiro. 2005. *Death by a Thousand Cuts: The Fight over Taxing Inherited Wealth*. Princeton: Princeton University Press.

Hacker, Jacob and Paul Pierson. 2002. "Business Power and Social Policy: Employers and the Formation of the American Welfare State," *Politics and Society* 30: 277–325.

2010. "Winner-Take-All-Politics: Public Policy, Political Organization, and the Precipitous Rise of Top Incomes in the United States," *Politics and Society* 38 (2): 152–204.

Hall, Peter. 2014. "How Growth Regimes Evolve in the Developed Democracies." Paper presented to the Annual Meeting of the European Political Science Association.

Kato, Junko. 2003. *Regressive Taxation and the Welfare State*. New York: Cambridge University Press.

Kaufman, Robert. 2009. "The Political Effects of Inequality in Latin America: Some Inconvenient Facts," *Comparative Politics* 41(3): 359–379.

Korpi, Walter. 2006. "Power Resources and Employer-Centered Approaches in Explanations of Welfare States and Varieties of Capitalism," *World Politics* 58(2): 167–206.

LAPOP. 2012. *Americas Barometer Core Questionnaire*. Nashville: Latin America Public Opinion Project, Vanderbilt University.

Lindblom, Charles. 1977. *Politics and Markets: The World's Political Economic Systems*. New York: Basic Books.

Luna, Juan Pablo. 2010. "Segmented Party Voter Linkages in Latin America: The Case of the UDI," *Journal of Latin American Studies* 42(2): 325–356.

Meltzer, Allan and Scott Richard. 1981. "A Rational Theory of the Size of Government," *Journal of Political Economy* 89(5): 914–927

Miliband, Ralph. 1969. *The State and Capitalist Society*. New York: Basic Books.

Mills, C. Wright. 1956. *The Power Elite*. Oxford: Oxford University Press.

Piketty, Thomas and Emmanuel Saez, 2006. "How Progressive is the US Federal Tax System?" NBER Working Paper 12404.

Piketty, Thomas, Emmanuel Saez, and Stefanie Stantcheva. 2013. "Optimal Taxation of Top Labor Incomes: A Tale of Three Elasticities," *American Economic Journal: Public Policy* 6(1): 230–271

Pribble, Jennifer. 2014. *Welfare and Party Politics in Latin America*. New York: Cambridge University Press.

Przeworski, Adam and Michael Wallerstein. 1988. "Structural Dependence of the State on Capital," *The American Political Science Review* 82(1): 11–29.

Makgetla, Itumeleng and Scott Shapiro. 2016. "Business and the South African Transition," unpublished ms., Yale University.

Schneider, Ben Ross. 2004. *Business Politics and the State in Twentieth-Century Latin America*. New York: Cambridge University Press.

2013. *Hierarchical Capitalism in Latin America*. New York: Cambridge University Press.

Steinmo, Sven. 1993. *Taxation and Democracy: Swedish, British, and American Approaches to Financing the Modern State*. New Haven: Yale University Press.

Wilensky, Harold. 2002. *Rich Democracies: Political Economy, Public Policy, and Performance*. Berkeley: University of California Press.

Winters, Jeffrey. 1996. *Power in Motion*. Ithaca: Cornell University Press.

2011. *Oligarchy*. New York: Cambridge University Press.

Wood, Elisabeth. 2000. *Forging Democracy from below: Insurgent Transitions in South Africa and El Salvador*. New York: Cambridge University Press.

Yadav, Vineeta. 2011. *Political Parties, Business Groups, and Corruption in Developing Countries*. Oxford: Oxford University Press.

8

Weak Liberalism and Weak Property Taxation in Latin America*

James E. Mahon, Jr.

Most discussions about Latin American tax systems lament their lack of progressivity. The concern is entirely justifiable. As highlighted in the Introduction to this volume, governments of this extraordinarily unequal region derive less revenue – compared to other regions of the world – from the two common forms of taxation that are most likely to be progressive in their incidence: personal income and property taxes (see also Mahon 2012). The fact that this situation still obtains after a generation of electoral democracy constitutes a problem for the economist's workhorse model of fiscal politics, the "median voter model," which expects poor majorities in a democracy to elect regimes that, by and large, tax the rich and spend on themselves (Meltzer and Richard 1981).

Yet this understates the gap between theory and reality. Along with electoral democracy, over the past two decades nearly all countries of the region have also institutionalized market-friendly macroeconomic policies and noninflationary fiscal management. However, although they are regularly labeled "neoliberal" by their critics on the left, most governments of the region fit the liberal profile better in terms of what the state *does not* do (e.g., operate major industries, inflate the currency, promote industrialization via trade barriers) than what it *does* (clarify and protect everyone's property rights, provide essential public goods efficiently). That is, governments that embrace free trade, welcome foreign investment, or align their foreign policy with Washington quite often also lack

* I thank Alberto Barreix, Richard Bird, Paula Consolini, Tasha Fairfield, Gustavo Flores-Macías, Stephen Kaplan, Robert Kaufman, Gabriel Ondetti, Ben Schneider, and Hillel Soifer for comments on earlier versions of this work.

independent judiciaries, regulation of monopolies, and the rule of law generally. This is not a new observation. De Soto notes that "the existence of prosperous enclaves in a sea of poverty conceals an abysmal retardation in a nation's capacity to create, respect, and make available formal property rights to a majority of its citizens" (2000, 75). (This failure to advance the positive or constructive agenda of liberalism, which includes items that require a capable state, has probably had a lot to do with the political unpopularity of the neoliberal project.)

The central puzzle comes into focus when we juxtapose these two observations. In a nutshell, the governments that have largely failed to tax the property or income of wealthy individuals (and redistribute relatively little income) also perform poorly, compared to the rest of the world, on common measures of the constructive aspects of liberalism, such as freedom to run a business and the reliable protection of property rights. In fact, they score more poorly, comparatively, than they do on indicators of democracy. In this sense they are better democrats than (neo)liberals.

This chapter proposes that this apparent paradox can be resolved by tracing the historical relationship of taxation and state formation. Personal income and property taxes, especially taxes on real estate, happen to be the same ones associated historically with the rise and maturation of liberal states in England and the United States, and in recent decades the world champions of wealth taxation are all notably liberal countries.[1] In post-Independence Latin America, these taxes were the preferred choice of liberals, too. But with weak administrations at their command and facing strong opposition from landlords, they failed. In a few countries, however, the old liberal blueprint succeeded in part. As Marcus Kurtz has shown (2013), in Chile and Uruguay key moments of early state capacity-building took the form of productive responses to coordination problems, responses that included elites taxing themselves – most importantly, through taxes on landed property. Where such advances in state consolidation were absent, limited, or reversed, state weakness persisted, facilitating domination by oligarchs and informal powers.

[1] In 1981, the only developing country in which wealth taxes made an important contribution to revenue was Singapore, where they provided 14% of all tax revenue or 2.6% of GDP; among OECD countries in 1988, the highest total contribution of net wealth and capital transfer taxes, 3.09% of GDP, could be found in Switzerland (Bird 1991, 323, 325). Across all countries for which we have good data, for all property taxes at all levels of government, the top-ranked countries by average revenue/GDP over the 2001–2010 period were the UK, Canada, France, Luxembourg, and the USA (ICTD database 2015: www.ictd.ac/dataset/grd/).

Thus, these historical patterns violate the expectations not only of the median-voter model but also of related ideas that link capital mobility – we are talking about *im*mobile capital, after all – to low levels of redistribution (Boix 2003). Instead, they suggest the utility of theories of oligarchy in thinking about Latin America's distinctiveness relative to the rest of the world, and of a fiscal-contract model in thinking about contrasts across the region. Regarding the latter, we need to recognize the generally accretive or layered character of both tax systems and state administrations. The legacy of state-building moments has survived in a broad correspondence between levels of property taxation, on one side, and the degree of adherence to the rule of law (especially among economic elites), on the other. In turn, weakness on the rule of law has posed more of an obstacle to the broad extension of property rights and business freedom – core elements of economic liberalism – than it has to electoral democracy. State capacity is the unacknowledged premise of the median-voter model, and its absence explains the model's lack of fit to most developing countries. In this light, we can appreciate that state capacity is probably an important reason why Uruguay and Chile are the only two countries that have seen unambiguously progressive tax reforms in the past decade.

This chapter draws together several literatures and addresses old, nagging questions. It builds upon recent studies of regional tax politics (Fairfield 2015a, b; Mahon et al. 2015), monographs on property taxation in the region (Jáuregui 2006; De Cesare 2016a), general works on oligarchy (Winters 2011), and historical work on state formation in Europe (Brewer 1989) and Latin America (Kurtz 2013; Soifer 2015). It is also informed by the work of tax specialists working in the region (e.g., Bird 2013; Bird and Zolt 2015) and important theoretical works on taxation and political development (Levi 1988; Timmons 2005; Besley and Persson 2011).

Four sections follow. The first section describes contemporary Latin America's distinctive tax profile of exceptionally weak property- and personal-income taxation. The second section describes one aspect of the region's political profile: the combination of relatively healthy electoral systems and relatively weak protection of property rights. The next, main section offers three kinds of evidence for a genetic connection between property taxes and liberal state formation in Latin America: contemporary political culture, administrative logic, and, most importantly, an historical narrative that ties early taxes on landed property (essentially, elite self-taxation) to the building of states capable of protecting property rights relatively broadly. After speculating about why general state capacity should be more important to property rights than to democracy, the chapter concludes.

THE DISTINCTIVENESS OF LATIN AMERICAN TAXATION

Compared to other regions, Latin America has a characteristic tax profile. The first half of Table 8.1 shows the percentages of total revenue supplied by income and consumption taxes for seven groups of countries for the 2000–2010 period, using the dataset compiled by the International Centre for Tax and Development (ICTD).[2] Looking down the last column, Latin America has the highest average ratio, and the contrast is quite strong with all other groups except the former Communist countries.[3] Turning to real estate taxes, according to the IDB, receipts from urban and rural property averaged only 0.37% of GDP in the 2000s – about half the amount collected by other developing countries, and only one-sixth of the average reported by the Organization for Economic Cooperation and Development (OECD).[4] In sum, two taxes that are considered the most likely to be strongly progressive in their impact – personal income and real estate taxes – are remarkably weak in Latin America, while consumption taxes, usually regressive on balance, play an important role.[5]

2 ICTD/UNU-WIDER, "Government Revenue Dataset," (version 1, 2015): www.wider.unu.edu/project/government-revenue-dataset.

3 Similar results are obtained from the dataset complied by the Inter-American Development Bank (IDB) and Inter-American Center for Tax Administration (Centro Interamericano de Administradores Tributarios, CIAT); see www.ciat.org/base-de-datos-de-recaudacion-bid-ciat/.

4 Latin American figures from De Cesare 2016a, 7, and Corbacho et al. 2013, 89, citing Sepúlveda and Martínez-Vázquez 2009. Comparisons from latter source. On Mexico, see Unda 2014.

5 The revenue share provided by the corporate income tax (CIT) is a poor indicator of taxation aimed at the rich, for two reasons. First, the final incidence of the CIT depends on competitive conditions (mainly, elasticities of substitution of the tax firm's output), whose assessment is quite complicated, as the literature from Harberger 1962 onward testifies. Second, even when rents from state-owned resource firms are not booked as CIT revenues, in Latin America this rubric often includes receipts from private natural resource firms, whose unusual rents the state tries to share via this tax, and MNC subsidiaries, which are weaker politically and have a greater stake in not avoiding CIT obligations in the host country. Now, it is true that in some countries the rate structure gives highly paid salaried workers (such as international soccer stars) a strong incentive to incorporate, thereby paying tax under the CIT. This indicates poor design and weak enforcement rather than CIT progressivity.

TABLE 8.1 *Total revenue and tax revenue by type of tax (% of GDP), general government*

Country/Region	Total Revenue	Total Tax Revenue (w/o Soc Sec)	(1) Personal Income Tax	(2a) Property Taxes	(2b) Real Estate Tax	(3) Corporate Income Tax	(4) Taxes on Goods and Services (domestic)	Ratio (4)/(1)
OECD Europe, ex-UK			22.63			11.47	41.47	1.83
			(19)			(19)	(19)	(19)
UK and Former British Settler Colonies			40.11			13.72	21.08	0.53
			(5)			(5)	(5)	(5)
British and Dutch Caribbean, Israel, and Japan			18.42			14.68	29.15	1.58
			(6)			(6)	(8)	(6)
Sub-Saharan Africa			12.03			9.51	30.42	2.53
			(34)			(33)	(38)	(34)
Eastern Europe and Eurasian ex-Communist			8.07			10.05	52.09	6.45
			(23)			(24)	(24)	(23)
South and East Asia			10.05			15.35	30.51	3.04
			(18)			(17)	(18)	(18)
Middle East and North Africa			6.08			9.07	17.73	2.92
			(11)			(9)	(15)	(11)
Latin America			4.41			12.36	45.66	10.36
			(13)			(12)	(18)	(13)*
Argentina	28.24	23.34	1.45	–	0.32	2.75	9.53	6.59
Bolivia	25.01	15.12	0.22	0.49	0.42	2.39	9.87	45.67
Brazil	32.82	26.59	2.31	1.14	0.49	3.28	14.02	6.07

(continued)

TABLE 8.1 *(continued)*

Country/Region	Total Revenue	Total Tax Revenue (w/o Soc Sec)	(1) Personal Income Tax	(2a) Property Taxes	(2b) Real Estate Tax	(3) Corporate Income Tax	(4) Taxes on Goods and Services (domestic)	Ratio (4)/(1)
Chile	26.61	19.11	1.32	-	0.55	5.45	9.80	7.43
Colombia	21.12	14.69	0.18	1.01	0.60	4.60	6.89	37.34
Costa Rica	20.21	13.51	1.18	0.78	0.25	2.31	8.17	6.91
Dom. Rep.	14.84	13.75	0.90	0.6	0.04	2.41	7.08	7.85
Ecuador	19.97	13.78	0.67	0.41	0.12	2.68	7.11	10.54
El Salvador	16.62	12.62	1.86	-	-	2.01	7.11	3.83
Guatemala	12.96	11.06	0.26	0.32	0.18	2.73	6.31	24.34
Mexico	19.55	10.03	2.31	-	0.19	2.35	3.98	1.73
Paraguay	19.06	12.09	0.0	0.23	-	2.07	7.52	N/A
Peru	16.98	14.16	1.62	0.29	0.19	2.96	7.36	4.54
Uruguay	27.50	19.99	1.65	-	0.76	2.19	11.18	6.79

NB: All estimates correspond to 2000–2010, except for real estate taxes (2010–2012). For regions, figures represent averages and the number of observations is shown in parenthesis.

* Average consumption tax percentage of total revenue divided by average personal income tax percentage of revenue for the 13 countries with data for both: Bol, Bra, Chi, Col, CR, DR, Gua, Hon, Mex, Pan, Par, Per, Uru.

Sources: For regional averages, International Centre for Tax and Development (ICTD) database, available at www.ictd.ac/en/about-ictd-government-revenue-dat aset. For Latin American countries, Inter-American Development Bank/ Centro Interamericano de Administradores Tributarios database 2014, except for real estate taxes; real estate tax estimate, De Cesare 2016a, fig. 1.1a (p. 2). Corporate income taxes for Chile exclude Codelco.

Table 8.1 also shows a larger global pattern in consumption and personal income taxes. We see a pattern that is the opposite of Latin America's in the UK and countries with a history as British settler colonies: they rely (for central government revenues) much more on personal income taxes, on average, than on consumption levies. In addition, across the global data set, where personal income taxation is fiscally important, property taxation (which includes real estate taxes) is more likely to also be important.

There are important differences across Latin America, but on the relative weight of personal income, real estate, and consumption taxes, the regional signature appears in nearly all countries. The greatest divergence within the region can be found in the overall levels of taxation and the fiscal importance of resource rents. On the first measure, Brazil and Argentina collect a much higher share of GDP in taxes than do, say, Mexico and Guatemala. On the second, as discussed by Monaldi in Chapter 2 of this volume, Venezuela and Bolivia rely the most on hydrocarbon-based income. The bottom half of Table 8.1 depicts total revenues, tax revenues, and revenues from various tax types as a percentage of GDP, over the period 2000–2010 (and 2010–2012 for real estate taxes), for Latin American countries. Total revenues and tax revenues vary widely, as do the weights of personal income tax or real estate taxes in GDP. Yet the highest Latin American figure for real estate tax revenue (Uruguay with 0.76%) is still less than half the OECD average cited earlier. And when we compare the ratio of consumption-tax to personal income-tax revenues across Latin America to the average ratios for other regions, we see that only one Latin American country (Mexico) manages (barely) to fall below the OECD-Europe average.[6] This is not just a function of low income: Mexico's ratio is also the only one that is lower (meaning, less relative dependence on consumption taxes versus the PIT) than the average of thirty-four countries from sub-Saharan Africa. All in all, while the countries of the region differ greatly in their overall tax burdens, they constitute an identifiable cluster with regard to their heavy reliance on consumption taxes and the weak presence of personal income and real estate taxes.

Over the past half-century, tax reforms have both confirmed this pattern and, more recently, slightly diverged from it. From the late

6 Mexico's unusually high PIT revenue figure is due in part to the tax's low income threshold (suggesting lesser progressivity): it was the only country in a twenty-country regional OECD study "where workers pay personal income tax at the average wage level" (OECD/CIAT/IDB 2016, 15).

1960s to the late 1990s, a "neoliberal" reform wave simplified tax codes, reduced rate progressivity, strengthened tax administration, cut trade duties, and, most notably, instituted or expanded the value-added tax (VAT) (Bird 1992; Shome 1995; Mahon 2004; Thirsk 1997; Keen and Simone 2004). In the next decade or so, governments adjusted these systems, sometimes adding heterodox taxes on financial transactions, while generally taking in more revenue relative to GDP (Focanti et al. 2013). However, several recent reforms mark a halting turn in a more progressive direction. Most notably, in Uruguay (2005–2006) and Chile (2014), reformers placed new emphasis on income taxes while seeking to expand revenue for broadly redistributive goals (Rius 2015; Fairfield 2015a).[7] It also appears that international financial institutions are now paying more attention to equity in their tax recommendations, as evidenced by a recent IDB publication (Corbacho et al. 2013) and the package adopted by the Honduran government under an IMF standby loan in 2014–2015.[8]

On balance, however, fiscal redistribution in the region is still relatively meager and takes place predominantly through spending (Molina 2006; Huber and Stephens 2012, ch. 6; CEPAL/Oxfam 2016).[9] However, regarding the latter, the well-known conditional cash transfer and non-contributory pension programs represent only a small fraction of social spending in the region, which is dominated by education, health, and (generally regressive) contributory pensions.[10] Meanwhile, the countries most identified with the "new left" (Venezuela, Bolivia, Ecuador) have funded new social programs mainly from resource rents rather than taxation of consumption or income. And new, high-quality studies of tax

[7] For an assessment of conditions favoring reform, see Mahon et al. (2015, 190–194). While Caro and Stein (2013) offer some evidence for a connection between the election of left parties and increases in tax revenue in the region, they do not link this to progressivity or redistribution.

[8] Progressive features in other recent reforms include the wealth tax in Colombia (2002, then renewed), as well as schedular capital income taxes or other measures in the Dominican Republic (2012), Mexico (2013), Colombia (2014), Honduras (2015), and Ecuador (2015) (CEPAL 2015; CEPAL/Oxfam 2016).

[9] We should not exaggerate the effect of the Uruguayan reform or the likely effect of the Chilean. In Uruguay, the new PIT brought in just over 15% of gross tax revenues in 2015. Uruguay, Ministerio de Economía y Finanzas, Datos, available at www.mef.gub.uy/540/1/mef/informacion-de-resultados-del-sector-publico-a-diciembre-de-2015.html, "Recaudación DGI." Rate increases passed in mid-2016 appear unlikely, at the time of this writing, to lift the tax's contribution above 20%.

[10] On the contribution of new programs to reducing inequality, see Lustig et al. (2013); for a skeptical view, Souza et al. (2014).

incidence based on official tax return data show that those in the top 1,000th of households pay modest effective tax rates in Chile, while in Brazil their rate is lower than what is paid by the salaried upper-middle class (Fairfield and Jorratt 2015; Wulff and Orair 2015). The region's distinctive fiscal profile remains largely intact.

BETTER DEMOCRATS THAN LIBERALS

At the same time as nearly all Latin American countries have come to be ruled by elected regimes, replaced peacefully at regular intervals, the region has also seen the rise of a "new left" that combines electoral and plebiscitarian democratic forms with a pronounced opposition to neoliberalism. In many respects these regimes resemble "illiberal democracies" in other parts of the world (Zakaria 2003). In other countries of the region, meanwhile, regular elections coexist with major deficits in state capacity, most flagrantly in the control of crime but also in the realm of competition policy and the regulation of monopolies. Electoral democracy appears to have been achieved before a fully functioning state, and the state's weak spots include areas that liberals value highly.

We can see evidence of this in Figure 8.1. Here, the vertical axis is a widely used indicator of democracy, the Polity IV variable "polity," rescaled to a 0–10 range. On the horizontal axis is the sum of two components of the Heritage index of economic freedom, one relating to freedom to start and operate a business, and the other to the protection of property rights. I chose these indicators in order to look past the usual signals of neoliberal policy commitments (e.g., tariff levels) to gauge those aspects of economic liberalism most closely dependent on the functioning of the state. All values are averages for 2000–2010. Most Latin American countries are labeled with three-letter codes, while all other countries are represented by a small number indicating their region or group, in the same order as in Table 8.1. The three Latin American countries that depend most on resource rents – Venezuela, Ecuador, and Bolivia – are represented only by the region number (4), since their revenue structure is anomalous. As we can see, while Latin America clumps near the top of the chart, at the highest values of democracy, the region shows more variation on the horizontal axis, centered at around the global mean on the economic freedom indicator.[11]

[11] This impression is not greatly affected by including the major hydrocarbon exporters.

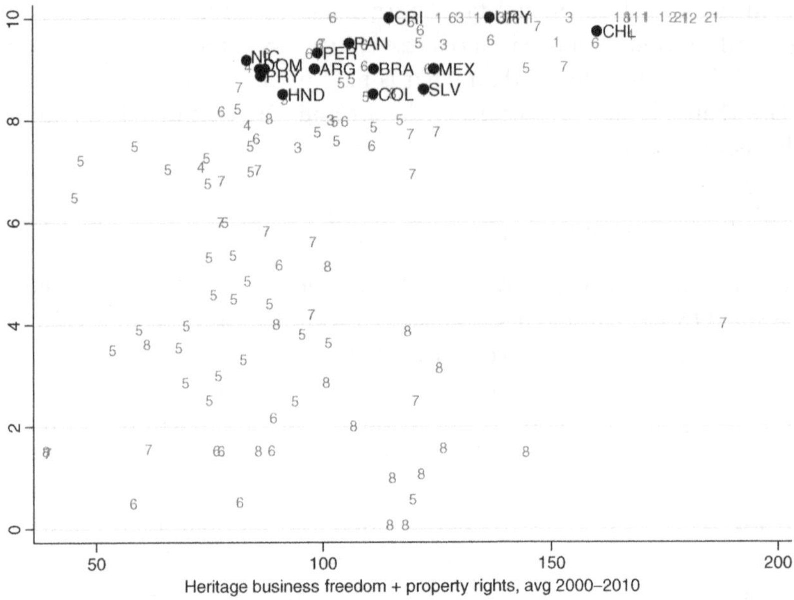

FIGURE 8.1 Relationship between democracy and liberalism
NB: Latin American countries, excluding Bolivia, Ecuador, and Venezuela (labeled), plus the rest of the world (numbers by region) on a Polity measure of democracy and the sum of two components from the Heritage index of economic freedom, business freedom, and property rights. Average of scores for 2000–2010. Regions: 1 = historic OECD Europe; 2 = UK and former British settler colonies; 3 = British and Dutch Caribbean, Japan, and Israel; 4 = Latin America; 5 = Sub-Saharan Africa; 6: Ex-Communist East Europe and Eurasia; 7 = South and East Asia; 8 = Middle East and North Africa. (Venezuela and Ecuador appear as "4" markers only, while Bolivia's "4" marker is partially hidden under the marker for Nicaragua.)
Sources: Polity IV, Marshall and Jaggers 2011; Heritage Foundation (2016)

Table 8.2 shows descriptive statistics and t-test results for different parts of the global sample on the democracy and economic liberalism measures appearing in Figure 8.1. T-tests (last column) show the difference plainly: for both Latin American groups, the test on the difference of means with the global remainder fails to reject the null for the economic liberalism variable, while rejecting it at the 99.99% level for democracy.

This pattern might surprise those who associate inequality with the undermining of democracy, or neoliberalism with the blinkered defense of property and business. Despite the region's social inequality and its governments' apparent inability to tax the rich, Latin America deviates significantly to the upside from the rest of the world on democracy, but sits

TABLE 8.2 *Descriptive statistics and t-tests for global, Latin America, and Latin America minus the three most hydrocarbon-revenue-dependent countries (Venezuela, Bolivia, Ecuador) on measures of democracy and economic liberalism*

Characteristic	Group or Sample	Obs	Mean	Standard Deviation	Median	Group Median Equals This Centile of Global Sample	t Statistic and 95% Confidence Interval for Difference of Means*
Economic Liberalism	Global	153	111.1	35.9	103.8	–	–
	Latin Am.	18	103.3	22.3	98.7	42.5	1.43 −8.95 to 26.6
	Latin Am. w/o hydrocarbon countries	15	107.9	21.5	105.9	52	0.55 −9.67 to 16.7
Democracy	Global	147	6.92	3.10	8	–	–
	Latin Am.	18	8.95	0.707	9	61–66	−7.1 −2.97 to −1.67
	Latin Am. w/o hydrocarbon countries	15	9.15	0.484	9	61–66	−8.20 −3.08 to −1.88

NB: Democracy = Polity IV "Polity" rescaled to 0–10, average for years 2000–2010 (Marshall and Jaggers 2011)

Economic Liberalism = Heritage business freedom + Heritage property rights, average 2000–2010

* test on separate groups, global mean does not include Latin Am. cases

right near the global mean on aspects of state performance concerned with operating a business or protecting property. In other words, by these measures Latin American governments are better democrats than economic liberals.

CONNECTING WEAK PROPERTY TAXATION AND WEAK LIBERALISM

What might explain this unusual combination? This section presents three kinds of evidence for a genetic connection between property taxation and liberalism. One can be found in contemporary elite political culture and another in the administrative requirements of property taxes. The third, related to the other two, comes from the region's post-Independence history, when many liberal leaders saw land taxation as the ideal fiscal foundation for their new states, yet generally failed to institute it. As we will see, the exceptions to this regional norm illustrate the connection as well.

Let us begin in the realm of political culture, with a particularly colorful example. Mireille Abelin describes a 2006 controversy in Argentina, which arose when Buenos Aires provincial tax officials tried to confiscate a late-model BMW whose owners had failed to pay property tax on it. By locking themselves in the car for seven hours while declaring that officials would have to seize them along with the vehicle, the owners created a local spectacle and sparked a national conversation. Behind their complaints of "fiscal terrorism" lay a distinctive attitude toward direct taxation, evidently shared by many in their gated community but not, as they discovered, in the working-class neighborhoods nearby, whose residents turned out in vociferous support for the authorities (2012, 329–333). Considering the incident in historical context, Abelin concludes that " the Argentine state was unable to instill in its elite subjects an ontological feeling of indebtedness, one materialized in the practice of taxation, that in Western Europe had derived from the state's successful self-fashioning as an exceptional protector of "collective rights" and a sovereign entity worthy of sacrifice."

She describes the result as a kind of "liberalism without governmentality" (2012, 348). Governmentality (here, the internalization of behavioral norms by a disciplined, liberal subject) arises from the broad acceptance of the state's role in solving coordination problems, including those involved in protecting the rights of the elite.

Political culture aside, there are also practical connections between liberal governance and direct taxation. To take the most concrete example, taxes on real estate strike an asset that, in Latin America especially, is extraordinarily unequal in its ownership. It can be argued that where they are instituted correctly, such taxes depend on two very specific forms of state capacity, the land registry and the cadastral survey, thus advancing, in tandem, the security of landed property and the tax revenue derived from it (Besley and Persson 2011, 130). In practice, though, cadastral surveys have often been incomplete or poorly maintained, while assessments have been eroded by inflation, and their updating blocked by political and legal opposition.[12] Historically, land registries accompanied tax assessment, but many registries were operated privately and their use was voluntary (Erba 2008; De Cesare 2016a, 11).

Post-Independence history offers the most persuasive evidence for a causal connection between land taxes and liberal states. In the first generation, liberal idealists sought to enact a philosophy that, in tax matters, revered the example of England after the Glorious Revolution, in which parliamentary supremacy derived, in part, from the revenue importance of the land tax (Brewer 1989, 99–100, 147). They favored the "direct contribution," which was basically a proportional property tax (Burgin 1946, 47–48, 188–189; Adelman 1999, 98; Centeno 2002, 158; Rhi 2005, 119; Pinto Bernal 2012, 54).[13] For example, regarding the Sucre government's intentions in newly founded Bolivia, Millington notes, "the idea behind direct taxes … was that, because they came proportionally out of each citizen's wealth, the citizens would demand accountability from the state concerning the use to which tax revenues were being put" (1992, 3–4; for similar sentiments in Mexico, Pinto Bernal 2012, 57). Merchants often preferred this tax to the colonial monopolies and *alcabala*. In regions that had avoided the administrative disruptions of the Independence wars, such as Jalisco, conditions for its success seemed promising (Serrano 2006, 187–189). Nevertheless, in Jalisco and most other places, the tax failed due to opposition from big landlords, general poverty, and the lack of cadastral surveys (or other ways to assess property) (Burgin 1946, 190; Santilli 2010, 45, 55; Soifer

[12] At the negative end of this spectrum, the 2012 tax reform in the Dominican Republic included changes to the country's practically inexistent tax on real property. Lacking a cadastral survey base, and given the centralized administration and destination of the tax, the tax authority invites filers to go online and calculate their tax in two steps. First, they enter the size, type, and location of their buildings into a form, which then spits out their value. They then go to a different page (on the same root menu) and enter their ID number (the tax is based on the total value attributable to one owner) to get their tax liability. Until reform reaches this part of the Dominican state, the reader can perform the first step at this site: https://dgii.gov.do/servicios/consultas/Paginas/ConsultaInmobiliaria.aspx

[13] This excludes one kind of direct tax: the head tax (*capitación*) on indigenous households.

2015, 101; Sánchez Román 2014, 2). Tenenbaum suggests that "much of the reasoning behind the adoption of centralism in the 1830s in so many countries was its tacit promise to avoid [land] taxation" (1986, 48).[14] Meanwhile, where liberal ideology was less influential, as in imperial Brazil, direct taxation was rarely even tried. Topik argues that there were "no appreciable wealth, income, or land taxes at the Federal level" at mid-century and only a few Brazilian states levied relatively insignificant land taxes (1988, 127). An 1883 imperial government report on fiscal policy stated that direct taxation of property was not under consideration (Hanley 2012, 4; Lieberman 2003, 118).[15] And even after a revolution in Mexico, well-organized rural elites blocked Obregón's attempt to decree a federal property tax (Unda 2016, 3–6).

As a result, the main pillar in the fiscal edifice of nineteenth-century Latin American states was an indirect and regressive tax, the import tariff. In fact, for most of the so called "liberal" period after about 1860, Latin America had the highest average tariff rates in the world, largely because tariffs were the easiest and, to the landowning elite, the most politically acceptable tax (Márquez 2005; Coatsworth and Williamson 2004, 221, 231).

There were two kinds of exceptions to this pattern. First, many countries did manage to achieve greater success at property taxation by around 1900, above all on urban property, although inflation would again reduce its real revenue contribution as assessments lagged. This taxation generally took place at the subnational level, mainly in the states or provinces. Argentina's 1853 constitution granted direct taxation power exclusively to the provinces, and Buenos Aires used it to greatest effect (Santilli 2010, 54–57; Herrera and Ferraro 2013, 174–176). Late in the century the Federal District in Mexico did likewise (Soifer 2015, 171). Elsewhere, however, the same pattern of liberal hope and failure at the national level could be found provincially (Pinto Bernal 2012, 61–72; Rodríguez 2014, 22; on the determinants of real estate taxation in Mexico, since 1982 devolved to municipalities, see Unda 2014).

Second, and most important here, national governments in Chile and Uruguay did impose significant (direct) taxation of property and

[14] Tortella observes that the situation was similar in Spain at this time: regarding "systematic evasion" of land tax in the mid-nineteenth century, he says the offenders were "the important people" with political clout and large holdings (2000: 182).

[15] De Cesare contradicts Topik and the other authors, tracing the Brazilian land tax to 1808 in the empire and 1891 in the republic (2016b: 39–40).

inheritances.[16] Chile established an effective land tax the earliest, by mid-century. In 1861, 31,000 properties were assessed for tax (Soifer 2015, 164). Although the revenue contribution from property tax declined under pressure from the nitrate boom later on, by the 1920s it was even stronger than before, thanks to a combination of central-government direction and local assessment (Soifer 2015, 165). In Uruguay, property taxes made up almost 13% of national tax revenue by the fiscal years 1902–1905, with business taxes contributing another 6% and inheritance taxes 1.4% (Finch 1981, table 4.1, 93). Batlle then fought to increase the fiscal importance of the *contribución inmobilaria* as part of a long struggle with powerful landowners, one that outlived him. By the 1920s its level of revenue from real estate taxes was anomalously high for the region (Finch 1981, 94–96; Bulmer-Thomas 1994, 181).

Much like post-1688 England, in both countries the imposition of taxes on land and other property accompanied a process of liberal, elite-controlled state-building. Kurtz argues that because elites lacked serious regional rifts and dominated societies of formally free labor, they could regard state-building as the solution to a collective action problem. "The Chilean elite," he comments, "was capable of taxing itself *–in advance*" to fund wars of conquest (2013, 90; emphasis in original). In Uruguay, the solution involved the definition – in favor of the largest landholders – of rural property rights (2013, 117–122). Regarding the states thus constructed, he summarizes,

> such strong institutions were initially the product of elite action and were only created where elites could cooperate around their mutual interests while guaranteeing the exclusion of other actors from the polity. That is, strong institutions were built before the social question became pressing. Indeed, elites risked their construction precisely because their control by middle- and/or working-class political actors was not anticipated. (2013, 178)

Even Batlle's precocious statism in Uruguay arrived well before the expansion of the franchise or the mobilization of workers into politics, so that "the social question was answered... long before it was posed from below" (2013, 205). And just as importantly, in contrast to Argentina, in Chile and Uruguay the public administration did not subsequently become sufficiently politicized so as to undermine its internal norms and coherence (2013, 222).

It is important not to overstate this. As in the rest of the region, during these years the most important revenue sources in Chile and Uruguay were

[16] After the federalization of Buenos Aires city in 1880, its substantial property tax income – which had represented 75% of the provincial total in 1872–passed from the provincial to national government (Oszlak 1985, 221; Santilli 2010, 57).

in fact the regressive ones – import tariffs, excises on staple goods, and inflation. (Spending was less regressive, especially as in both countries it funded a significant expansion of public education.) Thus, their pattern conforms to what we would expect from an oligarchy, almost as well as did the revenue bases of Brazil or Argentina at the time. True, it took more state capacity to tax landed property than it did to place duties on imports, or issue paper money, or revive the colonial *alcabala*.[17] But these states (like most states in Europe at that time) could not be called strong. The fundamental bias toward landlords showed up in the choice of trade taxes: export duties, which impacted rural production directly, were everywhere much less important than tariffs on widely consumed imports, even though both taxes were equally easy to collect at the ports (Oszlak 1985, 189; Soifer 2015, 162; Finch 1981, 93).

Nevertheless, we can make the following connection. The two countries that appear as most liberal (to the right) in Figure 8.1 are also the ones distinguished by historical processes of state consolidation linked to taxes on property, especially real estate. The states formed when they solved coordination problems for the elite, and part of the solution was that elites taxed themselves. Their distinctiveness endured, in what Kurtz sees as a path-dependent phenomenon – see Ondetti, Chapter 4 in this volume, for a discussion – when broad statist coalitions came to power in the aftermath of the Great Depression, and the core administrative structure was in each case able to withstand (or emerge stronger from) neoliberal military regimes later on (2013, 152–156, 214–215).[18]

Why should we expect the relationship to have persisted? On the one hand, we can see contemporary examples that follow a similar political logic – as in Colombia, where a "war tax" on wealth was imposed by a right-wing hero and used to build up the security forces, complete with mechanisms of oversight by members of the economic elite (Flores-Mac ías 2014). On the other hand, the connection should have been confounded by a host of complications – structural (federal versus unitary)

[17] It also took more capacity than reviving the colonial head tax on indigenous communities (at least when this was done soon after Independence), since this had come to be viewed as a customary price for recognition of their communal property by the state (Jáuregui 2006, 35).

[18] The expansion of the state's size and the scope of its activities would not necessarily undermine its effectiveness at basic liberal functions. See Mahon (2014) or the ranking of, say, The Netherlands in the World Economic Forum's Global Competitiveness Index: https://www.weforum.org/reports/the-global-competitveness-report-2018

differences, the inflationary erosion of property tax bases,[19] and contention over tax policy in democracies (as in contemporary Chile). Yet a rough correspondence does appear in recent data. Figure 8.2 plots real estate taxes as a percentage of GDP against the measure used above, the sum of the business freedom and property rights components of the Heritage economic freedom index.[20]

FIGURE 8.2 Real estate taxes as a percentage of GDP against the sum of Heritage business freedom and Heritage property rights (components of the Economic Freedom Index), averages for 2010–2012
NB: from De Cesare 2016a, fig. 1.1a

[19] De Cesare and her co-authors describe a variety of causes for the slippages and unfulfilled potential of the real estate tax in the region: incomplete or outdated cadastral surveys (common); outdated property assessments (very common); weak enforcement; a multiplicity of exemptions; and politicians' reluctance or outright refusal to reform or even collect the tax. Yet relative success was found in a few places, such as Belo Horizonte and Bogotá. In particular, see De Cesare 2016a, 3–12; and, in the same volume, Montaña 2016, 100; Román 2016a: 136; Román 2016b, 186, 192; and Barrera 2016, 207–209.

[20] A plot of real estate taxes against the sum of three components of the World Bank World Governance Indicators (rule of law, regulatory quality, and control of corruption) shows a similar pattern, while the democracy measure used above (Polity IV), largely because of its lack of variation in the sample, shows no correlation. Details on request.

LATIN AMERICAN TAXATION AND THEORIES OF FISCAL POLITICS

How do these patterns conform to the expectations of different theories of fiscal politics? As noted earlier, the widely used median-voter model would lead us to expect much more redistribution than we see – although in fairness, recent innovations in social spending and (in a few countries) progressive taxation have brought the region slightly closer to its predictions. Adding a premise of capital mobility (Boix 2003), although obviously plausible, does not actually explain the low levels of taxation on immobile real estate, nor does it square with the region's rather average levels of corporate income tax revenue (Table 4.2).[21] Following Scheve and Stasavage (2016), we might instead point to the lack of the distinctive combination of democracy and mass conscription that brought highly progressive income taxation to the combatant countries of the twentieth-century world wars (135–169). Still, many Latin American countries have had both democracy and a military draft, and in practice the rich and well-connected manage to avoid the latter (Rouquié 1987, 94–97; Torres 2011), just like they probably pay income tax at significantly lower rates than do those in the upper-middle deciles who are subject to withholding (Wulff and Orair 2015). In a way that is compatible with Fairfield's analysis (Chapter 5), the contrast between Latin America and other regions is best explained by positing oligarchical domination in the region (Winters 2011), under which members of economic elites avoid taxes while capturing substantial benefits of state spending, even under democracy (e.g., Best 1976, 50; Sokoloff and Zolt 2007). But this theory does not capture the variation across the region, in which Chile and Uruguay stand out. Here, the apparent genetic connection between greater state capacity and the early taxation of land recalls the model of the "fiscal contract."

This model requires a bit of explanation. It begins from two plausible premises: agents pay their taxes at lower political cost when they enjoy corresponding benefits themselves; and politicians seek both to maximize revenue and minimize political costs, in the interest of securing or expanding their rule (Levi 1988; Timmons 2005). The model's historical archetype, from early modern Europe, begins with the pressing need for ever-increasing revenue due to recurrent warfare (Levi 1988). It does not

[21] While we should suspect that this could be due to revenue from corporations in the mining sector, the pattern of company income taxes across Latin America in Table 8.1 suggests that this is only part of the answer.

prescribe a temporal order to innovations on taxation or governance. Formally, Besley and Persson (2011) model the "fiscal capacity" to gather tax revenue and the "legal capacity" to protect property rights as pure complements. The authors do not describe any actual transactions and note that the presence of the relationship is merely consistent with the data.[22] Yet this is not necessarily unrealistic: Wallis argues that local property taxes in the USA are benefit taxes, funding local public goods that enhance property values, and that it is this diffuse boon rather than a formal bargain that persuades owners to pay (2001, 141).

The fiscal-contract model thus offers a way to account for differences in state capacity by connecting them to historical paths of public finance. No Latin American states have been the perfectly capable instrument assumed by median-voter theory, and the most important moments of state formation involve not redistribution (the main object of taxation under the median-voter model) but rather a process by which a ruling group used taxation to solve a coordination problem – above all, to pay for war. In general, although a basic level of state capacity is a prerequisite for productive "contracts," additions to capacity can also be the result of bargains that grant taxpayers compensation in the form of policies and institutions they desire. Given the tendency of tax reforms and new institutions to layer themselves upon older ones, the aggregate result of a series of negotiations like this would be a pattern in which a tax structure roughly corresponds to spending, policies, or institutional characteristics whose origins lay in implicit or explicit exchanges for revenue, sometimes far in the past. This implies that the shape of a country's tax system could have a counterpart in the institutional capacities – or incapacities – of its government. The tests on contemporary data appear to confirm this.

THE USES OF STATE CAPACITY

Perhaps it should not surprise us that areas of a state administration developed a century ago for one set of tasks should provide a resource for facing current challenges. Part of what it means to be a capable administrative body is to evolve with the times. Censuses and property assessments are updated; budget-makers adopt new computer software

[22] A key difference is that under "legal capacity" they consider only the prevention of expropriation of one private agent by another. They mention but do not model the creation of limits on state incursions on private property (Besley and Persson 2011, 11, 162–164).

and storage options; and relevant ministries create web portals that offer detailed transparency on expenditures and internet sites that allow businesses small and large to file their value-added taxes remotely. What did state capacity have to do with the fact that Uruguay and Chile were also the two countries in which unambiguously progressive tax reforms were implemented in 2006 and 2014?

In each case, reformers deployed the considerable competence of their fiscal administrations. The Uruguayan tax authority (DGI) prepared credible incidence estimates for the 2006 tax package and thus helped weaken opposition from those who perceived themselves as "middle class" (Rius 2015, 73–75). In Chile, protesters championed reforms that would hand several percent of GDP to the country's tax agency, thence to be spent by the state on expanding education. This demand would have been almost inconceivable in Mexico, given widespread popular doubts regarding the competence of the corresponding ministries in that country.

An important question remains, however. Thinking about indicators of governance, why should effective economic liberalism be more closely associated with state capacity than is electoral democracy? Here the answer must be speculative, but one contrast seems obvious. Electoral authorities constitute discrete, relatively small administrative bodies whose performance is limited in time and scope, highly visible to news media and the voting public, and routinely observed by international experts. Reforms of electoral law regularly borrow from international best practices, usually without nationalistic qualms (on campaign finance, see Casas-Zamora and Zovatto 2015, 7). Elites who expect to govern under an electoral mandate have a direct stake in the legitimacy of election results. Protecting the property rights of those without wealth or political connections is another matter. Leaving aside the depredations of organized crime and corrupt police forces, many countries' weak patent enforcement and compromised regulatory authorities leave new market entrants unprotected against opportunistic theft and noncompliance by crony capitalists and established firms. The region's overloaded, inaccessible, and pliable judicial systems aid incumbent players with wealth and influence, as cases drag on for decades and money can often buy a favorable decision. (The same courts that privilege rich defendants against the poor tend to favor them when the tax authority is the claimant.) And all this takes place continuously, largely out of the public eye. Of course, this is part of a larger failure of democratic government. It is arguably just the property-rights side of what Guillermo O'Donnell called "low-intensity citizenship" (1993, 1361), which happens to show up in the handful of governance indicators we have consulted here.

CONCLUSION

This chapter has argued that two apparently distinct puzzles about Latin America are actually related. The first consists of the fact that this socially unequal yet mostly democratic region shows very low levels of progressive personal income and property taxation. The second notes that despite the apparent power of the Latin American rich to escape taxation, property rights protection is relatively weak there. It proposes that intraregional differences in the history of taxation and state formation give us an account of how weak property taxation is the counterpart to weak protection of property rights and low subjective levels of business freedom. While oligarchic domination and regressive taxation remained the norm in the region's early history, in Chile and Uruguay state formation took place as elites solved collective action problems by empowering the state and, to some extent at least, taxing their own property. Not coincidentally, perhaps, today Chile and Uruguay also stand out as exceptions to a regional prevalence of electorally democratic but (on key measures) economically illiberal regimes. They are also the only places where major progressive tax reforms have been implemented successfully in the past ten years. And general state capacity, it appears, is much more important to the everyday provision of the rule of law, including liberal priorities such as the broad protection of property rights, than it is to electoral democracy.

References

Abelin, Mireille. 2012. "'Entrenched in the BMW': Argentine Elites and the Terror of Fiscal Obligation," *Public Culture* 24(2):329–56.

Adelman, Jeremy. 1999. *Republic of Capital: Buenos Aires and the Legal Transformation of the Atlantic World*. Stanford: Stanford University Press.

Barrera, Saúl. 2016. "Perú," in Cláudia De Cesare (ed.), *Sistemas del Impuesto Predial*. Cambridge, MA: Lincoln Institute of Land Policy, 195–220.

Besley, Timothy and Torsten Persson. 2011. *Pillars of Prosperity: The Political Economics of Development Clusters*. Princeton: Princeton University Press.

Best, Michael. 1976. "Political Power and Tax Revenues in Central America," *Journal of Development Economics* 3(1): 49–82.

Bird, Richard. 1991. "The Taxation of Personal Wealth in International Perspective," *Canadian Public Policy/Analyse de Politiques* 17(3): 322–334.

1992. "Tax Reform in Latin America: A Review of Some Recent Experiences," *Latin American Research Review* 27: 7–36.

2013. "Taxation and Development: What Have We Learned from Fifty Years of Research?" *IDS Working Papers* 427: 1–19.

Bird, Richard and Eric Zolt. 2015. "Fiscal Contracting in Latin America," *World Development* 67: 323–335.

Boix, Carles. 2003. *Democracy and Redistribution.* Cambridge: Cambridge University Press.

Brewer, John. 1989. *The Sinews of Power: War, Money, and the English State, 1688–1783.* New York: Knopf.

Bulmer-Thomas, Victor. 1994. *The Economic History of Latin America since Independence.* Cambridge: Cambridge University Press.

Burgin, Miron. 1946. *The Economic Aspects of Argentine Federalism, 1820–1852.* Cambridge, MA: Harvard University Press.

Campello, Daniela and Cesar Zucco. 2015. "Merit, Chance, and the International Determinants of Government Success," Working Paper, Getúlio Vargas Foundation, Rio de Janeiro.

Caro, Lorena and Ernesto Stein. 2013. "Ideology and Taxation in Latin America," Inter-American Development Bank Working Paper 407. Washington, DC: IDB (May).

Casas-Zamora, Kevin and Daniel Zovatto. 2015. "The Cost of Democracy: Campaign Finance Regulation in Latin America," Policy Brief, Latin America Initiative, Brookings Institution, Washington DC (July).

Centeno, Miguel. 2002. *Blood and Debt: War and the Nation-State in Latin America.* University Park: Penn State Press.

CEPAL. 2015. *Panorama Fiscal de América Latina y el Caribe 2015: dilemas y espacios de políticas.* Santiago, Chile (March).

Coatsworth, John and Jeffrey Williamson. 2004. "Always Protectionist? Latin American Tariffs from Independence to the Great Depression," *Journal of Latin American Studies* 36(May): 205–232.

CEPAL/Oxfam. 2016. "Tributación para un Crecimiento Inclusivo," Comisión Económica para América Latina y el Caribe, Santiago, Chile (March).

Corbacho, Ana, Vicente Freites, and Eduardo Lora (eds.). 2013. *More than Revenue: Taxation as Development Tool.* Washington, DC: Inter-American Development Bank.

De Cesare, Cláudia. 2016a. "Relevancia del Impuesto Inmobilario," in Cláudia De Cesare (ed.), *Sistemas del Impuesto Predial.* Cambridge, MA: Lincoln Institute of Land Policy, 1–12.

2016b. "Brasil," in Cláudia De Cesare (ed.), *Sistemas del Impuesto Predial.* Cambridge, MA: Lincoln Institute of Land Policy, 37–76.

De Soto, Hernando. 2000. *The Mystery of Capital: Why Capitalism Triumphs in the West and Fails Everywhere Else.* New York: Basic Books.

Erba, Diago. 2008. *El Catastro Territorial en América Latina y el Caribe.* Cambridge, MA: Lincoln Institute for Land Policy.

Fairfield, Tasha. 2015a. "The Political Economy of Progressive Tax Reform in Chile," in James Mahon, Marcelo Bergman, and Cynthia Arnson (eds.),

Progressive Tax Reform and Equality in Latin America. Washington, DC: Woodrow Wilson International Center for Scholars, 30–56.

2015b. *Private Wealth and Public Revenue: Business power and tax politics in Latin America*. New York: Cambridge University Press.

Fairfield, Tasha. and Michel Jorratt. 2015. "Top Income Shares, Business Profits, and Effective Tax Rates in Contemporary Chile," *Review of Income and Wealth* 62(S1): 120–144.

Finch, Martin. 1981. *A Political Economy of Uruguay since 1870*. New York: St. Martin's Press.

Flores-Macías, Gustavo. 2014. "Financing Security through Elite Taxation: The Case of Colombia's 'Democratic Security Taxes,'" *Studies in Comparative International Development* 49(4): 477–500.

Focanti, Diego, Mark Hallerberg, and Carlos Scartascini. 2013. "Tax Reforms in Latin America in an Era of Democracy," IDB Working Paper 457. Washington, DC: Inter-American Development Bank.

Hanley, Anne. 2012. "A Failure to Deliver: Municipal Poverty and the Provision of Public Services in Imperial São Paulo, Brazil 1822–1889," *Journal of Urban History* 39(3): 513–535.

Harberger, Arnold C. 1962. "The Incidence of the Corporation Income Tax Source," *Journal of Political Economy* 70(3; Jun.): 215–240.

Heritage Foundation. 2016. "Index of Economic Freedom," historical data (Washington, DC: Heritage Fdn.). Available at www.heritage.org/index/download.

Herrera, Claudia and Agustín Ferraro. 2013. "Friends' Tax: Patronage, Fiscality, and State Building in Argentina and Spain," in Miguel Centeno and Agustín Ferraro (eds.), *State and Nation Making in Latin America and Spain: Republics of the Possible*. New York: Cambridge University Press, 157–180.

Huber, Evelyne and John Stephens. 2012. *Democracy and the Left: Social Policy and Inequality in Latin America*. Chicago: University of Chicago Press.

Jáuregui, Luis. 2006. "'De Re Tributaria': ¿Qué Son las Contribuciones Directas?" in Luis Jáuregui (ed.), *De Riqueza e Inequidad: el Problema de las Contribuciones Directas en América Latina, Siglo XIX*. México City: Instituto Mora, 9–46.

Keen, Michael and Alejandro Simone. 2004. "Tax Policy in Developing Countries: Some Lessons from the 1990s and Some Challenges Ahead," in Sanjeev Gupta, Benedict Clements, and Gabriela Inchauste (eds.), *Helping Countries Develop: The Role of Fiscal Policy*. Washington, DC: International Monetary Fund, 302–352.

Kurtz, Marcus. 2013. *Latin American State-building in Comparative Perspective: Social Foundations of Institutional Order*. New York: Cambridge University Press.

Levi, Margaret. 1988. *Of Rule and Revenue*. Berkeley: University of California.

Lieberman, Evan. 2003. *Race and Regionalism in the Politics of Taxation in Brazil and South Africa*. Cambridge: Cambridge University Press.

Lustig, Nora, Luis López-Calva, and Eduardo Ortiz-Juárez. 2013. "Deconstructing the decline in inequality in Latin America." World Bank Policy Research Working Paper (6552).

Mahon, James. 2004. "Causes of Tax Reform in Latin America," *Latin American Research Review* 37: 3–30.

2012. "Tax Incidence and Tax Reforms in Latin America," Woodrow Wilson Center Update on the Americas (November).

2014. "Economic Freedom and the Size of Government," *Challenge* 57: 1(Jan–Feb).

Mahon, James, Marcelo Bergman, and Cynthia Arnson. 2015. "The Political Economy of Tax Reform in Latin America – Comparative Context and Policy Debates," in Mahon, Bergman, and Arnson (eds.), *Progressive Tax Reform and Equality in Latin America*. Washington, DC: Woodrow Wilson International Center for Scholars, 1–29.

Márquez, Graciela. 2005. "Aranceles a la Importación y Finanzas Públicas: Del Porfiriato a la Crisis de 1929," in Luis Aboites and Luis Jáuregui (eds.), *Penuria sin Fin: Historia de los Impuestos en México Siglos XVIII-XX*. México City: Instituto Mora, 141–160.

Marshall, Monty and Keith Jaggers. 2011. *Polity IV Dataset* [Computer file; version p4v2010], College Park, MD: Center for International Development and Conflict Management, University of Maryland.

Meltzer, Allan and Scott Richard. 1981. "A Rational Theory of the Size of Government," *Journal of Political Economy* 89: 914–927.

Millington, Thomas. 1992. *Debt Politics after Independence: The Funding Conflict in Bolivia*. Gainesville: University Press of Florida.

Molina, Carlos (ed.). 2006. *Universalismo Básico: Una Nueva Política Social para América Latina*. Washington, DC: Inter-American Development Bank.

Montaña, Magda. 2016. "Colombia," in Cláudia De Cesare (ed.), *Sistemas del Impuesto Predial*. Cambridge, MA: Lincoln Institute of Land Policy, 99–122.

O'Donnell, Guillermo. 1993. "On the State, Democratization and Some Conceptual Problems: A Latin American View with Glances at Some Post-communist Countries," *World Development* 21(8), 1355–1369.

OECD/CIAT/IDB. 2016. *Taxing Wages in Latin* America *and the Caribbean*. Paris: OECD Publishing.

Oszlak, Oscar. 1985. *La Formación del Estado Argentino*. Buenos Aires: Belgrano.

Pinto Bernal, José. 2012. "Los Orígenes del Impuesto Directo y Progresivo en América Latina," *Historia y Sociedad* (Medellín) 23: 53–77.

Rhi, María José. 2005. "'¿Cómo Aventurarse a Perder lo que Existe?': Una Reflexión sobre el Voluntarismo Fiscal Mexicano del Siglo XIX," in Luis Aboites and Luis Jáuregui (eds.), *Penuria sin Fin: Historia de los Impuestos en México Siglos XVIII-XX*. México City: Instituto Mora, 115–140.

Rius, Andrés. 2015. "The Uruguayan Tax Reform of 2006: Why Did It Not Fail?" in Mahon, Bergman, and Arnson (eds.), *Progressive Tax Reform and*

Equality in Latin America. Washington, DC: Woodrow Wilson International Center for Scholars, 64–100.

Rodríguez, Pablo. 2014. "Comprendiendo a Leviatán: El Estudio Fiscal como Clave para Analizar la Formación de los Estados Hispanoamericanos en el Siglo XIX," *Revista de Historia* 69: 13–26.

Román, Marcela. 2016a. "Costa Rica," in Cláudia De Cesare (ed.), *Sistemas del Impuesto Predial*. Cambridge, MA: Lincoln Institute of Land Policy, 123–148.

2016b. "Guatemala," in C. De Cesare (ed.), *Sistemas del Impuesto Predial*. Cambridge, MA: Lincoln Institute of Land Policy.

Rouquié, A. 1987. *The Military and the State in Latin America*. Berkeley: University of California Press.

Sánchez Román, José. 2014. "Impuestos y Terratenientes en la Argentina: Un Balance," *Anuario del Instituto de Historia Argentina* 14:2–17.

Santilli, Daniel. 2010. "El Papel de la Tributación en la Formación del Estado: La Contribución Directa en el Siglo XIX en Buenos Aires," *América Latina en la Historia Económica* 33: 30–63.

Scheve, Kenneth and David Stasavage. 2016. *Taxing the Rich: A History of Fiscal Fairness in the United States and Europe*. Princeton: Princeton University Press.

Sepúlveda, Cristian and Jorge Martinez-Vazquez. 2009. "Property Taxation in Latin-America: An Assessment and Options for Reform," in CEPAL-GTZ conference, "Relaciones intergubernamentales y descentralización en América Latina." Santiago, Chile: November.

Serrano, José. 2006. "Contribuciones Directas y Reformas Fiscales en las Regiones de México, 1820–1836," in Luis Jáuregui (ed.), *De Riqueza e Inequidad: el Problema de las Contribuciones Directas en América Latina, Siglo XIX*. México City: Instituto Mora, 183–224.

Shome, Partasarathi. 1995. "Tax Reform in Latin America," *Finance and Development* 32(1) (March): 14–16.

Soifer, Hillel. 2015. *State Building in Latin America*. New York: Cambridge University Press.

Sokoloff, Kenneth and Eric Zolt. 2007. "Inequality and the Evolution of Institutions of Taxation: Evidence from the Economic History of the Americas," in Sebastian Edwards, Gerardo Esquivel, and Graciela Márquez (eds.), *The Decline of Latin American Economies: Growth, Institutions and Crises*. Chicago: University of Chicago Press, 83–136.

Souza, Pedro, Marcelo Medeiros, and Fabio Castro. 2014. "Top Incomes in Brazil: Preliminary Results" (October 23). Available at SSRN: https://papers.ssrn.com/sol3/papers.cfm?abstract_id=2511314

Tenenbaum, Barbara. 1986. *The Politics of Penury: Debt and Taxes in Mexico, 1821–1856*. Albuquerque: University of New Mexico Press.

Thirsk, Wayne. 1997. "Overview: The Substance and Process of Tax Reform in Eight Developing Countries," in Wayne Thirsk (ed.), *Tax Reform in Developing Countries*. World Bank Sectoral and Regional Studies, Washington, DC: World Bank, 1–32.

Timmons, Jeffrey. 2005. "The Fiscal Contract: States, Taxes, and Public Services," *World Politics* 57: 530–567.

Topik, Steven. 1988. "Brazil and Mexico Compared, 1888–1910," in Joseph Love and Nils Jacobsen (eds.), *Guiding the Invisible Hand: Economic Liberalism and the State in Latin American History*. New York: Praeger, 117–144.

Torres, J. E. 2011. "Colombia's 'Obligatory' Military Service: The Arbitrary Role of Class Disparity," *Colombia Reports* (25 July).

Tortella, Gabriel. 2000. *The Development of Modern Spain: An Economic History of the Nineteenth and Twentieth Centuries*, trans. V. Herr. Cambridge, MA: Harvard University Press.

Unda, Mónica. 2014. "Una Hacienda Local Pobre: Los Determinantes de la Recaudación Predial en México," Working Paper, Lincoln Institute for Land Policy.

2016. "A Tale of Two Taxes: The Diverging Fates of the Federal Property and Income Tax Decrees in Post-revolutionary México." *Investigaciones de Historia Económica- Economic History Research* 13(2): 107–116.

UN-ECLAC (United Nations Economic Commission for Latin América and the Caribbean). 2013. *Fiscal Panorama of Latin America and the Caribbean 2013: Tax Reform and Renewal of the Fiscal Covenant*. Santiago: CEPAL (February).

Uruguay, Ministerio de Economía y Finanzas. 2016. *Datos*, "Recaudación DGI."

Wallis, John. 2001. "A History of the Property Tax in America," in Wallace Oates (ed.), *Property Taxation and Local Government Finance*. Cambridge, MA: Lincoln Institute for Land Policy, 123–147.

Winters, Jeffrey. 2011. *Oligarchy*. New York: John Wiley and Sons.

Wulff, Sérgio and Rodrigo Orair. 2015. "Tributação e distribuição da renda no Brasil: novas evidências a partir das declarações tributárias das pessoas físicas," One Pager Portuguese 312, International Policy Centre for Inclusive Growth.

Zakaria, Fareed. 2003. *The Future of Freedom: Illiberal Democracy at Home and Abroad*. New York: Norton.

9

Preferences for Redistribution and Tax Burdens in Latin America

Juan A. Bogliaccini and Juan Pablo Luna

Diverse studies of the political economy of tax composition across middle-income countries have found that Latin American economies tax upper-income groups much less than do other developing regions, such as East Asia and Eastern Europe (i.e., Di John 2006; Mahon, Chapter 8 in this volume). As the Introduction to this volume suggests, this finding is consistent with the relatively low redistributive capacity Latin American states display when compared to advanced capitalist societies. Sharp within-region differences remain even during periods of significant inequality reduction in the region, such as during the most recent decade (see Lustig and Pereira 2016). Against this backdrop, this chapter analyzes cross-national differences in how distributive preferences map onto class and political attitudes.

Latin America is a heterogeneous region in terms of the strength and stability of democratic institutions and party system configurations (Mainwaring and Scully 2010; Kitschelt et al. 2010). However, the resilience of democratic rule in the region during the last three decades is also historically unprecedented. As Mahon highlights (Chapter 8 in this volume), the region thus combines stable democratic rule and high inequality, in a context where significant – though comparatively marginal – reductions in inequality occurred during the last decade and a half. The region is also characterized by diversity in party system configuration, programmatic structure and stability, and state capacity (Kurtz 2013; Soifer 2015). These characteristics, in a context of high inequality, affect the degree to which distributive preferences are consistent with objective class position, and are subsequently translated (or not) into political ideology, vote choice, and, eventually, effectively enforced public policy.

Authors continue to debate the relative impact of progressive taxation and social spending versus the impact of economic growth in reducing inequality in a context of increasing human capital and the unfolding of the so-called "commodity boom" circa 2005–2015 (Huber and Stephens 2012; Lustig and Pereira 2016). As Ondetti's, Schneider's, and Hallerberg and Scartascini's chapters (4, 5, and 6, respectively) suggest, there has been a tendency to increase taxation levels and social expenditure throughout the region, although at different paces. Policy innovations also might have reshaped redistributive preferences in the region, particularly in cases where the (usually progressive) middle class has been taxed to fund the expansion of social assistance to poorer segments of the population.

Overall, however, the region is characterized by states that redistribute less than their European and North American counterparts (see Lustig and Pereira 2016; Mahon, Chapter 8 in this volume). That is, the gap between market income and income after taxes and transfers is substantially smaller in Latin America. There are several possible explanations for this result, including weak state capacity, as suggested earlier (Soifer 2015); elites' instrumental and structural power in Latin American societies (Bogliaccini and Luna 2016; Fairfield 2015 and Chapter 7 in this volume); economic informality and the role of illegal enterprises in generating revenue (Dargent et al. 2017); the lack of programmatic structure in Latin American party systems linking societal preferences to policy output (Kitschelt et al. 2010); the resources curse (Ross 1999; Maloney et al. 2002; Monaldi, Chapter 2 in this volume); differences in tax morale within the region and across regions (Alm and Torgler 2006; Bergman, Chapter 3 in this volume); the perceived linkages between crime and inequality (Morgan and Kelly 2010; Alesina and Giuliano 2011); or "false consciousness" on the part of the poor (Haggard and Kaufman 2016). These various explanations each posit different causal mechanisms to elucidate the weak redistributive role that Latin American states play.

This chapter explores the role of three hypothesized causes, by working around the scant comparative public opinion data on Latin American citizens' preferences and opinions regarding taxation. Our empirical exploration partially taps into the structure of societal preferences regarding taxation and explores the extent to which distributive preferences in the region are structured by political ideology, economic well-being, and class position. In contrast to previous work that examined attitudes toward redistribution (e.g., Blofield and Luna 2011; Haggard and Kaufman 2016), we explore support for progressive taxation.

Furthermore, in doing so, we avoid "earmark" questions that assess respondents' willingness to increase taxes for a particular type of spending (e.g., public education, pensions, health, environmental improvements, and increased budget allocated to public safety). Although focusing only on nonearmarked public-opinion questions restricts our analytical exercise to a single survey item included in the AmericasBarometer, this limitation pays off in terms of obtaining a purer attitude measure regarding tax distribution between the rich and the poor.

In addition, and, by analyzing indirect reports on tax enforcement, also drawn from the AmericasBarometer data – which contribute to circumventing indicator problems related to social desirability biases – we provide a comparative assessment of the role of state capacity in extracting resources from society through VAT taxes in contemporary Latin America.[1] Specifically, the question we use asks respondents how often they receive a formal receipt while shopping at a local store.

Our analysis is admittedly exploratory and descriptive. As such, we cannot determine which of various possible causes explains why public opinion is not consistent with objective conditions, nor can we determine whether capacity or political will accounts for weak enforcement. Our exploration is further limited by the availability of data on taxation, and also by the (at best) partial causal role societal preferences and state capacity might play in shaping net levels of taxation and effective resource extraction, as well as their role in implementing progressive redistribution.

The analysis points toward three conclusions about the region. First, Latin American countries exhibit a low level of tax collection enforcement, which is consistent with its low levels of overall state capacity as compared to Europe and the United States. Second, preferences regarding taxation should be interpreted as being formed in such low-enforcement contexts. Third, with the data at hand, we fail to identify a region-wide preference structure regarding redistribution. The heterogeneity of observed preferences likely relates to countries' heterogeneous configurations and over-time trajectories in terms of inequality levels (and shapes), the stability of democratic institutions, and state capacity.

The lack of a systematic relationship between class position and redistributive preferences is thus a central finding of our work. Differences in attitudes toward redistribution linked to short-term pocketbook evaluations

[1] It is worth noting that nonenforcement of the VAT tax might end up having, by default, progressive results (see Holland (2015) for an argument on forbearance as an implicit redistributive policy).

are observed in a very diverse group of cases, and yet the causal mechanisms underpinning that correlation might differ sharply across cases. We also observe a very weak empirical relationship between political beliefs and redistributive preferences.

The chapter is organized as follows. We first explore theoretical arguments regarding distributive preferences that might be relevant to our case. Subsequently, we describe the structure of public opinion concerning redistribution and its relationship to political ideology, self-perceived economic well-being, and class position in ten Latin American countries. We then present an indicator of VAT enforcement in Latin America to briefly analyze the levels of tax enforcement across the region. The last section presents our conclusions.

PREFERENCES FOR REDISTRIBUTION AND TAXATION

There is a well-established literature on individual preferences for redistribution, mostly in the traditions of political science, economics, and psychology. However, most available research focuses on the developed world. Meltzer and Richard's influential article proposed that those with below-median incomes would at least favor some degree of redistribution while those with incomes above the median would not (Meltzer and Richard 1981). In this well-known model, individuals only care about their consumption (income). Therefore, an increase in income inequality is expected to produce greater public support for redistribution. More importantly, in a context in which citizens regularly vote their preferences (i.e., democracy), inequality is expected to yield redistribution.

That assumption is pivotal in influential works that address the relationship between inequality and regime transitions such as Boix (2003) and Acemoglu and Robinson (2006). However, many important disconfirmations and qualifications to Meltzer and Richard have appeared over the last three decades (cf. Cramer and Kaufman 2011; Blofield 2011 for evidence regarding Latin America; Bartels 2008; Przeworski 2010; Gilens 2012; Ansell and Samuels 2014; Luna 2014; Campello 2015; Haggard and Kaufman 2016).

The literature that relates levels of societal inequality to preferences concerning redistribution is particularly important for the Latin American case. Some studies support Meltzer and Richard's assumption. However, others tend to disconfirm that conclusion. Bénabou (2000) finds that popular support for welfare-enhancing redistribution will fall in response to increases in inequality. Kelly and Enns (2010), while looking at the

United States, claim that the public mood (an indicator of public opinion preferences over time) tends to counterbalance the ideological outputs of government, which is consistent with the stasis model proposed by Erikson et al. (2002). Luttig's work (2013) on public opinion in the United States supports Kelly and Enns' findings (2010). Kenworthy and McCall (2008), on the basis of a cross-sectional analysis of countries included in the Luxemburg Income Study, find that greater market inequality will tend to produce greater redistributive program generosity. Their finding contradicts those of Cramer and Kaufman (2011) and Blofield and Luna (2011) for Latin America. Lupu and Pontusson (2011), in turn, claim that the median voter's distributive preferences are driven not by the level of inequality, but by its shape. In this regard, they claim that the relative distance between middle-income voters, low-income voters, and high-income voters determines, ceteris paribus, the likelihood of observing a median-voter redistributive coalition (low- and middle-income voters) or a pro-status quo coalition (middle- and high-income voters). More recently, Holland (2018) argues that in truncated welfare states (i.e., welfare states that do not reach the poor and informal sectors) poor voters do not support redistributive efforts because they do not expect social policy to benefit them.

Both the perception of economic well-being and that of individuals' own economic situation (the latter usually tied to opportunities for upward mobility) are short-term factors that have repeatedly been reported as significant determinants of redistributive preferences in Latin America (Gaviria et al. 2007; Morgan and Kelly 2013). There is also an established literature on the link between attitudes toward redistribution and the position of each individual on the socioeconomic ladder, following Meltzer and Richard (1981). Some of these studies link individual preferences for redistribution to the nature of social mobility in society (Alesina and La Ferrara 2005; Bénabou and Ok 2001). Bénabou and Ok, for instance, argue that the poor might support the status quo (instead of redistribution) when they expect themselves or their offspring to achieve upward mobility. A related strand in the literature stresses the important effect of individuals' self-perceived social position on their attitudes toward redistribution, while claiming that those self-perceptions can change in response to short-term economic factors. Dallinger (2010) finds that citizens do not react directly to actual levels of inequality, but to relative levels of prosperity. Therefore, individuals in rich societies tend to define the market as the place where they can secure their income, and thus end up assigning lesser responsibility to the state's redistributive policies. In other words, preferences concerning social policy change according to economic context. It is only when wage fairness fails, Dillinger finds, that equality is expected to be realized by the state. In the same vein, Margalit (2013) finds that preferences regarding redistribution are, in the short term, strongly affected by changes in individuals' own economic circumstances, with the loss of employment having a major effect. Nevertheless, prior ideological commitments were found to remain an important factor in any account of individual policy preferences. Relatedly, Doyle (2015) argues that in countries where poor segments of the population receive large amounts of wire-transfers from abroad ("remesas") and thus do better economically, redistributive pressure on the state is significantly lessened.

In highly unequal societies, such as those in Latin America, social distance might impact distributive preferences through different individual-level mechanisms. For instance, inequality might shape the demand side of the representation equation by inducing a series of psychological effects at the individual level. Accordingly, high inequality might contribute to consolidating cognitive biases that could be consequential for political preference formation (see Shapiro 2002). "Empathy" and "physical distance" gulfs might emerge among individuals living immersed in different and segregated socioeconomic settings (Shapiro 2002). Those cognitive gulfs distort the translation of the effects of inequality into political preferences across segregated settings – for instance, by making differences among localities or social groups invisible (and therefore, nonconsequential for political action). Different "framing" effects could also contribute to the emergence of distinct foci of attention across social settings and groups, whose preference formation is primed, once again, in a socially segmented fashion. Overall, these processes make it more difficult for parties to engage in distributive preference formation and mobilization across social groups. Last, but not least, the capacity of powerful economic interests to lobby the political system and shape media discourse also plays a role in shaping policy output in a direction that serves the interests of the better-off members of society (see Gilens 2012; Bartels 2008).

Framing effects are also relevant for understanding elite behavior, which is the focus of another series of works (see particularly Reis 2011). Such research illustrates how elite preferences in high-inequality contexts and even in the presence of increasing security concerns continue to be strongly regressive. The latter defies O'Donnell's (1996) hypothesis regarding the possibility of a new redistributive pact to alleviate poverty emerging in Latin America under threats to elites from increasing criminality. Indeed, evidence on the recent success of the Colombian security tax clearly suggests that the levy on Colombian elites was only viable due to the government's earmarking strategy (Rodríguez 2011; Flores-Macías 2015).

The abovementioned individual-level arguments are consistent with a more abstract argument, which claims that system justifying ideologies held by the poor weaken support for social change and redistribution of resources (Jost and Thompson 2000; Jost and Hunyady 2005). In line with this reasoning, Chong et al. (2001) claim that people are more likely to recognize their own self-interest, and to act upon it, when their stakes in the policy realm are clearly identifiable, or in cases in which they have been primed to think about the personal costs and benefits of the policy (increased taxation in this case). Political parties, as well as other vehicles of political socialization such as trade unions and social movement leadership, might be crucial in providing an effective framing of redistributive claims. Although democratic contestation is far from being a sufficient cause for the effective operation of those representative vehicles, it is obviously a necessary condition for this mechanism to ensue (Huber and Stephens 2012).

State capacity has also been argued to affect effective tax extraction, while low levels of extractive capacity feed back into low levels of state capacity (Centeno 2002; Kurtz 2013; Soifer 2013 and 2015). However, as Soifer shows through his proposed state capacity ranking (2015), intraregional distances and positions in terms of such capacities have remained rather stable during the twentieth century, while, as we will show, redistributive preferences lack a clear structure. In this regard, it is important to recall that for theoretical regime transition models to hold empirically (Boix 2003; Acemoglu and Robinson 2006), elites should anticipate that under a democratic regime the state should be able to tax and expropriate the rich. Such capacity is nontrivial and is one that has been largely absent in the majority of Latin American cases throughout the region's history. Indeed, in a recent argument about land reform (a critical process for effective redistribution in highly unequal societies), Albertus (2015) claims that elite expropriation by the state is virtually impossible under a democratic regime, and has been more often associated with autocratic rule and inter-elite conflict.

In turn, according to Holland (2015), state weakness does not always explain weak enforcement. Instead, Latin America's elites would choose not to enforce policies that would hurt the economic interests of subaltern social sectors, thus implementing "covert" transfers that could also pay off electorally. In these cases, nonenforcement might yield redistribution, though in an informal and probably uneven and arbitrary manner. In part due to weak state capacity, VAT taxes have been central for tax extraction in Latin America. Whereas VAT generally produces regressive results, as Mahon discusses in Chapter 8 of this volume (see also Mahon 2011), the benefits of nonenforcement are not always transferred to lower-class consumers (e.g., merchants might keep for themselves much of the revenue associated with the VAT). Although we cannot sort this out empirically, and we expect that observed patterns might change across time and space, below we compute three tax-enforcement indexes, considering the entire sample for each country and that corresponding to the poorest 40% and 20%, in order to identify patterns of variance regarding VAT enforcement across social strata.

Finally, the structure of redistributive preferences may respond to the partisan divide as a component of left–right self-placement or even the programmatic structuration of party systems. In Latin America, there is great heterogeneity regarding both proposed factors. In particular, with respect to left–right self-placement, Chile and Uruguay stand out, with values almost twice as strong as than the regional average (Alcántara Sáez and Luna 2004; Luna and Zechmeister 2005; Kitschelt et al. 2010). A similar situation occurs with respect to programmatic structuration, where these two countries have the most programmatically structured party systems in the region (Kitschelt et al. 2010; Samuels and Zucco 2014).

Against the backdrop of these works, it is not possible to derive an internally coherent set of hypotheses regarding tax preferences in a context of high inequality, sustained democratic contestation (around three decades), and relatively weak state capacity. Moreover, the region is also highly heterogeneous. However, it is possible to identify a series of theoretically relevant factors, whose empirical leverage can then be gauged empirically (even if only in an initial exploratory effort). First, we should look at the relationship between tax preferences and social class. Second, we should also explore the impact of short-term economic well-being on tax preferences. Third, we should analyze to what extent relevant political variables (e.g., ideology and preferences regarding the role of the state in leveling inequality) provide structure to citizens' redistributive preferences. Ideally, we would like to map tax preferences onto partisanship, but, given the low number of Latin Americans that identify themselves with a political party, available operationalizations of partisanship would greatly reduce the number of observations available for analysis. Finally, even in cases in which public opinion favors redistribution and the political system reflects those preferences and translates them into public policy, the state's actual capacity to enforce the tax code is also critical in shaping redistributive outcomes. Although our indicator of VAT enforcement is not directly related to demand-side arguments regarding tax preferences, we use it to explore the distribution of state capacity for tax enforcement in Latin America.

OPERATIONALIZATION AND EMPIRICAL STRATEGY

To describe the social and political structure of redistributive preferences in Latin America, we analyze cross-national variations regarding the relation between redistributive preferences, class position, self-perceptions of economic well-being, and political attitudes such as political ideology and the role of the state in leveling inequality. To pursue this analysis, we rely on LAPOP 2014 data, and analyze nationally representative samples for Argentina, Brazil, Chile, Colombia, Costa Rica, Guatemala, Mexico, Peru, Uruguay, and Venezuela.

In order to map the structure of preferences in each country, we create a dummy variable from responses to the SOC1 question, coding as 1, responses that reflect progressive tax preferences for each 100 pesos that rich people earn (options 1 and 2) from those earned by their poor counterparts. The remaining responses – preferences for nonredistributive or regressive options – are coded as 0.[2]

To map class positions we built two dummy variables drawing on the income quintiles distribution; one variable grouped the bottom three quintiles together, in order to compare the 60% of the population with lower incomes against the upper 40%; the other grouped the bottom four quintiles together, to compare the 80% of the population with lower incomes against the top-earning 20%. We do this because we know there are high levels of heterogeneity with regard to social structures across the region. However, as in any comparative effort, average

[2] SOC1 question wording: "For each 100 [local currency] that a rich and a poor person earn, how much do you think each should pay in taxes? (1) A rich person should pay 50 [local currency]; a poor person 20 [local currency], (2) A rich person should pay 40 [local currency]; a poor person 30 [local currency], (3) A rich person should pay 30 [local currency]; a poor person 30 [local currency]." We built a dummy variable in which options 1 and 2 are pooled and represent the progressive taxation preference, while option 3 represents the regressive taxation preference.

preferences are evaluated around central tendency measures as the average or the median citizen. We propose the abovementioned cuts, in spite of the blunt income data indicators in LAPOP surveys, in order to explore cutoffs at different points in the social ladder.

In order to test how self-perceived relative prosperity maps onto the structure of distributive preferences, we include in the analysis two variables that tap into economic well-being: pocketbook evaluations of the current economic situation in each country, and a retrospective pocketbook evaluation that compares the respondent's current situation to that of a year earlier.[3]

With respect to political preferences, we rely on the left–right identification scale (10-point format) and on preferences concerning the state role in leveling inequality.[4]

Using redistributive preferences as the dependent variable and the above-defined socioeconomic, political, and economic performance variables, we proceed to identify the presence (absence) of significant differences in redistributive preferences among groups defined by each independent variable. To be sure, the analysis is merely descriptive and based on ANOVA F tests (which assess the differences in group means and their determinants – within- and between-group variances). Although we address the directional effects of each variable only marginally in the analysis that follows, the distribution observed in each case is presented in the online appendix.[5]

On the basis of the results obtained for each series of independent variables (class, economic well-being, and political factors), we then compute a cluster analysis (details in Table A5 of the online appendix). From this, we derive a preliminary typology of the structure of distributive preferences for the region, based on specific preferences regarding progressive taxation.

Finally, in order to capture the state's ability to impose taxes, we focus on sales taxes, which rank at an intermediate level in terms of ease of collection (Soifer 2013). We use the question COER1, which asks respondents to assess (on a four-point scale) the likelihood they receive a receipt

[3] IDIO questions wording: "How would you describe your overall economic situation? Would you say that it is very good, good, neither good nor bad, bad or very bad?" (IDIO1); "Do you think that your economic situation is better than, the same as, or worse than it was 12 months ago?" (IDIO2).

[4] Variables L1 and ROS4 in LAPOP questionnaire.

[5] Online appendix available at http://flores-macias.government.cornell.edu/Data.html.

for a purchase in a neighborhood store.[6] This question was asked in eight countries for which we also have average VAT imposition and Gini coefficients.

RESULTS

a Mapping the Structure of Redistributive Preferences Regarding Taxation

With respect to individual predispositions to tax the rich at a higher rate than the poor, the regional support for progressive taxation averages at 76% of the population. The regional range is bounded by Chile (where 88% of respondents favor a progressive tax) at the upper limit and Venezuela (where almost 60% favor such a tax scheme) at the lower limit. Apart from Venezuela, three countries display figures below the Latin American average: Brazil (65%), Uruguay (68%), and, close to the regional average, Mexico (75%). The position of other cases can be observed in Table A1 of the online appendix. Although these differences are interesting, two qualifications apply.

First, the regional average is relatively high. Second, and more interesting from an analytic point of view, citizens' overall redistributive preferences seem to be triggered by contemporary or even relatively contingent events in each case. For instance, Chile has recently witnessed a wave of social mobilizations that have triggered the politicization of inequality in that country (Luna 2016). In turn, Uruguay, being one of the least unequal countries in the region, and having recently implemented a tax reform that increased the taxes on middle- and upper-middle class households, is among the cases where support for greater taxation of the wealthy is lowest. At higher levels of inequality, a similar situation might be found in Brazil. In turn, Venezuela's Bolivarian "revolution" might be associated with a "regressive" reaction. While the cases of Brazil, Uruguay, and Venezuela seem to be consistent with Kelly and Enns's argument about the public mood (an indicator of public opinion preferences over time) tending to counterbalance the ideological outputs of government (Kelly and Enns 2010), the case of Argentina seems inconsistent with this

6 COER question wording: "When you shop in a local store/shop in your neighborhood, even if you do not ask for it, would you receive a receipt/cash register receipt/invoice?" Response options are: (1) Always; (2) Frequently; (3) Rarely; (4) Never. The question was part of a set on state capacity proposed and discussed in Luna and Soifer (2015).

postulate. Although these speculations might be of interest, we instead focus our analysis on the relationship between attitudes toward taxation and the independent variables identified earlier.

We shall first look at the impact of class on taxation preferences. Table 9.1 displays the results obtained when using proxies for respondents' income levels. The first analysis asks whether significant differences in attitudes toward taxation exist between those in the top income quintile (richer 20%) and those in lower quintiles. The second analysis asks whether significant differences in attitudes toward taxation exist between the richest 40% of income earners and those in lower 60% of the population, Tables 9.1–9.3 also classify cases regarding the strength of pro-tax positions. We classify cases with a country average above the regional mean as displaying high redistributive preferences. The remaining cases are categorized as countries exhibiting a low redistributive preference.

When comparing the opinion of those in the top 20% versus those in the bottom 80%, three cases exhibit significant differences (Colombia, Guatemala, and Mexico). Those differences are consistently signed: poorer respondents prefer to have the rich pay relatively more taxes. This result holds in Guatemala and Mexico also when comparing the richest 40% of respondents to the rest of the sample. Furthermore, significant differences are observed for Argentina under this operationalization. Meanwhile, the case of Colombia does not show a significant difference between the attitudes of the top-earning 40% and the bottom 60%. The remaining cases show no significant differences under either of the two social class operationalizations.

Regarding individuals' evaluations of their recent economic situation, Table 9.1 shows significant between-group differences in four countries (Mexico, Guatemala, Costa Rica, and Argentina). In line with Dallinger's argument (2010), individuals who perceive their situation to have improved the most are less inclined to support an increase in the tax burden of the rich than are those who do not perceive their own economic situation to have improved.

However, also consistent with Margalit's argument (2013), the observed result differs if one considers short-term changes in individuals' perceived economic well-being. In Chile and Brazil, those who perceive themselves to have fared badly during the previous twelve months support greater taxes on the rich. By contrast, in Guatemala and Venezuela, those who perceive their economic situation to have improved favor increasing taxes. No significant differences were observed for the other countries.

TABLE 9.1 *Classification of countries by class, well-being, and ideology dimensions*

	High Redistributive Preferences	Low Redistributive Preferences
Class		
Class (20/80)		
Significant differences	*Colombia* *Guatemala*	*Mexico*
No significant differences	Argentina Chile Costa Rica Peru	Brazil Uruguay Venezuela
Class (40/60)		
Significant differences	*Argentina* *Guatemala*	*Mexico*
No significant differences	Chile Colombia Costa Rica Peru	Brazil Uruguay Venezuela
Well-being		
Self-perception of own overall economic situation		
Significant differences	*Argentina* *Costa Rica* *Guatemala*	*Mexico*
No significant differences	Chile Colombia Peru	Brazil Uruguay Venezuela
Self-perception of change in own overall economic situation (last 12 months)		
Significant differences	**Chile** *Guatemala*	**Brazil** *Venezuela*
No significant differences	Argentina Colombia Costa Rica Peru	Mexico Uruguay
Ideology		
Left–right auto-identification		
Significant differences	*Guatemala*	*Uruguay*
No significant differences	Argentina Chile Colombia Costa Rica Peru	Brazil Mexico Venezuela

(continued)

TABLE 9.1 *(continued)*

	High Redistributive Preferences	Low Redistributive Preferences
Role of the state regarding inequality		
Significant differences		*Brazil* *Mexico* *Uruguay*
No significant differences	Argentina Chile Colombia Costa Rica Guatemala Peru	Venezuela

NB: Country names in *italics* = leftist/state-oriented sectors support more redistribution; in bold = rightist / market-oriented sectors support more redistribution. Significance is assessed in Analysis of Variance (see online appendix). *For class*, variables represent income quintiles, comparing preferences of the richest 20% to those of poorer 80%; and richest 40% to poorer 60%. *For well-being*, variables represent (a) the self-perception of own economic well-being; and (b) the self-perception of change in own economic well-being from last year. High redistributive preferences are considered those above the regional mean (0.76). *For ideology*, variables represent of (a) the self-positioning on the right–left continuum; and (b) the opinion on the redistributive role of the state. High redistributive preferences are considered those above the regional mean (0.76).

Table 9.1 also shows that, with respect to political attitudes, only two countries (Guatemala and Uruguay) exhibit a significant relationship between leftist ideology and redistributive emphases. The table also shows that only in three countries (Brazil, Mexico, and Uruguay) do we find a significant relationship between support for a greater state role in redistributing resources to reduce inequality and preferences for redistribution via taxation. In sum, preferences for redistribution through taxes are, at a regional level, only marginally related to political ideology or to more general statements about the state's role in reducing social and economic inequality.

To summarize the observed trends regarding preferences in contemporary Latin America concerning taxing the wealthy, we ran a cluster analysis entering the observed results into the analysis. Figure 9.1 shows the resulting dendrogram, which clearly identifies four groups (Table A5 in the online appendix provides descriptive statistics). The first and most internally homogenous group comprises Argentina, Costa Rica, and Chile. In these three cases, preferences for taxing the rich are higher than the regional average. Yet, at the same time, and with the partial exception of Argentina, political ideology and class are not significantly related to

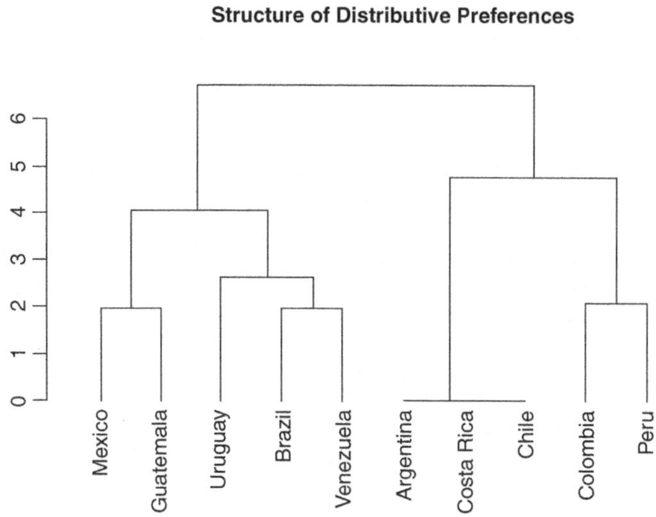

FIGURE 9.1 Dendogram for distributive preferences in Latin America

distributive preferences in these countries. Economic well-being is the only variable significantly related to distributive preferences in all three cases, which could be classified as displaying a highly redistributive (but unstructured) demand. The cases of Peru and Colombia also approximate that group, but displaying even lower levels of structure regarding taxation preferences ("highly redistributive (but completely unstructured) demand").

The cases of Mexico and Guatemala also display a significant degree of homogeneity in their observed patterns, and form a group we shall classify as cases with "structured preferences." Although the two countries differ in how much their citizens endorse taxing the rich (low preference in Mexico; high in Guatemala), they are the only countries in our sample that exhibit a significant relationship between distributive preference and all three variables analyzed here (i.e., class, economic well-being, and political ideology). A fourth group comprises Venezuela, Brazil, and, less strongly, Uruguay. These cases display low levels of preferred taxation, with some structuring. Whereas Brazil and Uruguay display a relationship between attitudes toward taxation and attitudes toward the role of the state in reducing inequality, attitudes toward taxation are significantly related to economic well-being in Venezuela and Brazil. Table 9.2 summarizes the configuration observed in each group.

TABLE 9.2 *Typology for redistributive preferences*

Type		Class	Economic Well-Being	Political Ideology	Overall Distributive Preference
Structured demand	Mexico	X	X	X	Low
	Guatemala	X	X	X	High
Low redistributive demand with a modicum of (political) structure	Uruguay			X	Low
	Brazil		X	X	Low
	Venezuela		X		Low
Highly redistributive (but completely unstructured) demand	Colombia	X			High
	Peru				High
Highly redistributive (but relatively unstructured) demand	Costa Rica		X		High
	Chile		X		High
	Argentina	X	X		High

Source: Authors based on LAPOP 2014 data

b Assessing the State Ability to Impose Taxes

We try to make sense of these results in the next and final section. First, however, we explore citizens' reports on VAT enforcement in each country. In order to capture the state's ability to impose taxes, we focus on sales taxes, which rank at an intermediate level in terms of ease of collection (Soifer 2013). We use the question COER1, which asks respondents in eight countries to assess (on a four-point scale) the likelihood they receive a receipt for a purchase in a neighborhood store.

Figure 9.2 displays the relationship between VAT rates and effective tax collection. As observed in the graph, most of the countries for which information is available report a very low level of enforcement irrespective of tax burden. Yet, Argentina, Uruguay, and especially Chile – which are also the cases that display higher levels of VAT – are the ones for which effective collection is greater (lower values in COER1 denotes a greater capacity for tax collection). These are the cases that are generally considered to have greater levels of state capacity in the region (see Kurtz 2013; Soifer 2015).

Finally, as reported in Table 9.3, there is no significant relationship in any of the countries studied between income class and effective tax collection. Individuals in the lower-income quintiles are not more or less likely to receive a store receipt than is the population as a whole. Indeed, the cross-national pairwise correlations for the three measures (entire sample, 60% poorer, 80% poorer) reach 0.99.

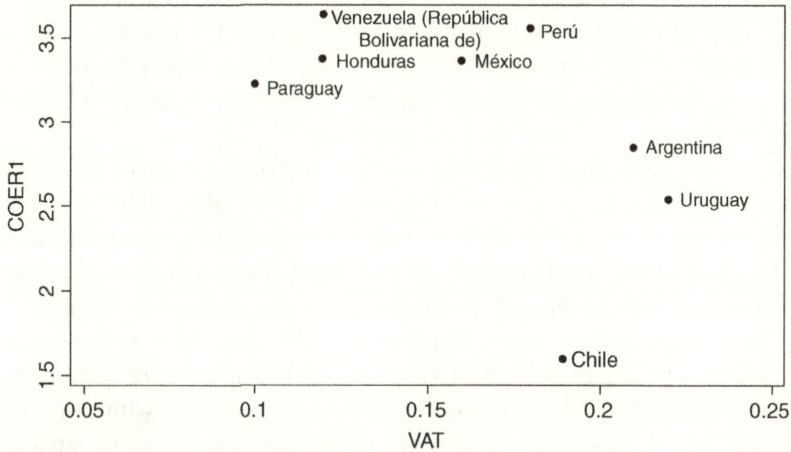

FIGURE 9.2 VAT level and effective tax collection
Source: ECLAC 2015 – CEPALSTAT and LAPOP 2014. NB: lower values in COER1 denotes a greater capacity for tax collection

TABLE 9.3 *Forbearance and predisposition to increase tax burden for redistribution*

	Effective Tax Collection	60% Poorer	80% Poorer
Mexico	3.36	3.43	3.39
Chile	1.60	1.61	1.61
Peru	3.55	3.6	3.58
Uruguay	2.54	2.62	2.55
Venezuela	3.63	3.73	3.69
Argentina	2.85	2.94	2.89

Source: LAPOP 2014

CONCLUSION

Overall, we can learn at least three things about the region from this analysis. First, Latin American countries exhibit a low level of tax collection enforcement, which is consistent with its low levels of overall state capacity as compared to Europe and the United States. Our evidence on VAT enforcement seems to suggest that state capacity plays a crucial mediating role in tax extraction in Latin America, and, thus, in the success of eventual redistributive efforts. In fact, three of the four cases where a greater redistributive effect was observed in Latin America circa 2010 (Lustig and Pereira 2016) are countries where respondents (indirectly) reported greater levels of VAT enforcement.

Second, preferences regarding taxation are formed in this lax enforcement context, which is important to point out given that such preferences are correlated with individuals' perceived utility of evading the tax – itself a function of both the benefit to the individual of not paying taxes and the individual's beliefs about the state's willingness to tolerate evasion.

Third, the analysis shows that the available data do not support the existence of a region-wide preference structure regarding redistribution, which is most likely linked to high regional heterogeneity with respect to inequality levels, stability of democratic institutions, and state capacity. Below we discuss in greater detail our findings with respect to whether the structure of distributive preferences is consistent with political ideology, self-perceived well-being, and class position.

The region does not exhibit a systematic relationship between class position and redistributive preferences. In the few cases where these preferences significantly differ by class, the poorest exhibit stronger redistributive preferences. This is inconsistent with arguments that attribute weak redistributive effort to the poor's "false consciousness" (Jost and Thompson 2000; Jost and Hunyady 2005), or with arguments about the presence of cognitive biases that influence political preference formation (Shapiro 2002). However, it is important to recall that in only four out of ten cases does class position significantly predict preferences toward taxation: Mexico, Guatemala, Colombia, and Argentina.

Differences in redistributive attitudes fueled by short-term pocketbook evaluations are present in a very diverse group of cases. Yet, the mechanisms behind this correlation might be sharply different across cases. Whereas in cases such as Brazil and Chile, those who have fared poorly in recent times support the imposition of greater taxes on the rich, in Argentina, Guatemala, México, and Costa Rica the opposite trend holds for those who consider themselves to be doing well. Thus, our findings at best only partially confirm Dallinger's (2010) and Margalit's (2013) findings.

The relationship between political beliefs and redistributive preferences is also quite weak. Only in Guatemala and Uruguay does left–right political self-identification predict preferences regarding taxation. While these results are consistent with levels of political-party ideological alignment in Uruguay and, therefore, with the political programmatic representation of distributive preferences, the data for Guatemala is less clearly explicable from this perspective. In turn, attitudes regarding the state's role in reducing inequality, which should be logically related to preferences for greater taxation of the rich, only significantly relate to the latter preferences in Mexico, Brazil, and Uruguay. These results are consistent with previous findings regarding the lack of programmatic structure in Latin American party systems. In sum, it is reasonable to posit that the lack of stable political parties with clear ideological positions, which characterizes many countries in the region, reduces the scope for finding a match between ideological self-identification and redistributive preferences.

If we compare the above-reported findings regarding citizens' attitudes toward taxation and the observed redistributive effects reported by Lustig and Pereira (2016), we find no systematic pattern. For instance, Argentina and Uruguay, which differ markedly in their levels of preferred taxation and on the observed structure of those preferences, are the two cases that exhibit the greatest level of redistribution in the region. They are followed by Brazil and Chile, but also by Mexico, whose observed configuration is also quite dissimilar to the former countries. At the other extreme, Colombia and Peru display low levels of redistribution, which seems consistent with their attitudinal configuration. Yet, Guatemala, a case with high demand for redistribution and high levels of political and social structuring of those preferences, also exhibits very meager (and comparable) results.

To sum up, this chapter essentially contributes a nonfinding, at least from a regional perspective. We do not necessarily regret this fact, which provides indirect evidence of the importance of alternative causal factors in shaping taxation and redistribution, as well as incomplete but suggestive evidence about the lack of theoretical grounds for pooling Latin American cases in statistical region-wide analyses of preferences for redistribution. Besides state capacity, the nature of elite bargaining and top-down policy design seem to be of primary importance. Of course, the validity of our nonfinding might be challenged by two sets of factors: the scarcity of data on pure preferences regarding taxation; and the nature of the empirical analysis we have pursued here. Regarding the latter, we could have, for instance, specified a multilevel regression analysis of the observed preferences for redistribution. Although we did pursue preliminary analysis in this direction, the results convinced us to pursue instead a more simple descriptive analysis. We nonetheless justify our methodological choices on the following grounds: first, we think it would have been misleading to concentrate on average regional effects before assessing the theoretical grounds for pooling cases. The preceding analysis seems to support our choices, as there seems not to be a reasonably coherent structure of preferences across the region. Second, we are interested in offering a preliminary typology of Latin American cases combining overall demand for progressive taxation with its potential determinants in terms of class position, self-perceived well-being, and political ideology, together with overall levels of country-level inequality.

References

Acemoglu, Daron and James A. Robinson. 2006. "Persistence of Power, Elites and Institutions." *NBER Working Paper* 12108. National Bureau of Economic Research.

Albertus, Michael. 2015. *Autocracy and Redistribution*. New York: Cambridge University Press.

Alcántara Sáez, Manuel and Juan Pablo Luna. 2004. "Ideología y competencia partidaria en dos post-transiciones: Chile y Uruguay en perspectiva comparada," *Revista de ciencia política (Santiago)* 24(1): 128–168.

Alesina, Alberto and Paola Giuliano. 2011. "Preferences for Redistribution," in Jess Benhabib, Alberto Bisin, and Matthew O. Jackson (eds.), *Handbook of Social Economics* (Vol. 1). Amsterdam: North-Holland, 93–131.

Alesina, Alberto and Eliana La Ferrara. 2005. "Preferences for Redistribution in the Land of Opportunities," *Journal of Public Economics* 89(5): 897–931.

Alm, James and Benno Torgler. 2006. "Culture Differences and Tax Morale in the United States and in Europe," *Journal of Economic Psychology* 27(2): 224–246.

Ansell, Ben and David Samuels. 2014 *Inequality and Democratization*. New York: Cambridge University Press.

Bartels, Larry. 2008. "The Irrational Electorate," *Wilson Quarterly* 32(4): 44–50.

Bénabou, Roland. 2000. "Unequal Societies: Income Distribution and the Social Contract," *American Economic Review* 90(1): 96–129.

Bénabou, Roland and Efe Ok. 2001. "Social Mobility and the Demand for Redistribution: The POUM Hypothesis," *Quarterly Journal of Economics* 116(2): 447–487.

Blofield, Merike (ed.). 2011. *The Great Gap: Inequality and the Politics of Redistribution in Latin America*. University Park: Penn State University Press.

Blofield, Merike, and Juan Pablo Luna. 2011. "Public Opinion on Income Inequalities in Latin America," in Marike Blofield (ed.), *The Great Gap: Inequality and the Politics of Redistribution in Latin America*. University Park: Penn State University Press, 147–81.

Bogliaccini, Juan A. and Juan Pablo Luna. 2016. "Deflecting my Burden, Hindering Redistribution: How Elites Influence Tax Legislation in Latin America." WIDER Working Paper No. 92/ 2016.

Boix, Carles. 2003. *Democracy and Redistribution*. New York: Cambridge University Press.

Campello, Daniela. 2015. *The Politics of Market Discipline in Latin America: Globalization and Democracy*. New York: Cambridge University Press.

Chong, Dennis, Jack Citrin, and Patricia Conley. 2001. "When Self-Interest Matters," *Political Psychology* 22(3): 541–570.

Cramer, Brian and Robert Kaufman. 2011. "Views of Economic Inequality in Latin America," *Comparative Political Studies* 44(9): 1206–1237.

Centeno, Miguel Angel. 2002. *Blood and Debt: War and the Nation-State in Latin America*. University Park: Penn State University Press.

Dallinger, Ursula. 2010. "Public Support for Redistribution: What Explains Cross-National Differences?" *Journal of European Social Policy* 20(4): 333–349.

Dargent, Eduardo, Andreas Feldmann, and Juan Pablo Luna. 2017. "Greater State Capacity, Lesser Stateness: Lessons from the Peruvian Commodity Boom," *Politics & Society* 45(1): 3–34.

Di John, Jonathan. 2006. *The Political Economy of Taxation and Tax Reform in Developing Countries*. Helsinki: Anthem Press and World Institute of Development Economic Research.

Doyle, David. 2015. "Remittances and Social Spending," *American Political Science Review* 109(4): 785–802.

ECLAC. 2015. CEPALSTAT, http://estadisticas.cepal.org/cepalstat/Portada.html ?idioma=english.

Erikson, Robert, Michael MacKuen, and James Stimson. 2002. *The Macro Polity*. New York: Cambridge University Press.

Fairfield, Tasha. 2015. *Private Wealth and Public Revenue*. New York: Cambridge University Press.

Flores-Macías, Gustavo. 2015. "The Political Economy of Colombia's 2012 and 2014 Fiscal Reforms," in James Mahon, Marcelo Bergman, and Cynthia Arnson (eds.), *Progressive Tax Reform and Equality in Latin America*. Washington, DC: Woodrow Wilson Center, 101–126.

Gaviria, Alejandro, Carol Graham, and Luis Braido. 2007. "Social Mobility and Preferences for Redistribution in Latin America," *Economía* 8(1): 55–96.

Gilens, Martin. 2012. *Affluence and Influence: Economic Inequality and Political Power in America*. Princeton: Princeton University Press.

Haggard, Stephan and Robert Kaufman. 2016. *Dictators and Democrats: Masses, Elites, and Regime Change*. Princeton: Princeton University Press.

Holland, Alisha. 2018. "Diminished Expectations: Redistributive Preferences in Truncated Welfare States," *World Politics* 70(4): 555–594.

Holland, Stephen. 2015. *Public Health Ethics*. New Jersey: John Wiley & Sons.

Huber, Evelyne and John Stephens. 2012. *Democracy and the Left: Social Policy and Inequality in Latin America*. Chicago: University of Chicago Press.

Jost, John and Orsolya Hunyady. 2005. "Antecedents and Consequences of System Justifying Ideologies," *Current Directions in Psychological Science* 14(5): 260–265.

Jost, John and Erik P. Thompson. 2000. "Group-based Dominance and Opposition to Equality as Independent Predictors of Self-esteem, Ethnocentrism, and Social Policy Attitudes among African Americans and European Americans," *Journal of Experimental Social Psychology* 36(3): 209–232.

Kelly, Nathan and Peter Enns. 2010. "Inequality and the Dynamics of Public Opinion: The Self-Reinforcing Link Between Economic Inequality and Mass Preferences," *American Journal of Political Science* 54(4): 855–870.

Kenworthy, Lane and Leslie McCall. 2008. "Inequality, Public Opinion, and Redistribution," *Socio-Economic Review* 6(1): 35–68.

Kitschelt, Herbert, Kirk Hawkins, Juan Pablo Luna, Guillermo Rosas, and Elizabeth Zechmeister. 2010. *Latin American Party Systems*. New York: Cambridge University Press.

Kurtz, Marcus. 2013. *Latin American State-Building in Comparative Perspective: Social Foundations of Institutional Order*. New York: Cambridge University Press.

Luna, Juan Pablo. 2016. "Chile's Crisis of Representation," *Journal of Democracy* 27(3): 129–138.

2014. *Segmented Representation: Political Party Strategies in Unequal Democracies*. Oxford: Oxford University Press.

Luna, Juan P. and Elizabeth Zechmeister. 2005. "Political Representation in Latin America: A Study of Elite-Mass Congruence in Nine Countries," *Comparative Political Studies* 38(4): 388–416.

Lupu, Noam and Jonas Pontusson. 2011. "The Structure of Inequality and the Politics of Redistribution," *American Political Science Review* 105(2): 316–336.

Lustig, Nora and Claudiney Pereira. 2016. "The Impact of the Tax System and Social Spending on Income Redistribution and Poverty Reduction in Latin America." *Hacienda Pública Española / Review of Public Economics* 219(4): 121–136.

Luttig, Matthew. 2013. "The Structure of Inequality and Americans' Attitudes Toward Redistribution," *Public Opinion Quarterly* 77(3): 811–821.

Mahon, James. 2011. "Tax Reform and Income Distribution in Latin America," in Marike Blofield (ed.), *The Great Gap: Inequality and the Politics of Redistribution in Latin America*. University Park: Penn State University Press, 313–347.

Mainwaring, Scott and Timothy Scully. *Democratic Governance in Latin America*. Palo Alto: Stanford University Press, 2010.

Maloney, William, Osmel Manzano, and Andrew Warner. 2002. "Missed Opportunities: Innovation and Resource-Based Growth in Latin America [with Comments]," *Economia* 3(1): 111–167.

Margalit, Yotam. 2013. "Explaining Social Policy Preferences: Evidence from the Great Recession," *American Political Science Review* 107(1): 80–103.

Morgan, Jana and Nathan J. Kelly. 2013. "Market Inequality and Redistribution in Latin America and the Caribbean," *Journal of Politics*, 75(3): 672–685.

2010. "Explaining Public Attitudes Toward Fighting Inequality in Latin America," *Poverty & Public Policy* 2(3): 79–111.

Meltzer, Allan and Scott Richard. 1981. "A Rational Theory of the Size of Government," *The Journal of Political Economy* 89(5): 914–927.

O'Donnell, Guillermo. 1996. "Illusions about Consolidation," *Journal of Democracy* 7(2): 34–51.

Przeworski, Adam. 2010. *Democracy and the Limits of Self-Government.* New York: Cambridge University Press.

Reis, Elisa. 2011. "Elite Perceptions of Poverty and Inequality in Brazil," in Merike Blofield (ed.), *The Great Gap: Poverty and Inequality in Latin America.* Penn State University Press, 89–108.

Rodríguez, Franco. 2011. "Internal Wars, Taxation, and State-Building." Masters Thesis, Northwestern University.

Ross, Michael. 1999. "The Political Economy of the Resource Curse," *World Politics* 51(2): 297–322.

Samuels, David and Cesar Zucco. 2014. "The Power of Partisanship in Brazil: Evidence from Survey Experiments," *American Journal of Political Science* 58(1): 212–225.

Shapiro, Ian. 2002. "Why the Poor Don't Soak the Rich," Daedalus 13(1): 118–128.

Soifer, Hillel David. 2013. "State Power and the Economic Origins of Democracy," *Studies in Comparative International Development* 48(1): 1–22.

2015. *State Building in Latin America.* New York: Cambridge University Press.

The Americas Barometer by the Latin American Public Opinion Project [LAPOP]. 2014. www.LapopSurveys.org.

10

Conclusion: Addressing Taxation's Political Challenges

Gustavo A. Flores-Macías

During the 1980s and 1990s, countries in Latin America carried out a wave of economic structural reforms as a response to the region's Debt Crisis, a process variously referred to as implementing the Washington Consensus or neoliberal reforms. Whatever the name, the consequence was clear: countries systematically moved to reduce the state's role in the economy. The solution to the debt crisis manifested in the form of privatizations, trade and capital liberalization, and the generalized reduction of government expenditures in the economy (Bird and Perry 1994).

Mediocre growth during the 1990s and 2000s has swung the pendulum back in the other direction, as governments realized that fiscal resources were required to provide a minimum level of public goods provision (Inter-American Development Bank 2013). The antistate dogmatism that often surrounded Latin American policy circles has gradually receded. Increasingly, there is recognition among finance ministries, think tanks, and international financial organizations that the provision of quality public goods requires higher levels of taxation to fund government public goods, from antipoverty programs to infrastructure to law enforcement (Brautigam et al. 2008).

Governments' current fiscal positions are not as dire as they were in the era of Latin America's bloated states before the 1980s debt crisis, but the end of the commodity boom has again put them in a vulnerable position. Debt has become more manageable, fiscal exceptions have receded, and government budgets are less strained. Fiscal discipline has become a priority, and reforms count among their main aims to increase equity and efficiency, and contribute toward growth and the reduction of inequality (Sánchez 2006).

However, as the book's Introduction points out, commodity business cycles continue to heavily influence the region's public budgets. For example, revenue from taxes and royalties in commodity-exporting countries dropped from almost 9% of GDP in 2011 to about 3% in 2016 (Melguizo 2017). To make matters worse, the growth in entitlement programs during the boom years has now become a problem for cash-strapped governments looking to cut expenditures. The bust in commodity prices poses a significant risk for governments' efforts to address income inequality, provide quality public goods, and generate growth (International Monetary Fund 2015).

More often than not, the obstacles to adopting necessary tax reforms to address the region's fiscal shortcomings are not technical. Technical solutions to the region's fiscal issues are known, but political obstacles make their implementation difficult. Fiscal quandaries therefore become important moments for policymakers to push for tax reforms (Mahon Jr. 2004; Hallerberg and Scartascini 2011). The aftermath of the commodity boom that ended in 2014 presents an opportunity for the region's governments to increase the tax burden, improve the tax structure, and promote tax neutrality – all of which would be politically unpalatable or unfeasible otherwise.

The findings in this volume show that commodity prices generate strong incentives for cycles of resource nationalism – encouraging certain governments to make poor tax decisions when entering into contracts – but also suggest that there is room for less structural factors to shape the levels and incidence of tax collection. In particular, factors including the strength of economic elites, the quality of government services in the fiscal exchange, patterns of economic incorporation, and compliance were found to account for variation in the levels of taxation. Electoral rules, interest groups, and public opinion play an important role in explaining differences in the tax structure, although there is some crossover between groups. This concluding chapter engages this set of findings and discusses their potential impact for Latin America. In particular, it discusses each factor's implications for the region's levels of taxation, the nature of its tax structure, and differences across countries. It suggests that the political factors studied in this volume can play an important role in making the adoption of fiscal reforms more likely and sustainable over time. The subsequent section offers a discussion of the tensions that exist among some of the main factors, namely between elites and the public and between path dependence and the role of government ideology. The final section seeks to contribute to the development of the taxation research agenda by offering relevant questions for future research.

WHAT EXPLAINS THE REGION'S LOW LEVELS OF TAXATION?

As the chapters in this volume have shown, most Latin American countries collect less in tax revenue than expected given their level of development. In particular, four main factors across chapters seem to play a central role in preventing greater fiscal extraction: the power of business groups, weak state capacity to generate compliance, personalistic electoral rules, and governments' low spending commitment.

A first factor shaping Latin American countries' comparatively low overall tax burden is the significant power of business elites, which is not uncommon elsewhere but takes on special relevance in Latin America where wealth is highly concentrated. As Fairfield (Chapter 7) notes, there are two main reasons why business groups enjoy significant influence over governments to prevent increases in the tax burden. The first is business groups' power, both structural – the ability to influence the economy through financial decisions, such as where to invest their capital – and instrumental – the ability to influence policy through lobbying, campaign donations, and access to policymakers and media, among other means. The second reason is the low salience that tax reforms tend to have for the average voter. Because the informal sector hovers around 50% of the labor force – with Bolivia, Colombia, Guatemala, Honduras, Nicaragua, Paraguay, and Peru at or above 60% (Holland and Schneider 2017) – large sectors of the population do not pay direct taxes in Latin America. Workers in the informal sector may care about indirect taxes such as the VAT, but changes in income tax rates are not of particular importance to them since their income is not withheld at the source and they tend not to file a tax return. Further, business elites can also manipulate public opinion by spinning reforms in a manner consistent with their goals or by sowing confusion as to the real incidence of a tax (Bartels 2005; Graetz and Shapiro 2005).

A second factor is weak state capacity, which has consequences for perceptions of fairness in the fiscal exchange and, in turn, compliance. As Bergman (Chapter 3) notes, low compliance has characterized the region even during periods of economic prosperity, such as the commodity boom between 2002 and 2014. This performance is especially worrisome given the technological advances and the increasing prevalence of electronic transactions, which have placed Latin America's tax authorities among the world's most advanced regarding electronic requirements for accounting and reporting – particularly in Argentina, Brazil, Colombia, and Mexico (KPMG 2017, 2). For example, Latin American countries have generally taken important steps toward making it easy to register with the tax authorities, often as part of the process of starting a business. In Argentina, Brazil, Chile, Colombia, the Dominican Republic, Ecuador, Mexico, and Peru, most taxpayers can only file tax returns electronically – in Chile, electronic filing has reached 97% (Crawford 2013, 52).

In spite of these advancements, low tax levels are a product of the deficit in the region regarding the construction and maintenance of up-to-date registries of taxpayers. Only about 23% of Latin America's population is registered as a taxpayer, compared to 59% in the OECD (Murdoch 2013, 17). According to the Inter-American Development Bank (2010), levels of registration of micro- and small businesses are also low. In Mexico, for example, about 70% of microbusinesses are not registered and pay no taxes, and only 63% of small and medium businesses are registered. In El Salvador, only 1% of all microbusinesses and 3% of all other businesses are registered.

Such low shares of registered taxpayers reflect the permanence of high levels of informal employment over the last decade, as well as governments' inability to incorporate more people into the formal taxpaying system. Although some countries have made a point of making it easier and more appealing for informal workers to declare taxes and have lightened companies' payroll burden in order to foster formal employment, as with Colombia's 2014 tax reform, this has not been the norm.[1]

Governments in the region have instead focused on collecting taxes among the captive formal taxpayers, which discourages compliance because of perceived unfairness in the system (Cummings et al. 2009). Tax compliance for direct taxes such as the personal income tax has remained very low, with evasion between 40% and 70% depending on the estimate.

In addition to deficient capacity, selective enforcement (Bergman 2009) – or what Holland (2016) has dubbed "forbearance" – also complicates the picture for extraction. Among the informal sectors, governments might not enforce tax laws because of the distributional consequences of enforcement, which can deprive informal workers of a way of earning a living and consumers of access to cheaper goods to make ends meet. Among the wealthy, governments may not enforce tax laws because of state capture, or the undue influence of business sectors at the expense of other social groups. As Bergman's and Fairfield's chapters suggest, both are prevalent in the region.

[1] For details on the Colombian case, see Flores-Macías (2015).

Third, the lack of tax neutrality has contributed to the region's low levels of taxation. Neutrality is especially important for Latin America because of its large informal sector outside the full reach of tax authorities. It helps achieve a broader tax base, which could in turn contribute to lowering existing tax rates. Neutrality can also contribute to perceptions of fairness, which play a role in encouraging compliance.

Contrary to expectations from other regions, tax neutrality does not appear to be determined by factors such as partisanship. In Europe and the United States, the distinction between left and right parties draws generally clear preferences regarding the incidence of taxation and the beneficiaries of government spending, with the left being fiscally expansive compared to the right. In Latin America, however, this distinction is not as clear, as Bogliaccini and Luna suggest in their chapter (9) on public opinion.

Instead, Hallerberg and Scartascini (Chapter 6) point to electoral rules, which can determine whether tax systems benefit particular groups in society or treat different sectors in a similar – or neutral – way. The more personalistic the electoral system, the more room there is for distortion in tax collection favoring some groups at the expense of others. In other words, the more electoral rules encourage politicians to focus on a narrow constituency rather than broader societal goals, the more they will seek to reward that narrow group.

In spite of the growing consensus that fiscal neutrality is desirable from an economic efficiency standpoint and should therefore promote growth, between 1990 and 2004 more reforms decreased neutrality than improved it. This trend highlights how political considerations can trump recognized best practices in tax policy. Because of the short-term political benefits, a majority of reforms are still adopted at the expense of broadening the tax base, equalizing tax rates across goods and income sources, and eliminating fiscal prerogatives for specific sectors. The findings are consistent with other research on the importance of political institutions for taxation, including studies that find that personalistic electoral systems are conducive to greater budget deficits (Hallerberg and Marier 2004).

A fourth factor contributing to the region's low tax burden is governments' low commitment to public spending due to the prevailing, outward-looking developmental model that seeks to keep business costs down to appeal to foreign investors. As Schneider (Chapter 5) shows, the material needs of certain industries that gain the upper hand in state–society relations can be an important determinant of the types of public goods provided by the government. Import- versus export-driven sectors or capital- versus labor-intensive industries will have different interests as to whether the government pays attention to spending in infrastructure or social security, or whether the government's main priority is to keep a low tax burden to attract foreign capital (Bird and McLure 1990; Saylor 2014).

Naturally, there is variation regarding governments' level of commitment to the export-oriented model, although most of the region embraced liberalization during the 1980s and 1990s. Against this backdrop, the example of Brazil is illustrative as an exception that was less committed to this model than most other Latin America countries. Following the inward-looking model of Import-Substitution Industrialization, as other countries with a sizable internal market did, Brazil began setting the foundations for increased spending that would generate the demand for tax resources. Between 1965 and 1970, the country's tax burden jumped from 15% to 25% of GDP in order to meet the military government's revenue requirements for industrial deepening.

As most countries backed away from this type of model as a response to the debt crisis of the 1980s, Brazil steadily increased its tax burden with the adoption of the 1988 Constitution, at least until the end of the Workers' Party (PT) rule in 2016. During this democratic period, the government responded to its constitutional obligation to invest in social programs by tripling social spending, as Schneider points out. In order to make this possible, Brazil's tax revenue as a share of GDP also increased significantly, from 25% to 35% of national output.

Ultimately, two key factors were responsible for making Brazil the Latin American country with the greatest ability to extract tax resources. The first is the adoption of spending mandates that required considerably more revenue than the government extracted at the time of the democratic transition. The mandate to provide education and healthcare – an earmark of sorts – generated strong incentives for increasing tax revenue in the context of the country's neo-developmentalist model (Schneider 2015).

The second factor is the federal government's incentives for municipal governments to raise taxes by setting limits to how much they could borrow. Both factors can comfortably travel to other settings, especially the second one. For instance, Mexico adopted legislation in 2016 to establish debt limits for states and municipalities (Agencia Notimex 2016) – rules that Brazil has had in place since 1999. This policy should increase the sustainability of public finance by encouraging federal units to collect more revenue from taxes.

These reforms did not come without costs, however. Brazil's governments engaged in patronage and pork-barrel politics in exchange for legislators' support for these reforms. They also had to compensate large corporations for their acquiescence through subsidies and preferential credits, going against the desirable tax neutrality discussed in Hallerberg and Scartascini's chapter. As recent corruption scandals reaching the highest government echelons suggest – including former president Lula da Silva (2002–2010), former speaker of the House of Representatives Eduardo Cunha (2015–2016), and President Michel Temer (2016–present) – quid pro quos outside the law might have been involved as well. Overall, however, the Brazilian experience shows that Latin American governments can leverage previously untapped tax resources by taking meaningful steps to meet legally protected social spending obligations.

What Explains the Region's Tax Structure?

The desire for progressivity is strong throughout the region, as Bogliaccini and Luna show in their chapter on public opinion. About 76% of survey respondents express a preference for progressive taxation. In fact, a majority of the population in all countries supports redistribution through the tax system, from Venezuela's 60% at the bottom to Chile's 88% at the top.

The structure and corresponding incidence of tax systems across the region differs considerably from this popular aspiration, however. Skewed tax burdens favoring regressive consumption taxes are also not exclusively a Latin American phenomenon, but the region performs worse than other parts of the world with similar levels of development, as Mahon (Chapter 8) highlights.[2] Even in places such as Chile, Colombia, and Uruguay, where tax reforms have made some progress toward increasing progressivity (Mahon Jr. et al. 2015), economic elites pay little in taxes compared to their share of income. In these three countries, the top 1% of earners pay an effective tax rate of 15% or less (Fairfield and Jorratt 2015; Alvaredo and Londoño 2013; Burdín et al. 2014, 40). In Mexico, where revenue from direct taxes is relatively high for Latin America, about half of income tax comes from salaried workers, whose contribution to national income is only 27%. Conversely, corporations

[2] Mexico is an exception in that its income taxes represent a greater share of total tax revenue than consumption taxes.

contribute 38% of income tax revenue, but represent 69% of national income (Unda Gutiérrez 2015, 85).

Naturally, there are important systemic factors that mediate the relationship between taxation preferences and policy outcomes, including the extent to which electoral rules translate preferences into congressional seats (Shugart and Carey 1992) and the nature of party systems (Flores-Macías 2010, 2012; Kaufman 2011; Kitschelt et al. 2010). There are also individual-level factors that can play a role in muddling the correspondence between people's preferences and voting behavior, including class position, ideology, and party ID. Although these factors would be expected to distort this relationship somewhat, the generalized reliance on indirect taxes and neglect of direct taxes in the region suggests that other more serious obstacles play a significant role.

Several chapters in the volume speak to the obstacles to realizing more progressive tax systems based on direct taxes, including those focusing on the power of interest groups, compliance and informality, state capacity, and commodity price cycles.[3] First, in a region where wealth is highly concentrated and the taxpayer base is fairly narrow, a key factor accounting for the prevalence of regressive taxes is the influence of the business sectors. Governments depend on this narrow base for attempts at increasing the progressivity of the system through direct taxes, but business elites begrudge having to carry the bulk of the fiscal burden. Moreover, the wealthiest sectors are also those best able to avoid additional tax obligations, whether through lobbyists to influence policymakers, accountants to find loopholes in the tax code, or lawyers to challenge their enforcement. They also have the wealth to gain favors from politicians in exchange for campaign donations and the personal access to top government officials to influence them directly. As Fairfield suggests in her chapter, whenever governments try to make the tax system more progressive, economic elites are often successful at spreading misinformation about the incidence of the proposed tax reform, controlling the agenda in the media, and threatening to take their investments elsewhere.

A second factor explaining the region's tax structure is state capacity. As Bergman's chapter highlights, governments in the region made important gains in compliance after carrying out modernizing reforms to update tax agencies' information technology systems and professionalize personnel. This allowed them to make progress in detecting evasion in

[3] Other factors not discussed in the volume may also come into play, including false consciousness by the poor (Kaufman and Haggard 2016).

consumption taxes such as the value-added tax, but other forms of evasion remain unaddressed.

Changes to the generally regressive structure of tax systems will be difficult as long as important deficiencies in the capacity to collect direct taxes remain. Currently, most countries rely on captive taxpayers who receive a salary and whose taxes are subtracted before they receive their paycheck. In most countries in the region, less than 10% of the population pays some form of personal income tax (IADB 2013). This in part is because income generated by small business, self-employed professionals, and on capital gains and dividends has remained elusive for governments, as Bergman notes. Additionally, the region's large underemployed sectors – close to 50% of the working-age population – remain hard to tax, although their share of national income is lower in comparative terms (Alm et al. 2005).

Taxing these sectors requires a series of capacity-improving reforms. Such reforms include generating and maintaining accurate property ownership records, as well as assessing, monitoring, and updating property values, as Mahon's chapter notes. The capacity to perform these tasks competently goes beyond the training of tax administrators or the ability to focus on a handful of large, captive taxpayers. Rather, it requires being able to identify and find the owners of property and wealth, present them with their tax dues, and enforce existing tax legislation. Strong courts and law enforcement institutions can make a difference in reversing the dismal number of cases prosecuted for tax evasion in the region. This type of capacity is still lacking, especially at the local level. However, adopting these reforms requires considerable political will.

Further, Latin American governments' inability to provide quality public goods represents an obstacle to increasing the share of income and property taxes. As Mahon's chapter shows, there is a strong correlation between adherence to the rule of law and property taxation, for example. Governments' failure to fulfill their part of the fiscal contract by providing quality public safety, infrastructure, and respect for property rights, to name a few government services, will continue to hinder the extraction of additional revenue via direct taxes.

It has been difficult for the region to break out of this equilibrium of low-quality public goods and low taxation. As both Mahon and Ondetti (Chapter 4) suggest in their chapters, there is considerable continuity in the taxation patterns that emerged early in the development of modern Latin American states. A diminished form of liberalism that has been replicated over time has perpetuated the region's weak governmentality –

the notion that citizens have a debt to the government as the legitimate body that solves collective action problems in society.

A final consideration working against sustained efforts to increase the progressivity of tax structures in the region is natural resource dependence. In commodity-exporting countries, commodity windfalls are relatively easy to tax, which reduced incentives to incur the enforcement and political costs associated with taxing noncaptive income and property. During the commodity boom, it was politically and administratively easier for governments in Argentina (a declining exporter), Bolivia, Brazil (a growing exporter), Colombia, Ecuador, Mexico, and Venezuela to increase taxes on hydrocarbons than direct taxes among the wealthy. As Monaldi notes in Chapter 2, governments opted for unilaterally modifying contracts on multinationals – which are often vilified in the popular imagination. The incentives brought about by commodity windfalls are cyclical, however, with greater incentives to tax as commodity prices decline.

These factors have become important impediments to the realization of the predictions of the Meltzer–Richard median-voter model (1981), which expected an increasingly redistributive tax system after the democratizing wave of the 1980s and 1990s.[4] This expectation is based on an emphasis on the adoption and deepening of democracy, focusing on the redistributive preferences of voters. However, the development of the liberal state – which does not necessarily occur alongside democratization – seems to be an important determinant of governments' ability to adopt direct taxes, as Mahon underscores in his chapter. Weak state capacity, powerful interest groups, and the use of taxes for goods other than redistribution, such as infrastructure or public safety, are all factors that contribute to the disconnect between the median-voter model's expectations and the permanence of regressive tax structures in the region over time (Besley and Persson 2014, 108; Flores-Macías 2018).

What Explains Variation Across Countries?

Although tax-collection levels are generally low across the region, there is variation in the region that can be accounted for. With tax levels at 33% of GDP, Brazil is noteworthy as the Latin American country that has managed to collect taxes in line with the expectation for its level of development. It is followed by Argentina and Uruguay at 27 and 28%,

[4] See also Boix (2003) and Acemoglu and Robinson (2006).

respectively. As Ondetti's and Schneider's chapters suggest, these countries' commitments to high levels of government spending – at or near 40% of GDP – have pushed for higher tax burdens, rather than the other way around. While in Brazil spending commitments were enshrined in the 1988 constitution, in Argentina they have been less institutionalized but clearly adhered to during the presidencies of Néstor Kirchner (2003–2007) and Cristina Fernández de Kirchner (2007–2015), and Uruguay has historically developed the region's most robust welfare state. Conversely, countries with much lower tax burdens, such as Mexico and Peru, have much lower spending commitments – around 20% of GDP.

Both Ondetti and Schneider show that the variation in government spending finds its roots in different patterns of interest group influence. For Schneider, the patterns of incorporation into the international system have at times shaped elites' incentives, such that taxation has followed elites' need to develop public goods conducive to furthering material gains. At its core, the politics of taxation is inevitably about generating winners and losers, and the prevailing mode of economic development can determine which sectors of society stand to benefit and their corresponding tax burden arrangement.

For Ondetti, the influence of business groups and the corresponding weakness of organized labor have contributed to keeping tax burdens relatively low in Chile and Mexico. In contrast, the weakness of conservative political sectors and the alliance between the labor movements, unions, and the left have resulted in greater taxation in Brazil. These patterns emerged due to earlier, drastic redistributive attempts in Chile and Mexico, which prompted a reaction among business sectors and made them very reluctant to turn over tax resources to the state. Because of the absence of comparable redistributive episodes in Brazil, business elites have not coalesced in the same fashion, allowing for greater tolerance for taxation.

Regarding variation in the tax structure, Fairfield's chapter suggest that differences in business groups' instrumental power account for differences in the extent to which countries adopted progressive reforms. Whereas strong instrumental power kept a lid on progressive reforms in Chile, business groups' weaker linkages with relevant parties gave way to more progressive reforms in Argentina, for example.

Another important factor explaining differences across countries is the quality of public goods, which is not necessarily correlated with the amount spent. For example, although Brazil's spending on public education is notoriously high, the same cannot be said for its quality. As Mahon's chapter suggests, differences in institutional strength are helpful to account for variation in the fiscal contract and, in turn, the ability to rely on direct tax burdens. Whereas Chile's and Uruguay's adoption of national property taxes followed the creation of an elite-driven liberal order with relatively strong institution for the region's standard (Kurtz 2013), the absence of institutions of similar quality elsewhere in the region undermined elites' tolerance to this form of direct taxation, with exceptions in places like Mexico City or Buenos Aires (Soifer 2015).

As this discussion highlights, many of the same political factors can contribute to both improving countries' levels of tax collection and increasing the tax structure's reliance on direct taxes. As the regions' governments become better at extracting direct taxes (and more willing to do so), the factors explaining levels and structures might diverge over time.

HORIZONTAL DEBATES: ON IDEOLOGY, PATH DEPENDENCE, ELITES, AND THE PUBLIC

While the previous discussion tackled the three main overarching questions that motivated this volume, in this section I address two main debates that cut across chapters. The first speaks to the role of agency versus path dependence, with an emphasis on whether ideology leads governments to depart from prevailing taxation patterns. The second deals with the role of elites versus the public, focusing on whether the public can play a role in shaping tax policy. These are areas that offer fruitful opportunities for further research.

Ideology and Path Dependence

This volume has offered insights suggesting both a stickiness in taxation patterns over time and room for governments to make a difference. In the first category are durable fiscal exchange arrangements that started early in the nineteenth and twentieth centuries and allowed for direct taxation among elites in exchange for strong institutions, as Mahon finds for Chile and Uruguay. The same can be said for the continuity in boom-and-bust patterns of commodity windfall dependence in resource rich countries, as Monaldi highlights for cases such as Venezuela. In the second category are governments' selective enforcement, which can have important consequences for extraction when directed at the wealthiest sectors, as

Bergman notes. Similarly, governments' decisions about public spending can make a difference in elevating tax burdens in the short to medium term, as in Brazil, as Schneider finds in his chapter.

Although there is a tension between these two factors, most of the chapters in this volume speak to the stickiness of low tax burdens, regressive tax structures, and the absence of tax neutrality. In this sense, most countries in the region appear to be in a low-quality equilibrium, slightly drifting upward over time, but far from catching up with countries with similar levels of development in other parts of the world.

One factor that seems to be in tension with the stickiness of taxation is governments' ideology. The literature in this regard has been mixed. On the one hand, there is cross-national evidence for ideology as a determinant of tax reform (Hallerberg and Scartascini 2011), as well as some subnational evidence (Machado and Stein 2012). Most recently, a systematic study of seventeen Latin American countries between 1990 and 2010 (Stein and Caro 2017) found that leftist governments were associated with increases in tax levels of up to 2.2% of GDP and in income taxes of 1.3% of GDP. Contrary to the finding that the left taxes more, however, Hart (2010) finds a role for ideology based on a panel-data study of nine countries, but points to right-of-center governments collecting more in taxes. He suggests that, since conservative governments are more willing to rely on indirect taxes, they can circumvent the obstacles to direct taxation and extract more. Other studies, such as Sakurai and Menezes-Filho's (2011) analysis of Brazilian municipalities, do not find a relationship between ideology and tax increases.

The chapters in the volume also have mixed findings in this regard. Several chapters point to a nuanced relationship between ideology and taxation. For example, Monaldi shows that governments' decisions about taxing hydrocarbons follow commodity price cycles in spite of strong ideological preferences. Although Argentina, Bolivia, Ecuador, and Venezuela increased tax rates considerably during the boom between 2002 and 2012 (Flores-Macías 2012), even leftist governments with clear statist agendas found themselves departing from their preferred ideological policy courses once the boom ended. They not only lowered taxes to attract investors but even formed joint ventures with the private sector in spite of their ideological commitment to the contrary. As others have found (Koivumaeki 2015; Weyland 2009), macroeconomic conditions and international cycles play a major role in explaining the adoption of statist policies, forcing the hand of even the most ideologically committed governments.

Similarly, Hallerberg and Scartascini do not find evidence for partisanship affecting the neutrality of reforms. This finding could be due to shared technocratic expertise in the ministries of finance across the region regardless of presidents' ideological orientation. It could also be that pork knows no political affiliations, and parties of all stripes are happy to engage in tax policies favoring narrow groups. Along these lines, and perhaps most surprising, is Bogliaccini and Luna's finding that party identification does not systematically structure public attitudes about progressivity across the region.

Rather, ideology appears to play a role not in the periodic turnover from one government to the next, but at critical junctures or key moments in history that determined whether a major reaction to redistributive efforts would take place in some countries but not others. According to Ondetti, in Chile it was the reaction to President Salvador Allende's Marxist economic policies that resulted in Pinochet's coup. In Mexico, the reaction to the expansion of statist policies in the 1960s and 1970s, culminating in the nationalization of the banking sector in 1982, resulted in great suspicion of the public sector among the business community. In Brazil, the absence of meaningful leftist redistributive threats obviated a reaction and led down a very different path. Once these new trajectories were set forth, however, changes in government seem to have only very gradually altered taxation, regardless of ideology.

The continuity in taxation patterns has been due in part to the institutional framework in place in these countries. For example, the Chilean leftist governments maintained a steady pro-market orientation because of constraints making change difficult in the aftermath of Pinochet's dictatorship, both in the economic sphere – e.g., central bank autonomy – and the political arena – e.g., the binomial electoral system, which generated a Congress typically divided roughly in half (González 2008). In contrast, the lack of comparable institutions provided greater room for a more radical left to develop elsewhere (Flores-Macías 2010; 2012).

The role ideology played in these key moments proved to be consequential for generations. For example, the Pinochet government's privatization of social security in Chile was coupled with a reduction in income taxes during the 1980s and 1990s (Pribble 2013; Garay 2016), which led to a decrease in the overall tax burdens. In the Mexican case, although some authors have pointed to resource dependence as the main explanation behind remarkably low levels of taxation (Elizondo 2014), the consensus among Mexican elites to maintain public spending at historical lows has impaired greater tax collection. Governments' commitment to the continuation of low expenditure policies, often coupled with ideological dogmatism regarding the role of the state in the economy, have maintained a low tax burden.

Other chapters allow for a more implicit role of ideology in giving continuity to current taxation trends. Fairfield's chapter, for example, points to the links that business elites develop with conservative parties as a vehicle for business groups' instrumental power. This implies variation across time and place regarding how much leverage business elites can exert over governments through ideologically likeminded politicians, among other channels.

In short, the chapters in this volume point to different perspectives regarding the extent to which ideology can play a role in breaking away from a particular taxation trajectory. Whereas the stickiness in levels and structure of taxation is a generally shared view throughout the volume, taken together the chapters suggests that ideology can be more consequential at key moments rather than consistently during the ebb and flow of the ideological tides from one administration to the next.

One possible reason for this discrepancy may be the relative compression of the political spectrum since the end of the Cold War. After the collapse of the Soviet bloc, leftist governments represented a lower redistributive threat, increasingly becoming government at different levels and adopting economic policies respectful of private property and fiscal responsibility. Although extreme cases of leftist redistribution in the region persist, as the presidencies of Hugo Chávez and Nicolás Maduro in Venezuela show, the left's economic policies can be characterized as center–left and have increasingly converged with those of the center-right regarding fiscal responsibility and keeping a lid on inflation.

As this discussion suggests, there is little consensus regarding the relationship between ideology and taxation. Further, existing research often presents contradictory findings, at times pointing to the left, others to the right, as correlated with greater extraction. Much more research is needed to understand whether ideology can play a role in moving countries away from their historical trends of low levels of taxation and regressive tax structures.

Elites and the Public

There is also tension in the literature as to whether the public can play an important role for taxation or whether elites are the dominant actor in the fiscal exchange. Although there is a broad literature on public opinion related to tax morale (Cummings et al. 2009), the role of the public's influence on taxation is often dismissed because of both elites' outsized influence and the difficulty in measuring public attitudes toward fiscal extraction.

Several of the contributions in this volume point to the power of elites in determining tax policy. For example, Fairfield's chapter frontally deals with how business sectors' leverage structural and instrumental power and offers a telling quote from a Chilean legislator confiding that he does not think any of his actions in the Budget Committee ever had an impact on whether people voted for him or not. Chapters by Mahon, Ondetti, and Schneider are consistent with this view, pointing to the lasting impact of elites as well. The importance of economic elites for setting tax policy is undeniable, but can the public also be consequential?

It may be the case that the public does not pay attention to taxes at all, as the legislator implies. More likely, however, public attitudes toward taxation are often expressed differently in the context of Latin America's weak democratic representation. When democratic institutions are perceived as ineffective, the public often relies on extra-institutional means, from street mobilization to the extreme of violence, rather than the ballot box to influence economic policies such as trade agreements or tax reforms. This often responds to the fact that in some countries, as in Venezuela, the trappings of a democracy might remain, but state institutions are captured by a small sector and few have confidence that elections are free and fair (Corrales and Penfold-Becerra 2011). In other places, such as in Mexico, elections might be generally free and fair at the national level, but subnational authoritarian enclaves continue to hinder representation (Gibson 2012; Giraudi 2015).

In other parts of the region, the public might be better represented, but there is a deficit in terms of programmatic structure that might link individual preferences with policy output (Kitschelt et al. 2010), and the issue of taxation is no exception. The chapter by Bogliaccini and Luna makes a contribution in this regard by highlighting the extent to which Latin American publics favor progressive taxation and noting the lack of structuration through political ideology, economic well-being, and class position. Instead, these attitudes toward redistribution appear to be a product of the high regional heterogeneity regarding inequality, economic perspectives, and partisan positions. In other words, our knowledge of what drives such strong preferences for redistribution remains very limited.

This does not mean that the public does not shape tax policy, but rather that further research is required to help understand this relationship.

There are notable examples in which governments have gone out of their way to try to understand public attitudes toward specific tax reforms, as with Jamaica's tax reforms during the 1980s and 1990s (Bahl 1997). There are also cases in which the public has derailed governments' attempts at adopting unpopular reforms, especially having to do with increases in regressive consumption tax rates, as with as the VAT in Mexico during the presidencies of Vicente Fox (2000–2006) and Felipe Calderón (2006–2012) (Flores-Macías 2018). Popular manifestations against proposed tax reforms have played a role in shaping both the level and structure of taxes, as with Bolivia's 2003 proposal to adopt an income tax (Fairfield 2013, 50; 2015b).[5]

Although it might be tempting to dismiss these manifestations as elite-driven, this view is inconsistent with the instances of successful public opposition to increases in the VAT, which is economic elites' preferred avenue for raising tax revenue. Rather, these examples suggest that fiscal policy is complex and many factors matter, with public attitudes being only one of them. Although the public will not organize every time, when it does it can translate attitudes into meaningful consequences for tax policy.

AVENUES FOR FUTURE RESEARCH ON THE POLITICS OF TAXATION

The tensions described above regarding the stickiness of taxation patterns over time and the factors that break from this path dependence, as well as the roles of elites and the public, lend themselves to fruitful avenues for future research. For example, there is much to do to improve our understanding of how elites and the public contribute to the politics of taxation. Latin America's high levels of inequality add urgency to governments' efforts to engage elites on the issue of taxes. Making resources available for government transfers is a required first step for addressing inequality, and perceptions of equity in the tax system can generate virtuous cycles of compliance across sectors (Cummings et al. 2009; Lledo et al. 2004; Prichard 2015).

While this might mean different levels of elite taxation depending on the country, governments across the region should adopt a combination of

[5] The public playing a role is even more common in the developed world. In the USA, for example, tax cuts enjoying broad popular support made possible reforms in 2001 and 2003 in spite of benefiting mostly the wealthiest sectors (Bartels 2005, 16).

strategies for achieving this goal, including following a gradual but steady approach to tax reforms (as in Chile in the early 2000s), linking reforms explicitly to generally held moral values such as equity (as in Uruguay's 2006 reform), identifying clear winners from reforms to rely on as champions (as in Colombia over the last two decades), and earmarking benefits (as in Mexico's 2013 reform) (Rius 2015; Romero 2015; Fairfield 2015a; Flores-Macías 2015). These experiences show that economic elites are a key factor in the political economy of taxation, and that there certainly is room for maneuver in terms of engaging them meaningfully in fiscal extraction.

There is also scope for research into how the influence of business elites can be countered. For example, business elites do not always form coherent groups with similar interests (Schneider 2004). Divisions often exist in terms of the fiscal treatment for importers and exporters, capital intensive and labor intensive, and the financial sector and the real sector (Castañeda 2017). Governments can often leverage such divisions to their advantage, as was the case in Uruguay's 2006 fiscal reform (Rius 2015). The case of Colombia's wealth taxes since 2002, for which different industries had different views depending on the difficulty in calculating the value of their assets, is another case in point (Flores-Macías 2015). Further, governments can also mobilize public opinion against business elites – which can become an easy target to vilify as opposing the interests of the people – as has been the case in Bolivia with President Evo Morales (2006–present) and Argentina during the administrations of Néstor Kirchner (2003–2007) and Cristina Fernández de Kirchner (2007–2015).

These efforts require political will from governments, but they can also leverage windows of opportunity. As noted in Hallerberg and Scartascini's chapter, economic crises are important moments to adopt tax reforms, not only because they inject governments with urgency to solve fiscal problems, but also because they make solutions more palatable for business elites. The recent increase in tax collection in Mexico following the sharp decline in oil prices in 2014 constitutes a good example. Although a fiscal reform promising a slight increase in tax collection was approved by Congress in 2013, President Enrique Peña Nieto (2012–2018) reversed much of the already-modest reform by executive decree that same year (Unda Gutiérrez 2015). When faced with the prospect of a significant budget shortfall from the steep drop in oil revenue in 2014, the Mexican government – which depends on revenue from hydrocarbons for a third of the federal budget – tightened oversight and managed to compensate for the foregone oil revenue. Further research into these political obstacles is much needed.

Another potentially fruitful avenue is one that studies the factors that help countries depart from historical patterns of taxation. A promising line of research deals with the factors that would improve the terms of fiscal exchange for citizens in order to strengthen the liberal state and, in turn, citizens' sense of obligation to reciprocate with resources. In particular, two avenues can deepen liberalism along these lines.

The first is by improving the provision of property rights by strengthening the judiciary and professionalizing the bureaucracy through a strict civil service meritocracy. Naturally there are political costs to doing so: enforcing property rights has important distributional consequences, especially among those groups in the informal sector who might otherwise find few opportunities in the formal sector, as Bergman (2009) and Holland (2016) suggest. Similarly, ending corruption in the links of the chain of property rights enforcement can also undermine an important form of patronage that represents votes for ruling parties. Examples consist of cleaning government registries where property ownership and values are recorded, establishing accountability mechanisms in the courts, and improving the capacity of prosecutors to collect evidence and bring solid cases against defendants. While these reforms take time, they are essential to the strengthening of the rule of law.

The second path is less structural, but perhaps equally consequential in eliciting society's acquiescence to shoulder a greater direct tax burden. This path focuses on generating clear value for taxpayers in exchange for their taxes by making explicit connections between direct taxes and the provision of specific public goods (Prichard 2015). Although improving the extent to which property rights are upheld would be ideal, taxpayers value a diversity of public goods that can also give them an interest in shouldering a greater tax burden. Recent examples include the adoption of increased taxes in Mexico after the government linked the additional revenue with spending in popular social programs including unemployment insurance (Unda Gutiérrez 2015; Romero 2015), and in Colombia after the government earmarked wealth taxes for public safety purposes (Flores-Macías 2015). The link between visible expenditures in public goods valued by the population, such as public safety, can play an important role in improving the perception of a fair fiscal exchange between taxpayers and the government.[6] As these perceptions improve, a virtuous

[6] For an example based on willingness to pay for public safety with evidence from Mexico, see Flores-Macías and Sánchez Talanquer (2018).

cycle can emerge in which society becomes increasingly willing to shoulder direct taxes in exchange for services that benefit them.

Although there are concerns about earmarking, earmarked taxes can also contribute to improving perceptions of the quality of the fiscal exchange. Criticism ranges from earmarking's potential rigidity to government's lack of credibility about spending commitments, but a main concern is about efficiency – or the distortions earmarks might generate in the economy (McCleary 1991). While these concerns are worth considering, earmarking tax revenue can also shape perceptions of how closely related taxpayers' burdens are to public goods that are important to them (Wallis 2001, 141; Flores-Macías 2018). In this regard, earmarked taxes can represent an important avenue to raise extraction, increase the share of direct taxes, and habituate people to paying taxes. This habituation would come at the expense of efficiency, but it may have long-lasting salutary effects.

Finally, the emphasis of most chapters in the volume was not on institutional factors, with the exception of that by Hallerberg and Scartascini. However, much remains to be done in terms of what makes certain institutions durable in some places but not others. For example, the adoption of fiscal rules, rainy day funds, and other accountability mechanisms to force governments' hands have been proposed in recent years (Eyraud et al. 2018), but we still have an incomplete understanding of the conditions under which governments tend to respect these rules.

CONCLUSION

Latin America has had its fair share of financial crises – both homegrown and imported from abroad – and their recurrence in the future is a distinct possibility. Unfortunately, future crises will not only bring about economic hardship, but their timing is seldom opportune for policymakers: rarely, if ever, do crises emerge at a desirable time. This book has therefore studied different political factors that can help inform the policymakers' toolkit beyond crisis-based perspectives.

As the chapters in this volume have shown, taxation is a complex issue where many different factors come into play. Understanding the politics of taxation can help address some of the region's most pressing needs, including public safety, education, healthcare, and infrastructure (Tsounta and Osueke 2014). Raising Latin America's tax burden to bring it in line with that of other countries with similar levels of development will require developing not just the technical expertise regarding which reforms to adopt, but also the knowledge of how to make them politically palatable. To the extent that reformers can identify strategies to make taxation politically feasible, they will also be making reforms sustainable.

In this sense, addressing the region's taxation challenges should not be a matter of ideological preconceptions about government size, but about marshaling the minimum necessary resources to promote growth and development. Making taxation politically feasible stands to make an important contribution for Latin America to enjoy better-quality public goods and escape the middle-income trap (Doner and Schneider 2016). Otherwise, low levels of taxation will sustain the current conditions of low public good provision, low redistribution, and low growth.

References

Acemoglu, Daron and James Robinson. 2006. *Economic Origins of Dictatorship and Democracy*. New York: Cambridge University Press.

Agencia Notimex. 2016. "Peña promulga la ley para regular deuda de estados y municipios; dará estabilidad al país, dice," *Animal Político*, April 27.

Alm, James, Jorge Martinez-Vasquez, and Sally Wallace (eds.). 2005. *Taxing the Hard to Tax: Lessons from Theory and Practice*. Bingley: Emerald Group.

Alvaredo, Facundo and Julieta Londoño. 2013. "High Incomes and Personal Taxation in a Developing Economy: Colombia 1993–2010." Commitment to Equity Working Paper 12.

Bahl, Roy. 1997. "The Jamaican Tax Reform: Its Design and Performance," in Wayne Thirsk (ed.), *Tax Reform in Developing Countries*. Washington, DC: World Bank, 167–231.

Bartels, Larry. 2005. "Homer Gets a Tax Cut: Inequality and Public Policy in the American Mind," *Perspectives on Politics* 3(1): 15–31.

Besley, Timothy and Torsten Persson. 2014. "Why Do Developing Countries Tax So Little?," *Journal of Economic Perspectives* 28(4): 99–120.

Bergman, Marcelo. 2009. *Tax Evasion and the Rule of Law in Latin America: The Political Economy of Cheating and Compliance in Argentina and Chile*. College Park: Penn State University Press.

Bird, Richard and Charles McLure. 1990. "The Personal Income Tax in an Inter-Dependent World," in Sijbren Cnossen and Richard Bird (eds.), *The Personal Income Tax: Phoenix from the Ashes?* Amsterdam: North-Holland, 235–255.

Bird, Richard and Guillermo Perry. 1994. "Tax Policy in Latin America: In Crisis and After," in Graham Bird and Ann Helwege (eds.), *Latin America's Economic Future*. London: Academic Press, 168–184.

Boix, Carles. 2003. *Democracy and Redistribution*. New York: Cambridge University Press.

Brautigam, Deborah, Odd-Helge Fjeldstad, and Mick Moore (eds.). 2008. *Taxation and State-Building in Developing Countries*. New York: Cambridge University Press.

Burdín, Gabriel, Fernando Esponda, and Andrea Vigorito. 2014. "Inequality and Top Incomes in Uruguay," World Top Incomes Database Working Paper 2014/1.

Castañeda, Néstor. 2017. "Business Coordination and Tax Politics," *Political Studies* 65(1): 122–143.

Corrales, Javier and Michael Penfold-Becerra. 2011. *Dragon in the Tropics: Hugo Chavez and the Political Economy of Revolution in Venezuela*. Washington, DC: Brookings Institution Press.

Crawford, David. 2013. *Detailed Guidelines for Improved Tax Administration in Latin* America *and the Caribbean, Chapter 7*. USAID/Deloitte Consulting LLP, August.

Cummings, Ronald, Jorge Martinez-Vasquez, Michael McKee, and Benno Torgler. 2009. "Tax Morale Affects Tax Compliance: Evidence from Surveys and an Artefactual Field Experiment," *Journal of Economic Behavior and Organization* 70(3): 447–457.

Doner, Richard and Benn Ross Schneider. 2016. "The Middle-Income Trap: More Politics than Economics," *World Politics* 68(4): 608–644.

Elizondo, Carlos. 2014. "Progresividad y eficacia en el gasto público en México: Precondición para una política recaudatoria efectiva," Woodrow Wilson Center Update on the Americas, March.

Eyraud, Luc, Xavier Debrun, Andrew Hodge, Victor Lledo, and Catherine Pattillo. 2018. "Second-Generation Fiscal Rules: Balancing Simplicity, Flexibility, and Enforceability," IMF Staff Discussion Note 18/04, Washington, DC: International Monetary Fund.

Fairfield, Tasha. 2013. "Going Where the Money Is: Strategies for Taxing Economic Elites in Unequal Democracies," *World Development* 47(7): 42–57.

Fairfield, Tasha. 2015a. "The Political Economy of Progressive Tax Reform in Chile," in James Mahon Jr., Marcelo Bergman, and Cynthia Arnson (eds.), *Progressive Tax Reform and Equality in Latin America*. Washington, DC: Woodrow Wilson International Center for Scholars, 30–56.

Fairfield, Tasha. 2015b. *Private Wealth and Public Revenue in Latin America: Business Power and Tax Politics*. New York: Cambridge University Press.

Fairfield, Tasha, and Michel Jorratt. 2015. "Top Income Shares, Business Profits, and Effective Tax Rates in Contemporary Chile," *Review of Income and Wealth*, doi:10.1111/roiw.12196.

Flores-Macías, Gustavo. 2010. "Statist vs. Pro-market: Explaining Leftist Governments' Economic Reforms in Latin America," *Comparative Politics* 42(4): 413–433.

2012. *After Neoliberalism? The Left and Economic Reforms in Latin America*. New York: Oxford University Press.

2014. "Financing Security through Elite Taxation: The Case of Colombia's Democratic Security Taxes," *Studies in Comparative International Development* 49(4): 477–500.

2015. "The Political Economy of Colombia's 2012 and 2014 Fiscal Reforms," in James Mahon Jr., Marcelo Bergman, and Cynthia Arnson (eds.), *Progressive Tax Reform and Equality in Latin America*. Washington, DC: Woodrow Wilson International Center for Scholars, 101–126.

2018. "Building Support for Taxation in Developing Countries: Experimental Evidence from Mexico," *World Development* 105(5): 13–24.

Garay, Candelaria. 2016. *Social Policy Expansion in Latin America*. New York: Cambridge University Press.

Gibson, Edward. 2012. *Boundary Control: Subnational Authoritarianism in Federal Democracies*. New York: Cambridge University Press.

Giraudi, Agustina. 2015. *Democrats and Autocrats: Pathways of Subnational Undemocratic Regime Continuity within Democratic Countries*. New York: Oxford University Press.

González, Francisco. 2008. *Dual Transitions from Authoritarian Rule: Institutionalized Regimes in Chile and Mexico*. Baltimore: Johns Hopkins University Press.

Graetz, Michael and Ian Shapiro. 2005. *Death by a Thousand Cuts: The Fight over Taxing Inherited Wealth*. Princeton: Princeton University Press.

Haggard, Stephan and Robert Kaufman. 2016. *Dictators and Democrats: Masses, Elites, and Regime Change*. Princeton: Princeton University Press.

Hallerberg, Mark and Patrick Marier. 2004. "Executive Authority, the Personal Vote, and Budget Discipline in Latin American and Caribbean Countries," *American Journal of Political Science* 48(3): 571–587.

Hallerberg, Mark and Carlos Scartascini. 2011. "Economic Crisis and Fiscal Reforms in Latin America," *IDB Working Paper* 82. Washington, DC: Inter-American Development Bank.

Hart, Austin. 2010. "Death of the Partisan? Globalization and Taxation in South America, 1990–2006," *Comparative Political Studies* 43(3): 304–28

Holland, Alisha. 2016. "Forbearance," *American Political Science Review* 110(2): 232–246.

Holland, Alisha and Ben Ross Schneider. 2017. "Easy and Hard Redistribution: The Political Economy of Welfare States in Latin America," *Perspectives on Politics* 15(4): 988–1006.

Inter-American Development Bank. 2013. *More than Revenue: Taxation as a Development Tool*. Washington, DC: IADB.

2010. *High Taxes and Evasion Eroding Economic Growth in Latin America and the Caribbean*. Washington, DC: IADB.

International Monetary Fund. 2015. *Fiscal Policy in Latin America: Lessons and Legacies of the Global Financial Crisis*. Washington, DC: IMF.

Kaufman, Robert. 2011. "The Political Left, the Export Boom, and the Populist Temptation," in Steven Levitsky and Kenneth Roberts (eds.), *Latin America's Left Turn*. Baltimore: Johns Hopkins University Press, 93–116.

Kitschelt, Herbert, Kirk Hawkins, Juan Pablo Luna, Guillermo Rosas, and Elizabeth Zechmeister. 2010. *Latin American Party Systems*. New York: Cambridge University Press.

Koivumaeki, Riita-Ilona. 2015. "Evading the Constraints of Globalization: Oil and Gas Nationalization in Venezuela and Bolivia," *Comparative Politics* 48 (1): 107–125.

KPMG. 2017. A Look Inside Tax Departments in Latin America and How They Are Adapting, KPMG Global Benchmarking Series, June: https://assets.kpmg/content/dam/kpmg/xx/pdf/2017/06/latam-benchmarking-survey-web.pdf.

Kurtz, Marcus. 2013. *Latin American State Building in Comparative Perspective: Social Foundations of Institutional Order*. New York: Cambridge University Press.

Lledo, Victor, Aaron Schneider, and Mick Moore. 2004. "Pro-poor Tax Reform in Latin America: A Critical Survey and Policy Recommendations," *IDS Working Paper* 221 (March).

Machado, Fabiana and Ernesto Stein. 2012. *The Rise of the Left and Increases in Tax Revenue: Evidence from Brazilian Municipalities*. Washington, DC: Inter-American Development Bank.

Mahon Jr., James. 2004. "Causes of Tax Reform in Latin America, 1977–95," *Latin American Research Review* 39(1): 3–30.

Mahon Jr., James, Marcelo Bergman, and Cynthia Arnson (eds.). 2015. *Progressive Tax Reform and Equality in Latin America*. Washington, DC: Woodrow Wilson International Center for Scholars.

McCleary, William. 1991. "The Earmarking of Government Revenue: A Review of Some World Bank Experience," *World Bank Observer* 6(1): 81–104.

Melguizo, Angel. 2017. "If We Want More Economic Growth in Latin America, We Need More and Better Taxes," *World Economic Forum on Latin America* (Blog), March 29: www.weforum.org/agenda/2017/03/if-we-want-more-economic-growth-in-latin-america-we-need-more-and-better-taxes/.

Meltzer, Allan and Scott Richard. 1981. "A Rational Theory of the Size of Government," *Journal of Political Economy* 89(5): 914–927.

Murdoch, Terry. 2013. *Detailed Guidelines for Improved Tax Administration in Latin America and the Caribbean, Chapter 5*. USAID/Deloitte Consulting LLP, August.

Pribble, Jennifer. 2013. *Welfare and Party Politics in Latin America*. New York: Cambridge University Press.

Prichard, Wilson. 2015. *Taxation, Responsiveness, and Accountability in Sub-Saharan Africa: The Dynamics of Tax Bargaining*. Cambridge: Cambridge University Press.

Rius, Andrés. 2015. "The Uruguayan Tax Reform of 2006: Why Didn't It Fail?," in James Mahon, Marcelo Bergman, and Cynthia Arnson (eds.), *Progressive Tax Reform and Equality in Latin America*. Washington, DC: Woodrow Wilson International Center for Scholars, 64–100.

Romero, Vidal. 2015. "The Political Economy of Progressive Tax Reforms in Mexico," in James Mahon, Marcelo Bergman, and Cynthia Arnson (eds.), *Progressive Tax Reform and Equality in Latin America*. Washington, DC: Woodrow Wilson International Center for Scholars, 161–188.

Sakurai, Sergio and Naercio Menezes-Filho. 2011. "Opportunistic and Partisan Election Cycles in Brazil: New Evidence at the Municipal Level," *Public Choice* 148(1): 233–247.

Sánchez, Omar. 2006. "Tax System Reform in Latin America: Domestic and International Causes," *Review of International Political Economy* 13(5): 772–801.

Saylor, Ryan. 2014. *State Building in Boom Times: Commodities and Coalitions in Latin America and Africa*. New York: Oxford University Press.

Schneider, Ben Ross. 2004. *Business Politics and the State in Twentieth-Century Latin America*. New York: Cambridge University Press.

2015. *Designing Industrial Policy in Latin America: Business-Government Relations and the New Developmentalism*. New York: Palgrave.

Soifer, Hillel David. 2015. *State Building in Latin America*. New York: Cambridge University Press.

Stein, Ernesto and Lorena Caro. 2017. "Ideology and Taxation in Latin America," *Economía* 17(2): 1–27.

Shugart, Matthew and John Carey. 1992. *Presidents and Assemblies: Constitutional Design and Electoral Dynamics*. New York: Cambridge University Press.

Toro, Francisco. 2015. "Venezuela's Collapse Has Nothing to Do with Oil Prices," Financial Times, February 9.

Tsounta, Evridiki and Anayochukwu Osueke. 2014. "What is Behind Latin America's Declining Inequality?" *IMF Working Paper* 14/124. Washington, DC: IMF.

Unda Gutiérrez, Mónica. 2015. "La reforma tributaria de 2013: los problemas de la Hacienda pública y la desigualdad en México," *Espiral: Estudios sobre estado y sociedad* 22(64): 69–99.

Wallis, John. 2001. "A History of the Property Tax in America," in Wallace Oates (ed.), *Property Taxation and Local Government Finance*. Cambridge, MA: Lincoln Institute for Land Policy, 123–147.

Weyland, Kurt. 2009. "The Rise of Latin America's Two Lefts: Insights from Rentier State Theory," *Comparative Politics* 41(2): 145–164.

World Bank. 2017. World Bank Development Indicators. Online Resource: https://databank.worldbank.org/data/source/world-development-indicators.

Index

Made in the USA
Coppell, TX
18 August 2025

53044009R00166